ADVANCED CIVILIZATIONS
OF PREHISTORIC AMERICA

ADVANCED CIVILIZATIONS OF PREHISTORIC AMERICA

The Lost Kingdoms of the Adena, Hopewell, Mississippians, and Anasazi

FRANK JOSEPH

Bear & Company
Rochester, Vermont • Toronto, Canada

Bear & Company
One Park Street
Rochester, Vermont 05767
www.BearandCompanyBooks.com

Bear & Company is a division of Inner Traditions International

Library of Congress Cataloging-in-Publication Data
Joseph, Frank.
  Advanced civilizations of prehistoric America : the lost kingdoms of the Adena,
Hopewell, Mississippians, and Anasazi / Frank Joseph.
    p. cm.
  Includes bibliographical references and index.
  Summary: "The examination of four great civilizations that existed before
Columbus's arrival in North America offers evidence of sustained contact between
the Old and New Worlds"—Provided by publisher.
  ISBN 978-1-59143-107-7
  1. Indians of North America—History. 2. North America—Civilization—
Indian influences. I. Title.
  E77.J785 2010
  970.004'97—dc22

2009034364

Printed and bound in the United States by Versa Press, Inc.

10 9 8 7 6 5 4

Text design by Jon Desautels and layout by Priscilla Baker
This book was typeset in Garamond Premier Pro with Copperplate and Gill Sans
used as display typefaces

All artwork and/or photographs are by the author unless otherwise noted.

To send correspondence to the author of this book, mail a first-class letter to the
author c/o Inner Traditions • Bear & Company, One Park Street, Rochester, VT
05767, and we will forward the communication.

To William R. Corliss and his more than thirty years of The Sourcebook Project, which has deepened our appreciation for and continues to widen our exploration of humanity and nature.

Putting your hand into a river, you simultaneously touch the last of what is passing and the first of what is coming.

LEONARDO DA VINCI

Contents

Introduction

Our Cultural Amnesia

The city had never experienced such an opulent funeral. As one organism, forty thousand men, women, and children put aside their everyday affairs to become participants in a drama of death and resurrection without precedent in the history of their far-flung population center.

Most waited silently in the early morning chill outside the 18-foot-high stockade, its unassailable exterior coated with a grainy plaster of pulverized mother-of-pearl, glinting pinkish white in the early dawn. These less privileged mourners clustered at the feet of gaunt watchtowers—five hundred twenty-three of them manned by sixteen hundred archers—spaced at regular, 20-foot intervals along two miles of the contiguous wall that parted them from high ceremonies taking place on the other side. These people were a world away from their short, brutal lives as farmers, artisans, and common laborers. As death separates the mundane from the supernatural, so this fortified enclosure stood as a forbidding border between the temporal and the eternal.

The surrounding ramparts embraced a pyramid 40 square acres at its base, greater than that of the Great Pyramid of Egypt. It was 1,037 feet long and 790 feet wide, with a total volume of approximately 21,690,000 cubic feet of earth, and it rose to over 150 feet in four terraces. These terraces supported wooden shrines with thatched roofs, identical to but smaller than a temple at the summit, which was 105 feet long, 48 feet wide, and 50 feet tall. The sacred area was directly reached

1

from ground level by a flight of broad steps, a grand stairway to heaven, ascending the entire southern flank of the gargantuan earthwork.

Upon the uppermost step of this flight stood a lone figure, a robed and plumed astronomer-priest, the personified interregnum of a vast empire that spread in every direction. From here, he could see wind-swept prairie grasslands stretching to the horizon and surrounding his five-mile-wide city like a wavy sea battering its encircling wall. Before him, to the south, sprawled 2,200 acres of urban development packed with family housing and markets amid 120 ceremonial earthworks fashioned into monumental cones, platforms, and linear mounds.

He squinted at the far-below oversized image of a falcon, depicted spread-eagle on the smoothed floor of the Grand Plaza, its 15-foot wingspan and twenty thousand or more marine-shell disk beads blazing in the torchlight of a hundred attendants alert for the priest's signal. These men waited in the shadow of the city's high wall, which kept the morning from entering this sacred precinct.

The astronomer-priest of the Cahokia culture (AD 1000) presides over the funeral of a deceased ruler.

The high priest looked to the west, ignoring the mighty river writhing like a mythic serpent not far beyond a place that future archaeologists would call Woodhenge. Some two hundred erect cedar posts, each 20 feet high and painted bright red, formed a circle 400 feet in diameter. A single pillar at its center was topped with a seat from which an observer could calculate solstices, equinoxes, cross-quarter days, and the rising of particular stars or constellations by using the posts like gun sights, aligning them against various sky phenomena. In so doing, an abundance of celestial information flooded this astronomical computer of cedar posts.

Yet the high priest atop his pyramid needed only one piece of heavenly news to set this day in motion. It came with the rising sun as conveyed by a large, blue banner waved back and forth in a long arc by the observer at Woodhenge.

The priest summoned an attendant from inside the temple to reply "message received" by waving another signal flag.

Next, a boy carried to the priest a heavy conch shell, a specimen of numerous trade goods imported from the far-off Bahamas. Now that the precise solar moment had arrived, the priest placed the ponderous shell to his lips and blew a long, hollow-sounding blast loud enough to echo across the 40-acre plaza.

The men far below suddenly threw their torches to the ground in the gathering morning light. Others, unseen in the shadows, set up constant drumming that reverberated even more powerfully against the surrounding wall, drowning out almost entirely the cries of multitudes mourning outside. About two hundred fifty young men and women were escorted by spear-wielding warriors to the image of the falcon, around which they were arranged in a semicircle, leaving a wide gap open to the east.

From that direction, four priests entered, carrying on their shoulders the corpse of a man in his mid-forties arrayed with the feathered crown and colorful robes of state. His pallbearers brought him to the marine-shell effigy, carefully resting his head on that of the stylized bird, with its wings and tail beneath his arms and legs—thereby arranging the man in the position of metaphysical transformation.

As the priests stepped back, some of the young men waiting in the semicircle around their dead ruler stretched forth their hands, which were swiftly lopped off by warriors armed with obsidian axes. Other sacrificial victims knelt unhesitatingly with bowed heads, offering them for decapitation. Their gushing bodies pitched toward the falcon bearing its dead king, while survivors were stabbed and strangled, their screams obscured by the incessant drumming. With the help of blood-spattered warriors, the priests collected every fleshy scrap of the mutilated remains—bodies, severed hands and heads—in piles around the falcon with its own royal corpse.

Once more, the conch shell sounded from atop the pyramid, silencing drummers and mourners alike. New attendants entered the Grand Plaza, bearing huge sheets and onerous rolls of hammered copper, which they set down near the honored deceased and his ritually killed retinue. More servants arrived, bearing clamshell hoes and shovels. With these primitive tools they set about working at once, digging enough soil to build a sepulchre.

Laboring day and night through relief teams, in less than a week they heaped a great earthwork over the scene, and fashioned it into a ridge-top mound resembling an elongated tent terminating at either end in a triangular configuration. Beneath this enduring mortuary, the nameless regent and his hundreds of slain retainers lay undisturbed for more than a thousand years.

How did I miss all that?

The event described here is not the fantasy of some fiction writer but actually occurred in western Illinois, across the Mississippi River from St. Louis, Missouri, at a place archaeologists call Cahokia. At the zenith of its metropolitan grandeur, around AD 1000, Cahokia's population was larger than that of contemporary London. In fact, it was greater than that of any city in the United States for the next eight hundred years, until Philadelphia reached the same population density after the turn of the nineteenth century.

How was it possible that such a place escaped my notice? In my youthful arrogance, I presumed I knew at least the broad outlines of history. But during all my education, I was never told anything about Cahokia. In my student years at Southern Illinois University the name was only fleetingly familiar because of a brown road sign that flashed by as I sped along I-64 on weekend road trips from the Carbondale campus to St. Louis: "Cahokia Mounds Exit." I presumed it must have been only an Indian cemetery, and went on my merry way, without giving it another thought.

Twenty years later, after reading for the first time about the Mississippian culture that flourished throughout the South and Midwest, I deliberately sought out the largest ceremonial center north of the Rio Grande River. I have since returned to that evocative site again and again on behalf of my books and magazine articles about ancient America.

But nothing compares with a first visit to the Cahokia pyramid. The impression it makes becomes even more potent when we realize that not only was it the centerpiece of the largest city of its time, but it was also the capital of a commercial empire that spread from the Upper Great Lakes region to the Gulf of Mexico. Cahokia was actually the hub of an even greater network of related city-states: the Mississippian culture, a loose confederation of like-minded pyramid-builders who dominated North America east of the Mississippi River.

Despite their prodigious accomplishments in social organization, monumental architecture, applied astronomy, large-scale agriculture, and urban planning, their society collapsed about one hundred years before the arrival of modern Europeans. It was all news to me. Throughout my school years, I was told that American history began when Christopher Columbus set foot on the beach at San Salvador. Prior to this seminal moment, my fellow students and I were told, the Aztecs and Mayas in Mexico and Peru's Incas had done something civilized, albeit backward, but no true civilization occurred in what would later become the United States. That was true enough, in a sense, because by the sixteenth century, tribes of Plains Indians occupied the New World north of the Rio Grande, although early pioneers were mystified by the enigmatic ruins of abandoned cities and atypical artifacts they occasionally encountered en route to the West.

But as the magnitude and fate of Cahokia and its precursors began to unfold, I was struck by some obvious, even disconcerting, though ignored conclusions—especially, that our civilization is not the first on this continent. Others have risen and fallen in North America several times long before our own. No civilization worthy of the name was ever created in a vacuum, incapable of affecting other societies greater or lesser than itself, often far removed from its own urban center. Shangri-la was a fable, but the lost civilizations of America were not. The seas, which today's mainstream archaeologists insist hermetically sealed off one ancient society from another before Columbus, were in fact superhighways humans rode from place to place, as proved more than once by Dr. Thor Heyerdahl. From the 1940s to the 1970s, the Norwegian archaeologist's faithful recreations of period ships operated by ancient Easter Islanders, Egyptians, Mesopotamians, and Peruvians demonstrated that mariners possessed a technology that enabled them to traverse the seas long before Columbus.

Contrary to his opponents, who still miss the point of his experiments, Heyerdahl proved not that voyagers from the ancient Old World sailed to the New, but that they had the means to do so. A people capable of constructing a massive pyramid and mastering at least the rudiments of astronomy could certainly build a transoceanic vessel and effectively guide its course using celestial navigation. Certainly, this same group who dealt constantly with the horrors of hand-to-hand combat would not have shrunk from the terror of the sea, particularly if tempted by the prospect of great riches or escape from overwhelming enemies. Conventional scholars argue that ancient peoples, such as the Egyptians or Chinese, whose civilizations stood much higher than

Polynesian society, for example, were somehow unable at least to duplicate the trans-Pacific catamarans operated by South Sea islanders.

Edmund J. Ladd, late curator of ethnology at Santa Fe's Museum of New Mexico, states:

> The mythology of the Melika, the "White People," tells us that we Native Americans came across the Bering Strait in small groups over a long period of time, perhaps even 35,000 years ago. If this is true, why couldn't others have come across later, or earlier? According to some, the Vikings came to Greenland (or Vineland) many years before Columbus. Artifacts found in archaeological sites along the West Coast give hints of earlier travel across the Pacific. . . . My point is that if we have some knowledge and documentation of all these early voyages from nearly all of the world, how many unknown or undocumented voyages might have occurred?[1]

As modern America is the product of overseas immigrants, so the four civilizations that preceded it were sparked by outside influences. First came the Adena in 1000 BC, their culture exploding full-blown between the Atlantic seaboard and the Mississippi River. For seventeen centuries, their material finesse ranged from massive earthworks and hill forts to dentistry and intricately designed tablets. They introduced pottery making, and were the first Americans to practice organized agriculture.

Around 300 BC, an entirely different people, the Hopewell, sprouted in the Ohio Valley. They built immense ceremonial centers, some of them connected by actual highways; they sculpted into a sacred landscape the effigies of great birds, lizards, and fantastic beasts; and they imported extraordinary quantities of luxury goods from the Gulf of Mexico to the Canadian shores of the Great Lakes. But in AD 400, the Hopewell suddenly became extinct, and the last of the Adena followed three centuries later.

A dark age of two hundred years ensued until city-states such as Cahokia erupted into existence throughout the Mississippi Valley. Yet shortly after AD 1300, they all lay in ruins. On the other side of the Mississippi River, contemporaneous Hohokam and Anasazi construction engineers laid out a vast irrigation network across the Southwest, where they raised monumental religious arenas and multistoried building complexes before vanishing into prehistory.

There are only a few books about the Mississippians or Anasazi available for nontechnical readers, fewer devoted to the Hopewell, and virtually none about the Adena. More important, nothing on the market describes these prehistoric cultures for what they really were: lost civilizations that rose and fell while Socrates lived in Greece and Charlemagne ruled continental Europe.

Their picture is somewhat obscured by an outmoded archaeology resistant to new discoveries, particularly those made by other disciplines that tend to jeopardize long-held academic dogma. A typical example is the Kensington Rune Stone, a granite boulder covered with Norse inscriptions dated to AD 1362 and found on a Minnesota farm in 1898. Consistently denigrated as a ludicrous hoax by establishment archaeologists, its pre-Columbian provenance has been affirmed repeatedly by professional geologists and epigraphers. As the renowned science writer Arthur C. Clarke noted, "When a distinguished scientist states that something is possible, he is almost certainly right. When he states that something is impossible, he is very probably wrong."[2]

Out of nowhere does such academic resistance arise more fiercely than from any suggestion of overseas visitors to our continent before 1492 from either the Occident or Orient. Even the foremost specialist in Southwest prehistory, Emil W. Haury, admitted, "[U]nfortunately, the archaeologist tends to think of his materials as cultural isolates, a state of mind that discourages relating people in geographically adjacent areas in a graded fashion."[3] Devoted as the defenders of pre-Columbian purity may be to their cause of cultural isolation, a growing body of fact, as convincing as it is abundant, and much of it authenticated by real scientists, leaves no doubt that ancient America was hardly sealed off from the rest of the world.

Notwithstanding crumbling paradigms, we must take into account to what extent these foreign influences were responsible for the advanced societies that flourished here so long ago. Did, in fact, those early civilizations entirely escape such alien impact, or were they actually indebted to contemporaneous forces from the Old World?

Answers presented in the following pages do not fit any preconceived theories, but instead emerge of their own accord from evidence that has accumulated as the story develops. The result is a mosaic of proofs that amount in the aggregate to a prehistoric drama as rich as it is unsuspected. It is offered here, in at least the general outlines of its totality and the controversial roots of its being, for the first time to modern readers. It is their legacy, part of their story as Americans. They may shine it as a new light on the deep past, or, should they choose not to shrink from disturbing parallels, use the past to illuminate their own time and that to come.

One

ADENA, FIRST CIVILIZERS
OF NORTH AMERICA

A warm breeze ruffled the surface of the water as I struggled to pull on my wet suit aboard our pitching pontoon boat overcrowded with deckhands, sonar and radio monitors, photographers, and coils and lines of rope and cable. Three other divers, some already half suited-up, huddled around a sonar operator, peering intently at his blinking scope.

"Sure looks unnatural," one of them exclaimed. "Maybe we found it this time," another said.

"You're almost directly on target," a distorted voice crackled over the receiver that our radioman held at the bow of the boat.

I squinted up into a bright sky to see the single-engine Cessna humming in an oval pattern about 2,000 feet overhead.

"But you're beginning to drift," the spotter pilot warned.

"Hear that?" the radioman asked our captain sitting at the helm.

"Nothing I can do about it until Doug gets back. Take a bearing between Korth farm in the west and Bartel's Landing in the east."

Our position lay in an area we previously avoided as unlikely, until a sonar hit brought us to the northwest quadrant of the figure 8–shaped lake—an area nearly three miles long and two miles wide—on this late spring afternoon.

At first sight, our vessel and its passengers might have seemed ordinary enough—save for a dozen scuba divers and news media cameramen aboard. Occasionally, our spotter plane swooped low over the flotilla of mixed pleasure craft to elicit a cheer from the several hundred spectators gathered on shore in expectation of our success. Well, at least the weather was cooperating for once.

Earlier attempts to search this singular body of water in the dead of a Midwestern winter—when we hoped in vain for exceptional underwater clarity—rivaled Antarctic expeditions for hardship. Those extreme adventures had been only part of many previous searches going back to the beginning of the twentieth century, when the lost pyramids of Rock Lake morphed from mythology into archaeology.

Pioneers trekking across southern Wisconsin during the 1820s first learned of them from Winnebago Indians living for time out of mind along the tamarack shores. A more ancient people were said to have venerated their lunar goddess at a sacred site long since engulfed by the waters that received their name from Tyranena, the Temple of the Moon. In native oral tradition, it and other sunken structures were referred to as "rock teepees," which lent themselves to the modern name Rock Lake.

For almost eighty years, they were dismissed as indigenous fantasy by the citizens of Lake Mills, the town that grew up nearby—until a severe drought in the summer of 1900 lowered water levels sufficiently to reveal at least one of the legendary pyramids. Its unexpected appearance was cut short by weeklong thunderstorms that ended drought conditions, but also brought disrepute to local observers, who were accused by neighboring townsmen of perpetuating a hoax.

Although most Lake Mills residents thereafter distanced themselves from the controversy, divers, professional scientists, and enthusiastic amateurs from across Wisconsin and beyond undertook the underwater exploration of Rock Lake for its elusive structures. Their search began in earnest during the 1930s, when Victor Taylor, a Lake Mills school teacher, arranged for state funds to look for sunken remains, without success.

Undaunted, other investigators took up the hunt where Taylor left off throughout the pre- and postwar periods and into the 1950s, 1960s, and 1970s. Occasionally, they caught glimpses of intriguing hulks lying in the murky depths, but nothing clear enough to convince the skeptics.

By 1987, I, too, had fallen victim to the quest, devoting myself almost full time over the next several years to its pursuit. After perhaps fifty diving expeditions at Rock Lake, under all kinds of conditions—some of them more hazardous than they should have been—I had interested enough fellow researchers to organize a thorough sonar sweep of the lake bottom. The new technology bore fruit almost at once, and we combined it with aerial observation to put our divers right on the target.

Now, in 1991, we felt we were on the verge of discovery. Douglas Gossage, a master diver from Lansing, Illinois, was the first over the side to verify the sonar contact visually. No one else would be allowed to dive there until he finished photographing it with his waterproof video camera. A filmy matrix floating "in solution" over the lake floor was highly sensitive to the slightest disturbance; one misplaced kick could conjure obscuring billows of silt that foiled all attempts at photography. We could not have a gaggle of excited divers spoiling a delicate operation that had been some four years in the making. They would have their chance, one by one, to descend to the structure after Doug completed its photographic documentation.

As the day's chief organizer, I would be the first diver after him to visit the target. I anxiously followed his air bubbles breaking the surface in a long line. He had already been down there at least thirty minutes, so we all assumed he must have been seeing something of significance. The sonar continued to reveal, beneath our keel, a large, solid, uniformly rectangular feature 60 feet beneath, where nothing of the kind was known to exist. No pier or harbor works could have been built this far from shore.

An iridescent-orange marker buoy abruptly popped to the surface about 20 feet from our pontoon boat. Ten minutes later, Doug's head appeared closer to the buoy. He looked around in surprise, almost annoyed that we had drifted farther than he expected. Tearing off his facemask and spitting out his mouthpiece, he yelled at us across the waves, "We're almost on top of it!"

Impatient for further explanations, I struggled into the rest of my wet suit, then fell backward off the deck into the water. Rising to the surface after my plunge, I kicked in the direction of Doug's marker buoy, as he wearily swam past toward our lurching pontoon boat. Rising waves made conversation difficult, so we exchanged hand signals instead—"Everything's okay." Reaching the buoy, I pulled down my facemask, bit onto the mouthpiece, and dived, following the yellow Mylar line secured to the bottom of the marker.

The growing turbulence at the surface transformed instantly into an emerald-green calm penetrated only by the bright yellow line that I circled and touched, though did not grasp, with my left hand. The taut line angled down into the depths, its unseen terminus vanishing beyond the 27-foot clarity of the water, unusually good for turbid Rock Lake.

At 30 feet down, my head, hands, and torso froze, though my legs and feet were still briefly comfortable as I descended through that boundary between the warm water sitting atop the colder realm beneath. This is the thermal clime, and it separates more than extreme water temperatures. The bright green lake grew suddenly dark, as well as frigid, making me feel as if I'd floated down into another dimension. Still guided in my descent by the yellow line, I tried to see where it ended on the bottom.

As my vision strove to adjust to the drastically dimmer light, directly below me spread what appeared to be a white, paved highway going across the brown, mud floor of the lake. Sinking to about 20 feet above the imagined road, I could see that it was not flat, but instead rose at a 15-degree angle to a central ridge with evenly sloping flanks on either side. Moments later, I came to rest atop the structure in a kneeling position on its uncut, undressed stones. Only its uppermost portion was visible. The rest lay concealed beneath silt and mud.

Everything about the structure bespoke human intent, from its symmetrical proportions to the triangular configurations at either end and its north-south orientation. Swimming over the top, I guessed the feature's overall length to be about 100 feet. More than anything else, it resembled an elongated tent. I kicked around the structure several times, until a comprehensive image of it was clear in my mind and my air ran out. I reached around to pull on the reserve tank valve, and my lungs gratefully refilled with air. Rising slowly to the surface, I glanced down again at our somber discovery fading in the diminishing visibility.

Back on the surface, I found myself surrounded by more than a dozen vessels—some of them belonging to the expedition—all crowded with excited men, women, children, and reporters. Television cameras followed my weary progress back to the pontoon boat, where we reaffirmed our protocol permitting one diver at a time to descend on the contact.

"Did you find the lost pyramids of Rock Lake?" a reporter yelled at me across the water.

"We found *something*," was all I could manage.

Even then, I was reluctant to believe that the monumental structure lying 60 feet beneath the surface had actually been built by human hands during what must have been very long ago, at a time when the bottom of Rock Lake was dry land. We later learned that a valley had been carved by a retreating glacier near the close of the last Ice Age, 10,000 years ago, when a small pond or tarn was deposited.

Due to isostatic rebound caused by retreating glaciers, Wisconsin's southern region fell at the rate of 1 foot per century, allowing a large river that formerly ran west to east just north of the little valley to spill into it. Water levels rose very slowly over time, until the river eventually emptied itself to become Rock Lake. At some early stage in this geologic process, when water levels were 60 feet lower than they are today, someone undertook to create what Winnebago Indians still remember as the Temple of the Moon.

That information helped to date it, according to James Scherz, professor of surveying and environmental studies at the University of

Wisconsin, Madison. He demonstrated that the structure sat near the lake's edge about three thousand years ago. Even so, his time frame seemed excessively ancient for the kind of social organization required to raise such a monument. Public works projects such as this one resulted only through a hierarchy of labor, building technology, and tool production and a uniform system of measurement exclusive to civilization.

As far as archaeologists knew, southern Wisconsin was sparsely inhabited by primitive hunter-gatherer tribes during the so-called Early Woodland Period, around the turn of the first millennium BC, before bow-and-arrow weapons were invented. Still, Professor Scherz pointed out, the geological evidence was clear and unequivocal. The sunken Temple of the Moon was no anomaly. Identical counterparts just as old still exist in Ohio, Kentucky, West Virginia, Pennsylvania, Maryland, and New York, and as far north as Heritage Park, Michigan. They are among the surviving infrastructure of North America's first civilization.

Archaeologists named it after the Adena plantation at Chillicothe owned by Ohio's sixth governor, Thomas Worthington. It was here that an unusual mound was professionally excavated in 1900 by William C. Mills. Grave goods he retrieved were unlike any artifacts from other ancient earthworks—in fact, he knew at once that the skillfully wrought pendants and ceremonial axes belonged to an entirely distinct culture. As director of the State Archaeological and Historical Society, Mills had no difficulty convincing fellow professionals that the structure he found represented a type site. It did indeed signify a whole new phase in our country's prehistory—the earliest phase of its kind.

As its investigation continued and expanded throughout the twentieth century, and especially when radiocarbon dating became available after 1949, the profound importance and strangeness of the Adena gradually emerged. The civilization showed no signs of development but seemed to appear full-blown around 1000 BC, largely in the Ohio Valley, although traces spread from the Atlantic seaboard to the Upper Midwest and the Minnesota shores of the Mississippi River. Carbon-14 dating also showed that the Adena was a particularly venerable civilization, expiring about AD 700 after seventeen centuries of existence. Such longevity speaks to its success.

These revealing time parameters were possible thanks to Willard F. Libby, professor of physical chemistry at the University of Chicago, who invented radiometric dating, which uses the naturally occurring radioisotope carbon-14 to determine the age of organic materials. Libby found that the radioactive decay of carbon-14 is equivalent to an exponential decay expressed in years going back as far as sixty centuries into the past from AD 1950. Radiocarbon dating additionally charted the developmental course the Adena followed from their abrupt emergence beginning three thousand years ago to their florescence some seven centuries later and gradual decline after AD 400.

But who were these people? Their identity had actually been known long before they were rediscovered by archaeologists in the early twentieth century. The first modern scholar to learn of these premiere civilizers was Henry Rowe Schoolcraft (1793–1864), one of early America's most important scientists and explorers. Schoolcraft's many achievements included his account—the first ever written—of an exploration of the Ozarks, and discovery of the source of the Mississippi River at Lake Itasca. The nearby Schoolcraft River, the first major tributary of the Mississippi, was named in his honor. Later, he was commissioned by Congress to write the most comprehensive reference work on Native America. The result was *Historical and Statistical Information Respecting the Indian Tribes of the United States* in six volumes, composed between 1851 and 1857. He was especially fitted to undertake such a challenge thanks to his years of first-hand experience with numerous Native American tribes as a leading ethnologist and years as an Indian agent fluent in Ojibwa. During his extensive travels across the continent, Schoolcraft learned from Delaware elders:

> [T]he oldest tribe of the United States, of which there is a distinct tradition, were the Alleghans. The term is perpetuated in the prin-

cipal chain of mountains traversing the country. This tribe, at an antique period, had the seat of their power in the Ohio Valley and its confluent streams, which were the sites of their numerous towns and villages.[1]

They may originally have borne the name of *Alli*, or *Alleg*, and hence the Indian versions, *Talligewi* and *Allegewi*. By adding to the radical of this word the particle *hany* or *ghany*, meaning "river," Schoolcraft described the principal scene of their residence, namely, the Allegeny, or "River of the Alleghans," now called "Ohio." The word "Ohio" is of Iroquois origin, and of a far later period, having been bestowed by them after their conquest of the country in alliance with the Lenapees or ancient Delawares.

Doubtless, these Alli or Alleg were the same people labeled Adena by Victorian Era archaeologists. In *The Mound Builders*, anthropologist Robert Silverberg observes that "this band of people of great size forced its way into the Ohio Valley about 1000 BC, it seems. . . . Perhaps there was a small elite of round-headed giants dominating and ruling an existing long-headed Ohio Valley population." John Heckewelder, among Moravian missionaries, engaged in converting the Delaware around Philadelphia, Ohio, during the early 1800s, wrote of the long-extinct Alleghans after learning about them from his Indian parishioners: "Many wonderful things were told of this famous people. They were said to have been remarkably tall and stout (i.e., robust), and there is a tradition that there were giants among them, people of much larger size than the tallest of the Lenape."[2]

Adena burials commonly yield the skeletal remains of both men and women of extraordinary stature, often well above 6 feet, occasionally approaching 7 feet. The sudden, unheralded appearance of the Adena following the previous and primitive Archaic Period represented a major break with the immediate past. Pottery making was unknown before the Adena, whose abilities had reached a high degree of skill from the outset of their existence, as attested by dozens of cord-decorated vessels retrieved mostly from burial mounds. These vessels are not crude, insignificant affairs. Some are more than 1 foot across and 18 inches deep, proof that the potter's art had already developed beyond its elementary stages. Other grave goods include smoking pipes decorated with mostly animal effigies; copper bracelets and necklaces; beads of semiprecious stone; and finely crafted chert axes and crescents.

But it was the several kinds of monuments they erected that made the greatest physical impression on America's ancient landscape. The structure lying on the bottom of Rock Lake belonged to what may have been many hundreds or maybe thousands of identical stone mounds that covered the eastern half of our continent from the Atlantic coast to the Mississippi River. Virtually all of them were dismantled by early settlers, who used the uncut but carefully chosen and heaped stone as handy quarries for the construction of wells and walls. All shared some basic features, which not only identify them as part of a common culture, but imply they were built at roughly the same time. If so, then the Adena were a very populous people.

In any case, every linear or ridgetop mound covered a long trench in which were laid varying numbers of honored dead with their burial accoutrements. Over them, stones selected for size were heaped and symmetrically organized into a tent-shaped structure resembling an elongated pyramid 102 feet long and 12 feet high and wide. Its orientation was either north-south or east-west, and each funerary mound, without exception, was built in close proximity to water—near a stream, on a river bank, on a lake shore, or at the sea coast. French fur traders traveling through Wisconsin in the late eighteenth century came upon a deserted lake that local Fox Indians avoided as the Hills of Death, a reference to numerous pyramids that dotted the shoreline. The French henceforward called the lake Butte des Morts, as it is still known today. The few stone mounds that survive are often overlooked as drumlins, heaps of gravel and rock debris left behind by retreating glaciers ten centuries ago.

Mainstream archaeologists still dismiss the Temple of the Moon in Rock Lake as a glacial remnant, even though underwater surveys completed by Professor Scherz in 1994 demonstrated that the structure lies in a perfect 1,500-foot alignment with another subsurface feature (Bass Rock Bar I) to the south and a freshwater spring due north. Thirty-eight years earlier, archaeologists gave road builders outside St. Paul, Indiana, the go-ahead to bulldoze a stone mound they were sure was only a drumlin. Yet, to a student at the state university, James H. Kellar, the formation seemed unnaturally symmetrical, so he dug into the structure before construction engineers could demolish it.

As he later reported, "The first hour of excavation settled any doubt there may have been regarding the origin of the stone pile." Thereafter known as the C. L. Lewis Stone Mound, it is a sepulchre containing fourteen separate human burials laid out on an east-west axis, together with the cremated remains of twenty-two other people covered by a beautifully woven grass mat. They were accompanied by dozens of copper ornaments and funeral offerings, including an impressive gorget (a political authority badge suspended around the neck), which Kellar recognized as a "diagnostic Adena form." The same burial yielded a ceremonial dagger. "The large blade exhibits exceptionally fine workmanship," Kellar remarked. "The material is light pink in color and is unlike any of the cherts or chalcedonies from any of the better-known aboriginal quarries."[3]

Recognition of the C. L. Lewis Stone Mound expanded the Adena's known borders beyond the Ohio Valley in all directions, and prompted archaeological reconsideration of similar structures previously ignored as natural formations. As was observed by William Webb and Raymond Baby, leading authorities on the Adena at the time of Kellar's find,

> From these investigations in New York, Maryland, Alabama, and Georgia, we must conclude that the cultural influence of Adena spread far beyond its area of concentration in the Ohio Valley, and was a potent influence on much of the eastern half of the United States about 800 years before the beginning of the Christian Era

and for perhaps 700 years thereafter. It is an easy prediction that the influence of this highly developed earthwork- and burial-mound-building people, who had the first agriculturally based economy in this country, will be detected over much of the eastern United States, as the knowledge of prehistory increases, and the data become better organized and integrated.[4]

Their prediction spread westward during the early twenty-first century, when two stone mounds were found on the Minnesota-Wisconsin border. The first one discovered had been inadvertently preserved (at least partially) a hundred years before, when Highway 61 was built along the banks of the Mississippi River skirting the small village of Camp Lacupolis. The structure was inadvertently covered over at its middle, allowing the southern and northern ends to protrude from either side about 10 feet beneath the road. One and a half miles east, in the wooded hills above the old riverboat town of Reads Landing, another stone mound has been largely overwhelmed by soil deposition sliding down the decline for the past several centuries, but its upper-most section is still plainly visible. Both structures are 102 feet long and located near dry streambeds that long ago flowed into the nearby Mississippi River. The Camp Lacupolis mound's orientation is north-south; its Reads Landing counterpart, east-west.

The Minnesota stone mounds are almost directly across the Father of Waters from a far-better-known site built by the Adena. At some period in their history, they arrived at Lake Pepin, as this section of the Mississippi came to be known. Although not really a lake, despite its name and appearance, it is actually the widest stretch of the river. Some two and a half miles across and twenty-two miles long, the thirty-eight square miles it covers must have seemed very special to these early visitors as the river suddenly opened up into an oceanlike vista.

Beginning about ten thousand years ago, at the end of the last Ice Age, the area in question had been created by a delta of the Chippewa River spreading across the gorge of the Mississippi at the southeastern end of the lake. Because of its steeper grade, the smaller Chippewa was able to bring in more glacial debris than the Mississippi could carry away. The delta became a natural dam, backing up waters to form Lake Pepin. Today, in addition to its great natural beauty, this area of the Mississippi River is one of the world's premiere bald eagle sanctuaries.

The magnificent predators must have been in even greater abundance here during preindustrial times. Now, as they likely did then, they congregate along the high bluffs on either bank to hunt fish that are abundant in the waters where the river broadens. The presence of so many birds of prey doubtless made a deep impression on the first visitors to Lake Pepin, to whom the eagle certainly meant great spiritual power. The large flocks of eagles must have convinced Adena explorers that this extraordinary stretch of the Mississippi River was a sacred area worthy of settlement.

At the northern entrance to Lake Pepin, early American pioneers were startled to find a far older effigy of gigantic proportions adorning a high hillside near Hagerstown. Local Dakota Sioux Indians knew nothing of the design, save that it had been created by an "alien people" some time very long ago. In 1902, Minnesota archaeologist Jacob V. Brower speculated, "[T]he intention seems to have been to represent a bow and

Fig. 1.1. Wisconsin's Crystal Eagle Mound

arrow drawn to shoot toward Lake Pepin. But some of the stones representing the bowstring are displaced." Although he was correct about the feature's orientation, it less resembles a bow and arrow than a white eagle flying toward Lake Pepin, where the sacred birds gathered around the holy shores of the Mississippi.

A signpost erected at the site by the state of Wisconsin reads:

> Modern archaeologists think the boulders may form a bird effigy, but no one has reached a definite conclusion. Although it is an old, well-known landmark, its origin and age are unknown, and it is not part of the Indian lore of this region. Boulder alignments made by Indians exist in other states, but this is the only one known in Wisconsin. Was it made by Indians? Is it a bow and arrow or a bird? It remains a mystery.

The colossal geoglyph still exists, although not in pristine form. Originally, it comprised what must have been tens of thousands of white crystals, each one about the size of a baseball, carried from all over the Midwest. Perhaps ancient visitors brought the rocks from throughout their far-flung commercial network. In any case, the Hagerstown effigy was a crystal eagle oriented precisely in the direction of Lake Pepin. Glistening in direct sunlight, it must have been visible for several miles. Even now, it can be seen from at least as far as Red Wing, on the Minnesota side of the river.

Over time, the geoglyph was robbed of its crystals. They were replaced with ordinary rocks, which are still laboriously whitewashed each year by members of a local Boy Scout troop to preserve a semblance of its original configuration. Though it hasn't maintained its authentic crystalline condition, at least something of the eagle effigy continues to survive.

Its only known counterpart is found, strangely enough, eight hundred airline miles away, in central Georgia, southeast of Atlanta, at the edge of the Oconee National Forest, in Putnam County, six and a half miles north of the small town of Eatonton. When Charles C. Jones Jr., an investigator for the Smithsonian Institution, visited the site in 1877, the geoglyph was located on a plantation, where it crowned a high ridge near the headwaters of the Little Glady Creek.

Jones found the Georgia eagle effigy mound

> . . . composed completely of white quartz rock gathered from the adjacent territory. Most of these boulders are of such size that they could have been transported by a single individual. For the removal of others, two or three persons would have been requisite. These boulders were carefully piled one above another, the interstices being filled with smaller fragments of milky quartz. Into the composition of the structure enters neither earth nor clay.[5]

He measured

> . . . the height of the tumulus at the breast of the bird being between 7 and 8 feet, its altitude thence decreasing toward the head and beak,

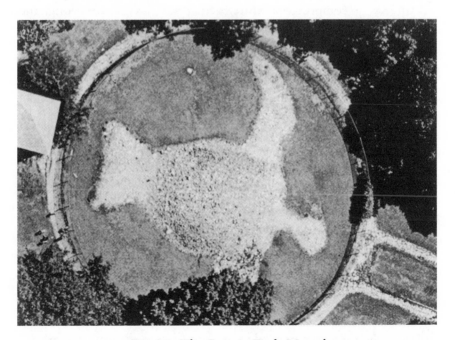

Fig. 1.2. The Georgia Eagle Mound

where it is not more than 2½ feet high, and also toward the extremity of the wings and tail, where it has an elevation of scarcely two feet. Measured from the head to the extremity of the tail, this structure is 102 feet long. The proportions of the head, neck, wings and tail are cleverly preserved. That this tumulus was designed to typify an eagle, we think may be affirmed with some degree of confidence. Its antiquity is evidently very considerable.[6]

Also in Putnam County, perhaps three miles north of the Eatonton zoomorph, Jones found another eagle effigy overlooking the Oconee River on a high ridge. "Like the former," he reported, "it is composed wholly of boulders of white quartz rock collected from the hill on which it stands. The entire length of the structure, from the crown of the head to the end of the tail, is 102 feet and 3 inches."

Although the three effigies are not identical in configuration, they have been standardized in all other respects, notwithstanding the enormous distances separating the Wisconsin site from that of Georgia. All three were composed of white rock crystal, are 102 feet long, and located on high ridges overlooking rivers. Even though the Oconee does not connect to the Mississippi, the widely separated geoglyphs appear to have been the expression of a single, common culture.

Yet it seems remarkable that Adena structures from the Upper Mississippi and the bottom of Rock Lake to Georgia should all have been built according to the same canon. This separated though rigidly adhered to conformity suggests a tightly unified society whose members did not gradually radiate outward from its heartland in the Ohio Valley, but instead marched in lock-step together from the Atlantic coast in large numbers, sweeping across the country all the way to the Mississippi River in a relatively short time. Yet if their literally thousands of stone mounds fell mostly to the construction needs of eighteenth- and nineteenth-century pioneers and farmers, the Allewegi earthworks suffered even more widespread devastation. All but a handful survive, yet excavation of their interiors opened unexpected panoramas on a lost world.

One of the most revealing of its kind was also among its most scandalous. The spectacular find was literally covered up, reburied by state officials, who allowed the earthwork to lapse into total neglect. When found some seventy years ago, it made headlines for months and was described by a feature article in prestigious *Scientific American* magazine. Yet today, the site is remembered only dimly by a handful of amateur antiquarians. Even most researchers in Ohio, where it is located, are unaware of its story.

It began in April 1939, when two mailmen interested in local prehistory examined a so-called Indian mound on the property of John Malsberry, just west of New Benton, in the northeastern part of the state, between Akron and Youngstown. Malsberry family members were early-nineteenth-century settlers in the area and the site's historic owners. They planted evergreen trees over a section of the mound, which was partially leveled for planting. Occupying a commanding position atop a hill overlooking the town of New Benton, the earthwork was almost 100 feet long, and stood 6 feet high.

The inquisitive mailmen alerted amateur archaeologists Willis H. Magrath and Roy Saltsman from neighboring Alliance to the curious structure that might, they speculated, contain a significant burial. After three weeks of laborious, careful digging, their suspicions were more than verified. The four men uncovered a tomb the likes of which had never been seen in America before and not met with since. Its reconstruction revealed that the heap of soil concealed the remains of a circular building originally 70 feet in diameter and nearly 20 feet high. Its perimeter was surrounded by a stone wall comprising large sandstone slabs set end to end. Behind this outer stone wall was another of timbers regularly interspersed with wooden pillars, only the burned stumps of which still survived.

A single entrance opening on the tomb's west side was wide enough to allow access for only one person at a time. Prehistoric visitors would have passed into a straight corridor about 30 feet long, flanked on either side by wooden posts. This corridor opened up into a central space occupied by a fire pit. Just beyond it lay the gigantic effigy of a spread eagle composed of white sandstone slabs laid on a slightly raised platform of molded clay. With a wingspan of 32 feet, the figure measured 16 feet from tail to its clearly beaked head that was aligned with the rising sun. An aperture engineered in the roof allowed a single ray of bright, late-morning light to illuminate the white figure, making it gleam in the darkness of the tomb.

Across the middle of the great eagle's north, or left, wing, and ceremoniously laid out, were the remains of a man. A human female skeleton reposed in the middle of the opposite wing. Both were stretched out on raised biers surrounded by rich burial offerings of copper, flint, and bone. These included a pair of spool-shaped copper earrings lined with buckskin; a platform pipe (the first found in northeastern Ohio); a musical instrument (a three-tube panpipe); and, most unique and curious of all, a hollow copper globe. Other burial offerings included quartz, jasper, chalcedony, mica, galena, bamboo, pipestone, banded slate, diorite, and hematite. Two smashed human skulls lay at the feet of the man; one at the woman's feet. A semicircular altar of rough stone stood southeast of the tomb's mid-point.

On the opposite side of the tomb, in the northwest, Magrath and Saltsman found another semicircular stone structure connected to a pair of walled rooms. Two smaller altars were in line with the man, and one with the woman, their number corresponding to the decapitated skulls present near each. Outside the corridor, on either side, were two bundle burials, and evidence of multiple cremation appeared in an organized arrangement on the north and south sides of the tomb.

On its north side, between the semicircular "shrine," or altar, and the eagle effigy's right wing was, according to Magrath, a "great stone grave." It contained the skeleton of an exceptionally large man. His skull measured in excess of 25 inches around, giving him a size-9 hat size. His thigh bones were nearly 21 inches in length. Although only his cranium and upper legs escaped destruction in the past by some ground-burrowing animal, they allowed subsequent investigators to determine that in life the man stood 6 feet, 10 inches. His was by far the largest of the tomb's seven skeletal remains.

Outside the bier lay a cylindrical column of dark organic matter, the remains of a food offering to the dead. Inside the "great stone grave" Magrath and Saltsman found what the *Youngstown Vindicator* described as an "odd five-legged swastika symbol"—a large, enigmatic glyph etched into a stone slab.

The enthusiastic amateurs immediately notified Dr. Richard Morgan, curator of archaeology at the Ohio State University Museum, where Magrath volunteered as a research associate and was already affiliated with the Society for American Archaeology. Dr. Morgan was interested in their discovery, and authorized a complete photographic study of it, supplemented by preliminary reports. Meanwhile, publicity generated by the opened mound attracted crowds of curious people, and too many of them began picking up souvenirs. Malsberry had his hands full trying to keep unwanted visitors away, and when an intact skull was trampled beneath the feet of a nighttime trespasser, the tomb was bulldozed for its own protection.

That was in 1939. No work has taken place there since. Most of its bizarre contents still lie buried beneath 3 feet of top cover, though the site itself has lapsed into virtually perfect obscurity. When *Ancient American* publisher Wayne May visited the North Benton location in 2002, he found it unmarked and undisturbed from the time of its pre–World War Two excavation. Yet the find made by Magrath and Saltsman was among the most extraordinary archaeological discoveries in the continental United States.

Of the three other stone avian effigy mounds in North America— those in Wisconsin and Georgia—the Eatonton, Georgia, figure bears the most striking resemblance to the North Benton eagle figure, defining a stylistic connection between both of these widely separated sites. The same people who built the Ohio burial mound appear to have been likewise responsible for the Georgia effigy, a parallel made all the more mysterious by the more than five hundred airline miles separating them.

Perhaps most peculiar of all the entombed artifacts was the hollow copper ball, an object too mysterious for explanation, but obviously the product of a technology beyond anything previously known in prehistoric Ohio.

Most Adena earthen structures were not only tombs, but also ceremonial centers and gathering places. The greatest survivor of them all is West Virginia's Grave Creek Mound, the largest conical earthwork in the United States, with an original diameter of 295 feet and standing 69 feet high. Approximately three million basketloads of soil, some 57 tons, went into the monument. It was encircled by a great moat of water 40 feet wide and 5 feet deep, giving the towering mound the appearance of an island in the sea. A causeway ran around the structure's base perimeter.

When treasure hunters dug into the mound during 1838, much of the archaeological evidence was lost. Enough escaped destruction, however, at least to provide a general understanding of its interior. A vertical pit dug from the top of the earthwork broke through the roof of a vault 12 feet long by 8 feet wide and 7 feet deep. Its walls were composed

Fig. 1.3. Grave Creek Mound in West Virginia (photograph by David Bornous, courtesy of Ancient American *magazine)*

of well-trimmed, upright logs that supported other timbers forming a ceiling. The vault had been hedged in and covered by loose stones, and contained two human skeletons, one of them surrounded by six hundred fifty seashell beads, plus a 6-inch long bone ornament.

An additional vertical pit sunk beneath the vault opened to another, virtually identical chamber 34 feet from the bottom of the mound. It enclosed just one skeleton of a man accompanied by more than two thousand disks finely cut from seashells, two hundred fifty pieces of mica, and seventeen bone beads, together with a collection of copper bracelets and rings weighing, altogether, 17 ounces. Doubtless this man and his two companions in the vault above must have been very special and powerful people to merit such an immense sepulchre, while the grave goods with which they were entombed bespoke the far-flung connections their culture enjoyed: seashells from the Gulf Coast, mica from the Carolinas, and copper from the Upper Great Lakes.

Grave Creek's close competitor in monumental drama is the Miamisburg Mound, the largest of its kind, in Ohio. Perched atop a 100-foot cliff, its base circumference measures 877 feet, with an original height of just under 70 feet, identical to its West Virginia counterpart, which it also resembles in its two burial vaults, one above the other. Construction engineers estimate that more than thirty-four hundred full-size dump truck loads would be required to duplicate the 54,000 cubic yards of earth that went into building the structure—a figure that helps us appreciate the magnitude of this material accomplishment by a preindustrial people.

Excavators in 1869 uncovered a layer of flat stones that overlapped like shingles to cover the roof of the upper burial vault; the tomb was found 24 feet beneath the apex. Similar evidence revealed that the Miamisburg Mound's exterior was originally faced entirely by stone, lending it a classic pyramid appearance.

Although smaller, the Criel Mound once stood as the centerpiece of a concentration of mounds and circular enclosures extending for eight miles along the upper terraces of the Kanawha River floodplain, in the vicinity of present-day South Charleston, West Virginia. Until the advent of the twentieth century, the sprawling complex comprised more than fifty mounds ranging in height from 3 to 35 feet. Their base diameters ranged from nearly 40 to 200 feet. The mounds were joined by ten circular earthworks, each one surrounding 1 to 30 acres, while an unrecorded number of stone mounds dotted the bluffs above the floodplain. Some eighty miles southwest of Grave Creek, precisely equidistant between two of the landscaped circles—each 556 feet across— the Criel Mound stood on a 173-foot base.

It lost some of its original 33-foot height when its top was leveled in 1840 to accommodate a judges' stand for horse races conducted around the base of the structure. During the next century, residential developers obliterated all the geometric circles and most of the mounds, save Criel and two others: the small Wilson Mound preserved in a nearby private cemetery, and an undersized specimen in neighboring Institute.

Before these losses, Criel Mound was excavated by Professor Cyrus Thomas of Washington D.C.'s Smithsonian Institution. In 1883 and 1884, he revealed an internal arrangement of log tombs covered by stones similar to other Adena burials, with the addition of abundant white ash, evidence of cremation. But Criel contained far more human skeletons: Two were found just under the top, and eleven more were discovered at the base, forming an unusual configuration. Ten skeletons had been laid out at precise intervals like the spokes of a wheel, their feet pointing toward the remains of an extraordinarily large man at the center of the circle they formed around him.

But Alleg accomplishments in monumental construction did not end with their prodigious mound-building program. When the first pioneers began crossing our continent two hundred years ago, they encountered a number of extensive, abandoned sites that local Indians claimed were built by a nonnative people exterminated in a series of wars long ago. These unusual locations, comprising stone walls of prodigious extent, dominated high hills with commanding vistas in all directions. To early Americans, fresh from their experiences in the War for Independence, the impressive structures were obviously designed as military installations. Hence, their designation as forts.

Much later, during the second half of the twentieth century, archaeologists were largely convinced that almost everything pre-Columbian was astronomically oriented somehow, and therefore insisted that the ramparts actually comprised celestial observatories built by the members of a family or two in their spare time.

A prime example of these ancient forts, now deemed observatories, survives not far from Lebanon, Ohio. Sprawling across a bluff 235 feet above the Little Miami River is a colossal network of stone ramparts covered with earth. Varying in height from 4 to 23 feet, the walls enclose 100 acres studded with conical mounds and crescent-shaped gateways. To level the top of the hill, raise these walls, and build interior mounds, prehistoric engineers moved an estimated 480,000 cubic yards of earth—enough material to fill a line of modern dump trucks stretching for more than two hundred miles. Clearly, such an immense public works project could have been undertaken only by a populous community whose members rated its massive construction as the utmost priority.

Fort Ancient, as it is known, is part of a state park comprising 764 acres of plant and animal life, and featuring two miles of trails through surrounding woodlands. The three and a half miles of walls left by an obviously gifted people define a gigantic precinct capable of enclosing perhaps twelve thousand people at a time. It is not known if such numbers ever assembled behind the enduring ramparts, but great multitudes certainly gathered there on certain occasions. Only a few burials took place within the enclosure, and these apparently contain the remains of dedicated sacrifices made when work was completed.

The site is made up of two main areas joined by a middle section connecting both with a limestone walkway. Extending for a quarter of a mile from the enclosure are parallel earthworks leading to a single, large mound.

Across the river, in a clearing, are limestone slabs arranged in the

35-foot-long configuration of a snake. A large, wood pole—a modern duplicate of the ancient original—stands at its head to cast a shadow along the length of the effigy on the morning of every summer solstice. An identical serpent image oriented to the winter solstice sunrise lies a short distance from the riverbank. Both effigies are currently on private property belonging to the Y.M.C.A.

According to official archaeological opinion, the impressive walls of Fort Ancient do not belong to an actual fort, as the first pioneer discoverers assumed, even though its modern name is still in use. The site, they argue, is a ceremonial sacred center never used for habitation or defense. Its master builders belonged to the Hopewell culture that began around 200 BC and came to an abrupt end six hundred years later. Still other academics claim the site isn't all that ancient either, but dates back only about ten centuries. Even the Hopewell are excluded as its builders to make way for "a Fort Ancient people," who supposedly perished through exposure to diseases brought by Spanish explorers in the 1500s. Few of these speculations find any material support; both radiometric dating and construction styles related to stone mound–building more certainly identify Fort Ancient and others like it as products of the Adena culture.

For example, Indian Fort Mountain—defended by eighteen walls, one of them 1,200 feet in length—three miles east of Berea, Kentucky, has been carbon dated to 580 BC, nearly four centuries prior to Hopewell beginnings. Another radiometric date from a different section of the site yielded the date AD 40. Doubtless, some archaeologists have mistaken tribal peoples who sometime later occupied Indian Fort Mountain and its affiliated structures for the Adena builders of the earthworks. Adding to the confusion are the overlapping time frames of the Hopewell and Adena: the latter raised their stone walls, while the former heaped up their own, very different earthworks.

Sadly for the advocates of Forth Ancient as an astronomical observatory, they are unable to point out any celestial alignments behind the walls. The crescent-shaped gateways there must have served other purposes. The precinct contrasts with the solar-oriented serpent effigies across the river. The discovery of a pavement near one of the walls in the narrowing middle section of the site, a feature found nowhere else in pre-Columbian North America, might have been a ritual path corresponding, perhaps, to the irregular gaps appearing in the enclosure, although we cannot rule out a military function: a causeway connecting long-decayed wood defense towers that once occupied the open gaps seen today. Finally, trees within the precinct were not cleared, making any kind of astronomical observations all the more difficult. There is a kind of plaza or open area near the south overlook, where general assemblies no doubt took place.

Fort Ancient actually represents one link in an extensive chain of stone enclosures spanning almost five hundred miles from the Mississippi and Ohio Rivers. At least fifteen similar, though smaller stone structures, all dating roughly to a common era, are known in southern Illinois, Indiana, Ohio, and Tennessee. Fort Hill, nearly fifty miles east of Fort Ancient, is practically as large. No one knows how many of these prehistoric ramparts, all located atop high bluffs overlooking rivers in thickly wooded areas, originally stood in the four-state region. Of their surviving number, Fort Ancient is the largest and most accessible.

Its counterpart may be visited just west of Manchester, in Coffee County, Tennessee. A small, but important and informative museum—imaginatively constructed in a building style of the ancient architects who designed Old Stone Fort—stands a few paces before the prehistoric entrance. The Adena built the original enclosure atop a near-island created by the confluence of two rivers. After the Duck cascades over a limestone-rich shelf of the western Cumberland Plateau, it approaches the Little Duck, and both drop 100 feet to scour deep gorges around the peninsula, causing thundering waterfalls and boiling whitewater rapids.

The site's northwestern walls skirt the Duck River for 1,394 feet, while its southeastern ramparts follow the Little Duck for more than

1,094 feet. These sections that parallel the rivers far below gradually move inward, away from both rivers, converging on each other in a pincerlike formation. Just before the walls meet at the northeastern half of the peninsula, they terminate to form a narrow entrance flanked on either side by two mounds. Referred to by archaeologists as *pedestals,* one is 35 feet across at the base; the other is 48 feet in diameter. They stand at the head of an L-shaped corridor running 120 feet into the fort.

The wall on the south runs almost perfectly straight for 2,116 feet, save to accommodate an outward bulge of the ridge. It and the northwestern and southeastern bulwarks are flanked by sections of open space at particularly steep proclivities where assault would not be possible. Enclosing more than 50 acres, the walls, averaging 4 to 6 feet in height, were built of a stone-earth matrix consisting of inner and outer layers of piled rocks and slabs filled in with a mix of soil, clay, and gravel. The result was an amazingly tough, artificial embankment that has endured, albeit in a ruinous condition, for the last fifteen hundred years.

Practically surrounding the fort is a deep ditch that gives the site a roughly rectangular outline. This prodigious moat, once as much as three-quarters mile long, is now a 4-foot dip. In other words, Old Stone Fort was long ago entirely surrounded by water, a condition afforded by the ditch connecting the Big and Little Duck Rivers. These construction details unquestionably define Old Stone Fort primarily as a military complex, notwithstanding current archaeological interpretation of it as a purely ceremonial arena or an astronomical observatory or both. If its low walls seem inadequate for defense, that is because they have lost much of their former ramparts over time. Examination of them shows that their ridges had been, according to the park's official guidebook, "worn down from traffic on top," most likely by warriors on regular patrol duty. The narrow, protected entrance; its "blind" (because L-shaped) corridor; and the absence of walls at inaccessible points self-evidently identify the entire site as an armed installation.

Its construction was undertaken around AD 80. During the next five centuries, the walls were built, repaired, and reconstructed. Then, just as suddenly as they appeared, the inhabitants quit the precinct around AD 550. These time parameters were confirmed in 1966, when the state of Tennessee commissioned investigators from the state university's department of anthropology to radiocarbon date charcoal found at the site. By so doing, they inadvertently demolished theories of "a Fort Ancient people" who were supposed to have flourished five centuries after Old Stone Fort, one of their alleged observatories, was abandoned.

Clearly, North America's so-called Indian mounds were not crude piles of dirt heaped up by primitive savages. They were instead expressions of applied geometry, materials handling, advance planning, design, an organized workforce, and construction skills—building feats to defy the passage of millennia, succumbing only to the greed and ignorance of modern developers. In these imposing structures alone, the Adena eminently met a number of qualifying criteria for traditional definitions of civilization: a system of weights and measures, division of labor, monumental architecture, and extensive commerce as evidenced by their grave goods from around the continent.

Adena cultural greatness is most apparent in these outsize public works projects, but it was not confined to such works. The same genius capable of raising such prodigious accomplishments as Grave Creek Mound or Fort Ancient was likewise adept at creating small-scale masterpieces of wonderful ingenuity. An extraordinary example was recovered from Indiana's C. L. Lewis Stone Mound. Excavators noticed that the skull belonging to one of the interred men featured a metal cap on his tooth. According to James Kellar, "A small copper object was found which was originally associated with an upper incisor fitted over the bottom to form a sheath-like covering."[7]

Subsequent examination revealed that the cap was not ornamental, but more resembled modern bridgework to hold the tooth in place. Archaeologists had discovered the oldest evidence of dentistry in the New World.

Somewhat more common finds include thirteen small, stone tablets recovered over the years from several widely separated Adena sites in Ohio, Kentucky, and West Virginia. Most were carved in fine-grained sandstone, but one is made of baked clay and another of limestone. The workmanship is of consistently high caliber, and the tablets are generally similar in style, but their differently executed, complex, interrelated designs imply a kind of lively expressionism or even geometrically abstract art hardly expected from prehistoric Americans. These tablets are all of a size to be held in the palm of the hand, because it seems they were also whetstones used for sharpening bone needles. It has been determined that the other engraved side was coated with paint, then impressed onto the skin of a person just initiated into a particular social group, perhaps a mystical cult or warrior class. The outlined figure was then pricked with the needle to make an identifiable tattoo.

This is no speculation: engravings of all thirteen tablets have paint residue. Pigments were produced from graphite, manganese dioxide, and red ochre, while sparkling, metallic gray was obtained from pulverized galena. Nor did the Adena neglect the plastic arts. During 1901, Ohio Historical Society archaeologists excavating Chillicothe's Burial Mound Number 21 found an extraordinary effigy pipe carved from local pipestone that had been quarried around the hills near Portsmouth. The

Fig. 1.4. Ink impression made by an Adena tablet (courtesy of Ancient American *magazine)*

10-inch-high figure is the realistic representation of a man dressed in what must be a faithful reproduction of Adena attire. Indeed, the pattern of his loin cloth seems similar to the dynamic designs associated with Adena tattooing tablets.

Remarkably, the figure depicts a clearly recognizable kind of deformity known as achondroplastic or chondrodystrophic dwarfism, a condition typified by a heavy-set, muscular body; stubby arms and knees; and a disproportionately oversized head. His swollen neck and limb joints portray, respectively, goiter and rachitis (rickets), common ailments suffered by chondrodystrophic dwarves. How such a person came to be portrayed is unknown, although another mound in Waverly, Ohio, did contain the skeleton of a dwarf, suggesting a particularly honored status. What the Adena actually thought of such people is beyond speculation, however. What we can know: the Chillicothe effigy pipe demonstrates that Adena artistic abilities were on par with their monumental building techniques.

The Adena were the first Americans to live in permanent settlements. Located near streams, these early villages were surrounded by circular earthen embankments about 5 feet high, and may have supported defensive works with stockades, although time has erased any trace of such conjectured walls. Family homes ranged from 15 to 45 feet in diameter with sectioned walls fastened to paired posts tilted outward and joined to other posts to form a conical-shaped roof, according to reconstructive research of archaeological investigators described by Baby and Webb. Domiciles were made of bark, dried grass, and wickerwork tied and perhaps sewn together.[8] The Adena were settled in such hamlets because they were also North America's first farmers. They cultivated plant foods including squash, sunflower, pumpkin, gourds, and possibly corn as part of their diet of raspberries, black walnuts, catfish, deer, elk, rabbit, turkey, grouse and rattlesnake, among others.[9]

In addition to their monumental construction and all that entailed, they developed agriculture, were familiar with astronomy, and mastered the fine arts. Although most of Adena culture has been

lost, archaeologists have succeeded in piecing together its broad outline from relatively few artifacts. These fragments nonetheless reveal
a populous society of settled farmers, far-ranging traders, innovative
artisans, and public works engineers who spread over the eastern half
of North America for seventeen hundred years. Their mystery, however, does not lie in their greatness or even in their demise.

Native American folk memory is replete with oral accounts of genocidal warfare during pre-Columbian times. Doubtless, these tribal recol-
lections refer to the extermination of enemy peoples through aggression
and assimilation. Survivors of such violence were absorbed into the victorious culture. By the time the first pioneers from Europe laid eyes
on the towering monument at West Virginia's Grave Creek during the
early nineteenth century, its builders had long since vanished into local
Indian lore.

Two

WHO WERE THE ADENA?

The real enigma of the Adena is their origin. They literally burst upon North America three thousand years ago as public works engineers, astronomers, and metalsmiths, the land's first farmers and potters. But they are far better remembered by a name inextricably linked with their most visible material achievement: the Mound Builders. Nothing in the development of America's Plains Indians, however, so much as suggests a connection.

For at least ten thousand years, the hunter-gatherers' way of life had reached its fixed plateau, as natural and venerable as it was rigidly conservative and unchanging. Then, around 1000 BC, an innovative and materially advanced people without precedent on our continent—culturally and physically removed from the indigenous residents—suddenly appeared in their midst. Even today, the pitifully few shreds of their material accomplishment highlight the Adena with bold relief against the backdrop of the Early Woodland Period during which they made their dramatic entrance into prehistory.

The Mound Builders stood out like aliens in the midst of tribal America's far more multitudinous native population. Their difference was deliberately accented by their preference for head elongation. Some male and female newborns of particular social classes—almost certainly ruling families and spiritual leaders—had their heads gently but firmly bound between a pair of cloth-covered cradle boards. As the infant

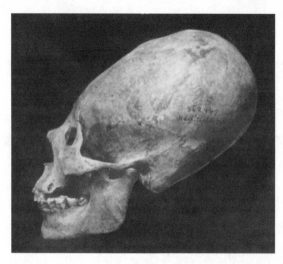

Fig. 2.1. A specimen of Adena head deformation

developed, its head grew into a desired, oblong shape, assuming its final configuration by middle childhood. The result was an ovoid skull, with the skin of the face pulled back so tightly that the eyes became crossed and extremely slanted, and the lips were withdrawn from the teeth.

Subjecting select young to such disfigurement was meant to distinguish them and their similarly deformed elite not only from the lower orders of their own people, but from outsiders as well. This form of identification was without precedent in the Ohio Valley, although Indian tribes, including the Chinookans of the Northwest and the Choctaw of the Southeast, copied Adena head binding much later. It was this practice that led Webb and Baby, the leading experts of their time, to speculate that the Adena must have traveled all the way to the Ohio Valley from the Valley of Mexico, where cranial elongation was all the rage among the Olmecs, the people who built Mexico's first high culture, beginning in the Veracruz area along the northeastern Atlantic coast. They introduced hieroglyphs, city planning, and all the other material arts associated with Mesoamerica.

Today, the Olmecs are perhaps most renowned for having created the colossal stone heads, some weighing as much as 20 tons, realistically portraying gruff-looking men wearing a kind of headgear suggesting the leather helmets of football players. Seventeen specimens, all of them buried, have been discovered so far. Carved from single blocks of volcanic basalt from the Tuxtlas Mountains, on the southeastern Veracruz Gulf coast in southcentral Mexico, they range in diameter from 10 feet to about 50 inches, but the characteristic that most concerns us here is their lack of any facial resemblance to forensic reconstructions of Adena crania. The former evidenced round, full, fleshy, thick-lipped features more reminiscent of West African blacks than of Native American Indians to most impartial observers. Adena heads (those not subjected to artificial deformation, that is) were precisely opposite: tall and lantern-jawed, with squarish ophryon, and beetling brows.

Although the Olmecs appear to have come into being as early as the late fourth millennium BC, more generally recognized are their most important event horizons at 1500 BC and 1200 BC. During both, they experienced major population and cultural surges, but by 400 BC, their civilization had collapsed. None of these defining time parameters coincide with Adena development, which begins in 1000 BC, experiences a florescence after 300 BC, enters a gradual decline around 100 BC, and terminates circa AD 700. Chronological comparisons between the Olmec and Adena do not fit.

Moreover, Adena artifacts bear no resemblance to anything in the Olmecs' material culture. The only commonality they seem to have shared was infant head binding, which is poor proof of connection, because numerous other peoples around the world—dynastic Egyptians, Australian natives of Tommen Island, Eskimo, Mayas, Incas, pre-Inca Peruvians, prehistoric Colombians, and so forth—engaged in the same practice. It is, in fact, the only evidence Webb and Baby submitted on behalf of their speculation for an Adena homeland in Mexico.

That they felt encouraged enough by the facts to search for Adena origins outside the Ohio Valley demonstrates the profound dissimilarity archaeologists observed between the Adena and the contemporaneous Woodland aborigines. Webb and Baby, nonetheless, undertook a proper course of action by endeavoring to find explanations outside North America when all lines of inquiry reached a dead end with the Plains Indians. Yet if Adena lineage cannot be traced back to Olmecs, then broadening our objectivity may reveal an ultimate source. Taking into account the unacknowledged maritime abilities of the ancients to extend their influences far beyond the limitations placed on them by conventional scholars, we may increase the number of possibilities for Adena origins by widening the search. From this vantage point of increased objectivity, we can observe what was taking place in the rest of the world when the Adena made their appearance, flourished, declined, and eventually disappeared. Parallels to their story, once freed from the nearsightedness of mainstream perspectives, might reveal the forces that brought the Adena into being and formed their culture.

Of all the major changes that transpired beyond the Americas just when the Adena arose circa 1000 BC, one event stands out: the simultaneous rise of the Kelts. Two hundred years earlier, they had been driven en masse from their primeval homelands in the Steppes of Central Russia—that fermenting cauldron of all Indo-European peoples—by catastrophic climate deterioration that was as severe as it seemed interminable. They were victims of a natural disaster that afflicted most of the earth's Northern Hemisphere, venting itself in conflagrations that incinerated the cities of Mycenaean Greece and Asia Minor, virtually depopulating much of the British Isles, and reducing Germany's Black Forest to a wasteland of ash and cinders. In far away China, the Shang Dynasty collapsed, while volcanoes of North America's Cascade Range erupted simultaneously, and asteroids the size of castles plunged into the Atlantic Ocean.

During 1997, an international convocation of leading geologists, astronomers, plant biologists, oceanographers, anthropologists, and archaeologists met in Cambridge, England, to answer a single question that had bedeviled scholars for more than a century: What brought the Bronze Age to its sudden and violent end? Economic or military theories had fallen short of a comprehensive explanation, but a consensus of interdisciplinary research at Fitzwilliam College showed that a massive comet made a close pass to our planet around the turn of the twelfth century BC. This comet rained down a barrage of meteoric material that shattered the high cultures of Europe and the Near East, shrouding their ruins with a dark age that lasted for the next three hundred years.

The global cataclysm had not spared the more remote, less civilized areas of the world. Relentlessly scourged by famine and drought, the Kelts fled from their devastated pasturelands in the Steppes to the less affected bogs and swamps of Poland. But population pressures that aggravated agricultural limitations and incessant hostility with resident tribes eventually prompted another mass migration—this time into southern Germany, where, around 1000 BC, the Kelts entered history as an identifiable people for the first time.

Archaeologists refer to this initial phase as the Hallstatt Period, named after one of the earliest known sites in Upper Austria's Salzkammergut, southeast of Salzburg. In 1843, Johan Georg Ramsauer, a salt mines manager, found an ancient cemetery near Lake Hallstatt. For the next twenty years, he employed careful excavation techniques and made detailed drawings of its 1,045 discovered burials.

During initial phases (Hallstatt A and B), the Kelts spread over Bavaria, Austria, Croatia, Slovenia, Switzerland, Bohemia, western Hungary, and parts of Slovakia. The first literary reference to them was made in 517 BC by the Greek historian Hecataeus of Miletus, who knew them as the *Keltoi,* after "barbarians," occupying Picardie, northeastern France, who called themselves Kelts. It was from this single branch that the rest of their ethnic group derived the name still applied to an entire people. How they referred to themselves in a pan-tribal sense, if they ever did, is not known. Although they were a composite of many tribes, they were never a politically unified people. Their commonalities were primarily racial, cultural, and linguistic, despite significant dialectical differences.

To the later Romans, they were the *Celtae,* and are still called Celts, even though the hard *k* in Kelt is more proper and less confusing than

Celt, which is also the name of a prehistoric tool of stone or metal that resembles a chisel or ax head. Keltic stock survives in the present-day peoples of Ireland, Scotland, Wales, and parts of the European continent, particularly in central Spain, northern France, the Netherlands, and Bavaria. Keltic languages are still spoken today in Irish and Scottish Gaelic, Welsh, Breton, and Manx. Seventh-century-BC Kelts who moved into France became the *Galli,* from *galno* for "strength." The English *Gaul* derives from the French *Gaule* and *Gaulois,* a rendering of Latin *Gallus.* Their description by the first-century-BC Greek geographer Diodorus Siculus could have been applied to the Kelts in general. He observed in his *Library of History,* "The Gauls are tall of body with rippling muscles and white of skin, and their hair is blond."

Poseidonius, a colleague of Diodorus Siculus, echoed the opinion of other classical writers, such as Strabo, Livy, Pausanias, and Florus, in portraying the Kelts as primitives given to extreme ferocity and cruel sacrificial practices. Early Keltic victories over the politically divided forces of Rome were attributed to the undoubted individual heroism of the barbarians as much as to their numerical superiority in combat. Another Greek contemporary of Diodorus Siculus, Dionysius of Halircarnassus, wrote that Keltic forces were less like armies than hordes. He writes:

> Their manner of fighting, being in large measure that of wild beasts and frenzied, was an erratic procedure, quite lacking in military science. Thus, at one moment, they would raise their swords aloft and smite after the manner of wild boars, throwing the whole weight of their bodies into the blow like hewers of wood, or men digging with hoes, and again they would deliver crosswise blows aimed at no target, as if they intended to cut to pieces the entire bodies of their adversaries, protective armor and all.[1]

In contrast to their barbarism on the battlefield, the Kelts were artisans of extraordinary skill. Manufacturing prodigious quantities of tools, weapons, luxury goods, and art objects—especially jewelry and metalwork—they bartered throughout Europe and the Near East. As early as pre-Roman times (Hallstatt B), their trade routes spanned Eurasia. This far-flung commerce has particular bearing on our investigation of prehistoric North America, because it represents an early clue to the mystery of Adena origins.

Even students of Keltic culture are mostly unfamiliar with Keltic maritime abilities, which made long-distance trade possible. The Kelts preferred vessel was the *curragh,* tanned animal hides stretched over wicker framework. These one- or two-man skiffs were eminently sturdy and seaworthy, so much so that they were still being made and sailed as late as the seventeenth century. Not surprisingly, the leather craft proved exceptionally resilient in rough water.

The late-ninth-century author of the Anglo-Saxon Chronicle told how "three Irishmen came to King Alfred in a boat without rudder from Ireland. . . . It was made of two and a half hides, and they carried with them food for seven days." The boat described here was a *coracle,* a larger version of the curragh, able to carry about a dozen people in the place of livestock alone or animals and other cargo.

Although coracles and curragh were the Kelts' most ubiquitous craft, they sailed substantially larger ships with tall masts of yards and cordage from which billowed leather sails. These held up against Atlantic Ocean winds far more successfully than the linen sails that equipped Mediterranean vessels. A single sail featured on Keltic merchantmen known as *birlinn* was sufficient to freight cargoes from the Hebrides to the Nile Delta and back again. Larger galleys were propelled by banks of forty oars, and held up to one hundred passengers and crew. The Kelts' maritime glory reached its height, however, in warships they fielded against Julius Caesar during the greatest naval battle he ever fought. In 55 BC, his attempted conquest of Britain was blocked by the presence of an immense Keltic navy. Veneti and Pretanian allies mustered two hundred twenty cruisers carrying sixty-six thousand men-at-arms.

In his *De Bello Gallico,* Caesar reported that the enemy warships were able to sail "upon the vast, open sea" (*vasto atque aperto mari*)[2] by tacking against contrary winds and riding out storms. The Keltic vessels, all of them larger than Roman counterparts held together with pegs and ropes, were stronger for their oak timbers fastened with iron nails and chains. They handled better and were more seaworthy, too, because the Veneti and Pretanian ships sacrificed cumbersome oars for stronger, steeper sides.

Even after the Roman occupation of Britain, Keltic marines known as *scotti* used their troopships to sack enemy coastal fortifications and take hundreds of prisoners at a time back across the Irish Sea to Dublin. Without doubt, the Kelts possessed deep-water vessels capacious enough to ferry tens of thousands of people across the Atlantic Ocean to North America. Such voyages were moreover in keeping with the Kelts' rambling nature. They were a restless people, always on the move, forever widening their trading networks, and fond of mass migration into new territories. Their renowned courage was not daunted by the sea; if anything, the oceans reinforced their religious beliefs, which included reincarnation.

As such, the Kelts' sudden expansion into Central Europe three thousand years ago and the no less abrupt debut of the Adena in the Ohio Valley at the same moment should at least prompt a comparison of these population groups to determine if something more than a temporal relationship existed between them. By so doing, the hidden forces that triggered the lost civilizations of America might be uncovered. From the beginning, on a fundamental level, parallels between European Kelts and American Adena show that the two are remarkably close. The former were described by contemporaneous Greek and Roman writers as tall and sturdy, with large heads, a characterization borne out by the well-preserved remains of a fifth-century-BC Keltic man found in an Irish bog. Recovered during 2004, he stood six feet, six inches tall in life. Nor was he an exception. Of the more than a thousand Keltic graves opened by Ramsauer in the nineteenth century, at least a third of the male skeletons were above average height.

So too, the Adena stood out from North America's indigenous populations with larger skulls, higher and broader foreheads, prominent jaws, and more pronounced cheekbones. Adena stature was much taller than that of the Plains Indians. Burial 54 in West Virginia's Cresap Mound belonged to an Adena man of remarkable stature: 7.04 feet. "All the long bones were heavy," observed Don Dragoo, Curator at the Carnegie Museum of Natural History's Section of Man, in Pittsburgh, "and possessed marked eminences for the attachment of muscles."[3] This is not to argue that Keltic and Adena skeletal remains are identical—they are not, but they are comparable. The skulls of both, for example, are brachycephalic—that is, relatively short or broad, with a width that is 80 percent or more of their length. Differences may be due to interbreeding that took place between foreign immigrants and indigenous peoples: the very few preserved human remains of the Adena might not represent an original genotype, but are almost certainly the later result of miscegenation, in which at least some of the Keltic genes survived.

The mid-twentieth-century archaeologist William A. Ritchie found that the earliest Adena skulls occur in New York State, suggesting a migration westward across our continent toward the Mississippi River. In other words, there was no Adena ethnogenesis in the Ohio Valley, from which its culture radiated outward across the lower Midwest. Instead, the

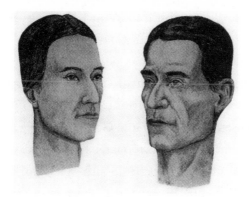

Fig. 2.2. Forensic facial and cranial reconstruction of a pair of Adena skulls (courtesy of Ancient American *magazine)*

progression of early to late brachycephalic skulls from east to west shows that the Adena entered America at the Atlantic Seaboard, then moved into the heartland of the country. This conclusion is underscored by a large number of stone chambers throughout northern New England.

Mainstream archaeologists argue that these are nothing more than root cellars dating back no earlier than colonial times, because their geographical distribution coincides with areas of European settlement during the seventeenth and eighteenth centuries. Though many if not most of the chambers date back to that period, others do not fit the colonial mold. The Pearson Chamber at Upton, Massachusetts, for example, is a 4-foot, 6-inch tall, 3-foot-wide stone corridor that runs for 20 feet into the side of a sloping hill. According to researchers J. W. Mavor Jr. and B. E. Dix, "five large adjacent boulders, each weighing 30 to 40 tons, form a portion of one of the walls. The chamber itself is a large stone 'beehive,' architecturally similar to some in Ireland and Scotland."[4]

Capped with a flat lintel, this beehive chamber itself rises 10 feet in a neatly corbelled form. Overall construction of the subterranean site is dry wall with local granite taken from bedrock and glacial boulders. Mavor and Dix were able to prove that the entrance and corridor had been deliberately aligned with an artificial stone mound on a ridge overlooking a valley and pond about a mile away. Suspicion of a relationship between the two structures revealed an orientation to sunset on the summer solstice. The most important Keltic deity was Belenus, "the shining one," a sun god, whose feast day was June 21.

The Pearson Chamber's astronomical alignment, to say nothing of its 30- or 40-ton stones, clearly disqualify it as a colonial root cellar, and its beehive design is a cultural fingerprint of the Kelts. Other stone chambers in Massachusetts, at Webster and Goshen, along with a Connecticut specimen near Montville, are far too large to ever have served as root cellars. A substantial stone chamber in South Woodstock, Vermont, has a floor measuring 10 feet by 19 feet and an entrance oriented to sunrise on the winter solstice. As the encyclopedist William R. Corliss observes,[5] "its very size militates against the root-cellar explanation."

Fig. 2.3. Three examples of New England's stone chambers (photographs by Scott A. Browne, courtesy of Ancient American *magazine)*

Scott A. Browne, in the June 2000 issue of *Ancient American* magazine, reports that around the turn of the nineteenth century a "Keltic dagger was found in Amesbury, Massachusetts, and in 1954 a badly encrusted bronze shield was pulled from the ocean at Marshfield, Massachusetts by a local fisherman."[6]

According to Andrew E. Rothovious, another *Ancient American* writer, "In the roster of North American sites that are not explicable in terms of mainstream archaeology, a high ranking has to be accorded to the Gungywamp Complex in southeastern Connecticut, which teams with puzzling stone-construction enigmas that hint of links with Keltic Europe." (See References, chapter 2). The location extends over some 300 acres in the northern part of the township of Groton to include buried chambers, walls, standing stones, three small stone bridges (each one marked by a standing stone), and circular foundations.

Rothovious continues:

> Unresolved as yet is the site's odd name, Gungywamp. It has suggested to be a Pequot or Mohican word meaning "place of ledges," or "swampy place," both of which accurately describe some parts of the site. It is also said to signify "church of the people" in Old Gaelic. In 1654, the fur trader, John Pynchon, at Springfield, in central Massachusetts, wrote to John Winthrop the Younger, governor of the New Haven colony, which stretched along the entire north shore of Long Island Sound, asking about "a stone wall and strong fort . . . made all of stone, which is newly discovered at or near Pequot"—as the Gungywamp area was then called—"there being many strange reports about it."[7]

What reply Winthrop Junior made to Pynchon, if any, is not known. In any case, Pynchon's inquiry in 1654 is clear proof that at least the major portion of the Gungywamp stonework antedates the coming of white settlement in the seventeenth century. I am convinced of the falsity of the archaeological establishment's dismissal of Gungywamp as a "Colonial" oddity and an "eccentric New

England farmstead." The site was never a farm. It is highly unsuitable for farming, and early settlers had neither leisure nor motive for erecting stonework follies in the wilderness.

Corliss concurs, "Actually, Gungywamp Hill is so heavily wooded and so far from reliable water that farmers probably avoided it anyway."[8] Rothovious continues:

> The first feature of interest is the large stone chamber, one of two intact ones remaining on the site. It is large enough to have 17 adult persons fit comfortably inside. Behind the huge boulder which forms the right-hand side of the entrance is a hidden, underground stone chamber of beehive shape. A stone tube 3.5 feet long and 9 inches in diameter focuses the sun's rays on the entrance of the hidden chamber on the days of the spring and fall equinoxes. The seven, one-ton slabs that form the chamber's roof are of a rock with a high density of garnet that appears to magnify the intensity of the sunlight that enters through the stone tube.
>
> Like all other shaped stones within the Gungywamp Complex, this one bears no signs of working with metal tools, rendering Colonial European origin extremely improbable.[9]

Better known than Gungywamp is Mystery Hill. Although renamed "America's Stonehenge," it shares little if anything in common with Britain's foremost Neolithic monument standing on the Salisbury Plain, but it does suggest a Keltic presence in southeastern New Hampshire. It, too, is a complex of chambers, passageways, standing stones, a stone circle, even a so-called sacrificial table—a rectangular slab with a groove running uniformly around the inside perimeter. Larger quarried slabs weigh from 2 to 50 tons, far heavier than anything required of a root cellar or equivalent Colonial structures.

An early-nineteenth-century farmer, Jonathan Pattee, was the earliest known owner of the site, and at least some of the structures owe their existence to him. Others do not, however, as borne out by a spread of radiocarbon dates taken at various locations throughout Mystery Hill, ranging 3,475 and 2,995 Years Before Present (YBP) to 1,250 YBP and AD 520. Though the earliest date precedes the start of Hallstatt A and the birth of the Adena by nearly five centuries, 2,995 YPB coincides perfectly with both seminal events. The older period probably reflects a preconstruction, Paleo-Indian presence in the area as shown from a campfire's charcoal deposits. The year AD 520 does not match any pertinent event horizon, but 1,250 YBP marks the close of the Adena culture.

These comparative dates of Keltic and Adena history occurring at Mystery Hill are reinforced by three inscribed stones discovered at the site. The first specimen, found in 1967, was engraved with an Iberic text dedicated to Bel—that is, Belenus, as translated by Dr. Barry Fell, president of the Epigraphic Society. Eight years later, he and the property owner, R. Stone, were investigating the same chamber in which the so-called Bel artifact was recovered when Stone found another tablet, this one in an adjacent wall. It read simply, *Dedicated to Bel.* Later, in 1975, while setting up a fallen monolith, workers noticed a Latin inscription on the side that had faced the ground. It read *XXXVIIII LA,* or "Day 39." During the Roman Era, Beltane, an annual festival dedicated to Bel, took place on the thirty-ninth day of each year. Appropriately, four upright monoliths in a circle of five are oriented nearby with the sun's position at the solstices; the fifth, or North Stone, marks the meridian. "The antiquity of Mystery Hill inscriptions could now be confidently set at about 800 to 600 BC," Fell concludes, "and it was clear that Goidelic [Gaelic-speaking] Kelts were the occupants at that date, and, in all probability, the builders, too." These proofs aside, the physical resemblance of northern New England's chambers to Keltic versions in Western Europe is, in many instances, extremely close.

As Corliss rightly observes, "If the Upton Chamber and its associated mounds were located in Europe, most archaeo-astronomers would not hesitate to declare that here was an ancient chamber built by an astronomy-wise culture." In any case, the mere discovery of these look-alikes where early Keltic settlement in North America would have most logically taken place—that is, not far from landfall on the Atlantic coast—tends to support their ancient authenticity.

Though none of New England's stone chambers may be identified as Adena, the hilltop enclosures within and without the Ohio Valley cannot escape such a designation. They were mostly raised during the Hopewell period, but differ so significantly from that culture that they cannot be associated with it. The forts' construction technique of intermixing stone and wood with earth is a recognizably Adena, not Hopewellian, building trait. Their resemblance to ancient Old World defensive works is especially pertinent to our examination of Western European influences operating in prehistoric North America.

Many Kelts resided in *oppida,* fortified settlements atop strategically located hills. An outer bulwark of stone slabs and earth-gravel filling in timbers was referred to by Caesar as a *murus Gallicus,* or "Gallic wall." The layout and even configuration of Germany's Heuneburg hill fort situated between two tributaries of the Danube is remarkably similar to Tennessee's Old Stone Fort embraced more closely on either side by the

Fig. 2.4. A Keltic hill fort in Bavaria, northwest of Munich

Big and Little Duck Rivers. Other *oppida* at Zavist in Bohemia, Ireland's Dun Ailinne, Mont Beuvray in France, Portugal's Citania de Sanfins, and Numantia in northeastern Spain are all much the same, and are often indistinguishable from their contemporary Adena counterparts.

Clearly, the same spirit of military construction was alive on both continents at the same time. No less remarkably similar are the mortuary structures that typified each people. The Adena are, after all, referred to as the Mound Builders. Their earthworks contained central, log-frame chambers for the dead surrounded by rough embankments of stone rubble. Keltic burial mounds featured precisely the same, otherwise unique internal arrangement, as exemplified at Vix, Chatillon-sur-Seine, in France; Germany's Hochdorf tomb, outside Stuttgart; and Magdalenenberg bei Villingen, Schwarzwald-Baar-Kreis.

Fig. 2.5. This on-site sketch of an Ohio Valley Adena burial mound as it was excavated during the mid-nineteenth-century documents the tomb's log-and-stone construction. This illustration is publicly displayed at Vienna's Voelkerkunde Museum.

Fig. 2.6. Excavation of a Keltic burial mound outside Saltzkammergut, Austria, reveals its log-and-stone construction.

The simultaneous appearance alone of externally similar earthworks among Adena and Kelts should warrant suspicions of at least some kind of a relationship between them. But when we learn how their apparent affinity extends inside the mounds to identically configured sepulchres, that relationship is no longer in doubt. These sepulchres join the oppida, or hill forts, and stone chambers on both sides of the Atlantic Ocean to argue persuasively for a Keltic-Adena connection.

A no less cogent correspondence appears in the Kelts' massive, rectangular precincts. Archaeologists are uncertain about the function—whether military, ceremonial, or sacred—of these complexes, and typically refer to them as sanctuaries. Writing of a well-preserved example at Buchenberg, Starnberg, in Bavaria, Salvatore Michael Trento, director of New York's Middletown Archaeological Research Center, describes how "the regularity of the ground plan indicates that strict specifications were used to lay out the sacred structures." The same standardized measurement is evident at virtually identical formations—even to their dimensions—within the Adena sphere of influence. Like their Keltic counterparts, the perfectly surveyed enclosures are invariably located near rivers, such as the 31-acre, 1,320-foot-long rectangle at the confluence of Sugar Creek and the White River in Ohio.

Comparison of these Keltic and Adena sites is made all the more remarkable by their rarity on both continents; in Western Europe, they were built only in southern Germany and Normandy during the fourth century BC, just when the same sacred spaces appeared in North America.

But even these convincing material parallels find additional support in one of the great but generally unrecognized mysteries of prehistoric America. As early-nineteenth-century pioneers began developing the Ohio Valley, they obliterated most Adena mounds they encountered during the process of clearing new farmlands. But some of these old earthworks revealed a surprise. When the venerable monuments gave way to shovel and plow, settlers occasionally left standing a primitive kind of furnace. On inspection, they found nodules of smelted iron inside, amid heaps of white ash, the result of very high temperatures. When questioned about the furnaces, local Indians claimed to know nothing about them or recalled tribal myths of the *Yam-Ko-Desh,* the "People of the Prairie," an ancient race of giants who built the mounds and were responsible for all kinds of strange magic that got them into genocidal trouble with ancestors of the Ojibwa.

Dismissing such folk traditions as so much childish fantasy, modern anthropologists and archaeologists emphatically deny that any Native Americans ever understood metallurgy, particularly iron working. Because their denial is an article of faith, no university-credentialed scientist in any related discipline has visited, much less seriously investigated, Ohio's alleged furnaces, thereby relinquishing the issue entirely into the hands of avocational antiquarians. These dedicated, if less accredited, amateurs have nonetheless uncovered sufficient evidence about the anomalous furnaces to warrant examination.

William Conner, a former reporter for Ohio's *Columbus Dispatch,* has been researching them since 1963. "I knew American archaeologists weren't world-class authorities on pit furnace iron making," he was quoted in *Ancient American* magazine[10] "because all of the known sites were in the Old World. So, I wrote to a British historian of metallurgy,

Leslie Aitchison. Studying photos and descriptions of the Overly furnace I sent him, Aitchison identified the remains as 'almost certainly' those of a pit furnace." The Overly Furnace that Conner mentions refers to just one of approximately one hundred thirty iron-producing pits scattered throughout south-central Ohio. Others may yet be found there.

"Neither the magnitude nor the capability of the prehistoric iron industry in America will ever be known, even approximately," declared Arlington Mallery, a professional engineer who investigated the ancient furnaces after World War II.[11] Although he did much to publicize the mystery, Mallery had his predecessors. Reporting for an 1820 issue of *Archaeologia Americana* magazine, Charles Atwater was the first observer to document the discovery of an indigenous furnace, when a conical mound near Cillicothe was demolished. Another excavated mound that had been built around one of the old, anomalous structures was described by F. W. Putnam in 1883.

"The long tunnels, or flues, as we are inclined to call them, still retain their form perfectly," he stated, "and on the floor of each is a layer of fine ashes." Some late-nineteenth-century antiquarians could not bring themselves to believe that the furnaces were actually iron smelters, but thought they were more likely signal beams. Clyde E. Keeler and Bennett E. Kelley, writing in a 1971 *NEARA Newsletter,* pointed out that the furnaces had often been discovered in mounds, because such a surrounding structure kept in heat and provided a ramp for laborers to carry bog-iron ore and fuel. Also, the sides of a surrounding wall or embankment allowed direct access into the furnaces. "Observation signal fires," they reasoned, "would never have been built five feet deep down in a furnace-like structure buried in a mound."

Many other smelters were found along stream banks, an improbable location for signal fires. The furnaces were not properly identified until 1949, when Mallery announced they were iron smelters. "When I climbed Spruce Hill to examine the ruins of the ancient stone wall there," he later recalled, "I came upon piles of ancient iron slag, and immediately began a search for the ancient iron furnaces in which the slag had been produced." Over the next two years, he and his associates found twenty smelters.

For the first and last time, mainstream archaeologists addressed the issue, insisting, without condescending to offer any contrary evidence, that Mallery had mistaken prehistoric furnaces for Colonial lime kilns. The identity of these furnaces as iron smelters is nonetheless beyond question, if only for their residue of charcoal, slag, green-glazed rocks, cinders, baked clay, thermally altered cobbles, and iron nodules—materials not generally found together in lime kilns. When not discovered inside mounds, the furnaces are commonly located along stream banks (handy for cooling and tempering processes), or on hill slopes to take advantage of windy conditions necessary for creating intense fires for high temperatures.

The pits themselves are simple affairs, oval-shaped, with a flue, as Putnam reported, extending upward from the top, either in the center or to one side. Many are either buried inside mounds or in close proximity to Adena earthworks, so their construction by the redoubtable Mound Builders seems certain. But when amateur archaeologists removed charcoal for radiocarbon analysis, they were surprised to learn that the furnaces were dated to AD 1640, plus or minus one hundred years. This period is especially troubling, because the mounds that enclosed the iron smelters were themselves dated to two thousand and more years ago.

The Ohio Valley had not been settled yet by the mid-seventeenth century, when only a handful of French fur traders visited the region. No evidence exists to show that they ever engaged in building smelters for making iron. A few Frenchmen could not have been responsible for at least one hundred thirty furnaces. Indeed, historical iron production did not even begin in the Ohio Valley until 1803. The buried smelters were as much a surprise to early American settlers as they were to local Indians, who were utterly unfamiliar with iron making or any form of metallurgy. Additional carbon-14 examination produced a still higher, no less unrealistic date for the furnaces: AD 1750.

Amateur archaeologists investigating the pits, lacking instruction in radiometric procedures, almost certainly removed materials improper for carbon-14 analysis, resulting in meaningless time parameters. Only after the furnaces are professionally assessed will Ohio's mysterious smelters find their correct dating via carbon testing. Until then, however, sufficient physical evidence is at hand to credibly establish the furnaces' provenance. Their design alone identifies them as ancient, because iron smelters used by American Colonists or sixteenth- and seventeenth-century Europeans in the New World were far more advanced than the specimens dug out of the mounds.

According to Conner,[12] "evidence is entirely lacking that these furnaces were built and operated by early Ohio pioneers. The technology represented by these furnaces was long obsolete in the early 1800s." The specific kind of metallurgy these furnaces serviced, however, leads directly to their makers, users, and origins. They were engaged in the production of something called *bog iron*.

As Corliss explains, "this is a variety of limonite [iron ore] found in bogs and swampy areas, where decaying vegetable matter acts upon iron salts to form spongy nodules and sheets of the ore." Much of Keltic life was conducted in and around bogs, where human sacrifices were made and bog iron was manufactured using precisely the same type of archaic smelters found throughout the Ohio Valley. In fact, the Kelts ushered in the Iron Age as skilled smiths, who produced weapons, tools, cauldrons, and various implements of the metal that replaced bronze. Iron was more valuable to them than gold, which served primarily decorative and religious purposes. "Much of the newly prepared metal was traded in the form of bars on the Continent," writes Miranda J. Green in *The Celtic World*. "In Britain, they were the so-called currency bars named after a passage in Caesar's *De Bello Gallico* (v. 12), where he refers to the Britons using iron bars as a form of currency."[13] At least one currency bar was removed from the Ohio Haskins' Mound, which also contained a furnace and an iron ax head. Mallery himself removed a 62-pound cast-iron bar from the Arledge Mound near Chillicothe, Ohio, in 1948.

Fig. 2.7. Arlington Mallery holds a long tube of iron slag he excavated from an Adena mound in the Ohio Valley.

When the dwarf effigy pipe cited in chapter 1 was removed from its burial mound, excavators found that "the specimen is covered with a deposit of iron ore, which appears in small blotches over the entire surface of the specimen, the one side of the face and body being more densely covered with it than the other parts of the pipe."[14]

The respected archaeologist Cyrus Thomas, reporting for an 1884 issue of *Science* magazine, described a triangular, North Carolina burial pit 48 feet long on each side, with a base of 32 feet, but especially remarkable for iron objects in the right hand of a male skeleton. Thomas was able to personally examine four of the "implements," ranging in length from 1.5 inches to 5 inches. This longest specimen "is, without doubt, part of the blade of a long, slender, cutting or thrusting weapon of some kind; as a sword, dagger, or large knife."[15] Other artifacts included a small iron chisel or celt, found under somewhat similar conditions in a mound in the same section. Thomas concluded:

[W]e cannot ascribe the presence of this metal to an intrusive burial. The people who dug the pit, deposited here their deceased chief or man of authority, and placed around him and those buried with him the pipes, celts, axes, engraved shell gorgets and other implements and ornaments, undoubtedly placed here also the pieces of iron. . . . That this burial pit was made by the same people who erected the mounds of this region cannot be doubted.

An Adena earthwork in the area, the Nelson Mound, yielded an iron celt and the fragment of an iron blade, according to Dr. Gunnar Thompson. He went on to state that "many of the ancient iron tools found in the Ohio Valley were manufactured by a process called *cladding*. Northern European smiths developed the process in which thin sheets of metal were welded together to form a tool of substantial strength. Tests at the Battelle Memorial Institute verified that Mallery's Ohio Valley artifacts were made by the *cladding* process that predated the 17th Century Colonial period."[16]

Many of the prehistoric smelters, which made such objects possible, were found at a prominent hill fort in Ohio's Ross County, where its collapsed walls, originally two miles long, amounted to some 200,000 tons of cut limestone. The prehistoric builders had carried this prodigious tonnage 400 feet up a steep incline from a nearby quarry. "For the furnaces at Spruce Hill to produce celadon glazes on sandstone, or hard-baked mortar," Conner argues, "metallurgical temperatures had to have been achieved in them. The sandstone itself is highly refractory [resistant to melting], so glazed surfaces on stone fragments at Spruce Hill must have come from the clay which is less refractory."[17]

Conner's discovery confirms antiquarian John Haywood's 1823 report concerning Spruce Hill: "On the inside of the wall there appears to have been a row of furnaces or smith's shops, where the cinders now lie many feet in depth."[18] Kelts worked the same kind of bog iron in smelters contemporary with and identical to furnaces discovered inside Adena mounds and hill forts, those ancient American oppida. "The Ohio pit furnaces," Conner believes, "are the most significant evidence for the pre-Columbian presence of Europeans in North America."[19]

Though skeptics may still dismiss Ohio's Keltic-style furnaces as nothing more than Colonial lime kilns that somehow managed to find their way inside three-thousand-year-old mounds, they are unable to deny the existence of at least one iron mine that was worked by ancient Americans. Their own colleagues, a Smithsonian Institution archaeologist, W. H. Holmes, and the city archaeologist for St. Louis, D. I. Bushnell, confirmed the pre-Columbian operation of an iron mine in Franklin County, near Leslie, Missouri. It had been brought to the attention of the Bureau of American Ethnology in early 1903 by modern miners, who suspended all further digging until their inadvertent discovery had been studied by scholars.

Acting on a report issued for the Bureau in April by Dr. S. W. Cox urging further investigation, Holmes, Bushnell, "and other St. Louis archaeologists" personally visited the site near the banks of Big Creek, a branch of the Bourbois River. They found that the prehistoric mine was around 100 feet wide, running approximately 150 feet long to a depth of about 20 feet. "As the work progressed," Holmes stated in the 1904 *Smithsonian Institution Annual Report,* "it was found that the ore had been fairly honeycombed by the ancient people, the passageways extending even below the present floor of the mine." The scientists recovered some one thousand stone mining tools—sledges, hammerheads, and wedges—that had been piled near the entrance. "It is apparent," Holmes wrote, "that the sledges could have had no other function than that of crushing and breaking up the solid masses of ore to be used in the manufacture of implements, or in opening new passageways through the ore body."[20] Although the Missouri mine lay outside the known cultural limits of the Adena, it was not so far removed from Mound Builders' country that its great importance would not have tempted them to cross the Mississippi River boundary for iron.

The ancient iron mine, smelters, and hill forts are echoed in tribal oral traditions. According to Dr. Gunnar Thompson,

Shawnee Chief Blackfoot retold an ancient legend of a race of white people who used iron tools and lived in Florida before the Spanish came. His tale was recorded during the 1800s and preserved in Henry Schoolcraft's *Indian Tribes of the United States.* An aging Cherokee chief, Oconostota, told antiquarians that bands of white people from across the Great Water had landed near the mouth of the Alabama River before moving inland. They built stone fortifications near the Highwassee River. After several years of warfare, the whites left the territory and settled in Kentucky.[21]

Kentucky was part of the Adena domain.

Three

THE KELTIC FINGERPRINT ON PREHISTORIC AMERICA

In Western Europe, beginning around 600 BC, the Kelts built a type of defended homestead known as a *broch*. In outward appearance, it resembled a single-tower castle or one of those squat smokestacks associated with nuclear power plants. Standing some 45 feet high, the dry-stone citadels employed a slightly tapering shape for structural strength, with walls 15 or more feet thick and a base diameter of about 40 feet. Each chieftain usually set himself up in such a fortress atop a prominence of some kind—a hill or cliff—from which he oversaw his tribal territories. The Romans documented more than five hundred such structures, most of them in Scotland and the western and northern islands.

Yet what appears to have been at least one Keltic broch stood in northern Ohio as late as the American Civil War. Early pioneers were awestruck by the Great Stone Stack, a massive tower made all the more commanding for its position near the edge of a hill ten miles from Newark, itself the site of truly gigantic earthworks. With its 500-square-foot base tapering upward to 45 feet, the Great Stone Stack shared a standard broch's dimensions and configuration. According to William Corliss, "the brochs are squat, massive, and lacking cement. The thick walls of the brochs consist of flattish stone slabs piled atop one another. These walls have to be thick to stand by themselves."[1]

His description matches exactly that of the Ohio structure. As some indication of its immense bulk, more than ten thousand wagonloads of stone were carried away from the stack when it was demolished in 1860 to build a dam at West Virginia's Tygart Lake. It was here, near the Monongahela River, in Marion County, that a prehistoric road ran for at least twelve miles between the Tygart Valley and Little Creek at Catawba. With an average width of 9 feet, construction consisted of macadamized stone and crushed mussel shell. Another 9-foot-wide road, this one at Corlea in central Ireland, dated from 148 BC, suggests a standardization of measurement the Kelts brought to North America, although their roads were made only of timbered planks.

The Kelts were themselves accomplished road builders, as evidenced by other examples south of Oldenburg, in German Lower Saxony. Parallels with the pre-Columbian Midwest go beyond these larger comparisons, however. Like many Adena, some Kelts, usually members of the druid priest class, practiced head elongation. The human head was, in fact, an object of cult infatuation for both people. Both were headhunters for whom decapitation secured honored trophies of victory in the field of battle. The esoteric side of such bloody business was the reciprocal, metaphysical belief that, as death cannot exist without life, so life cannot exist without death. This, at any rate, was the Keltic view.

The Roman historian, Livy (Titus Livius, 59 BC–AD 17) described in his *Ab Urbe Condita* how the Keltic Boii, after killing Postumus, a Roman consul, carried him to their chief temple, where his body was decapitated. The head was de-fleshed, and the skull was cleaned then mounted with gold to serve as a drinking cup in the honor of the gods. Human skull bowls have been retrieved from several Adena mounds, most notably at Kentucky's Fisher Site in Fayette County, where three were discovered in a single earthwork.

The Kelts were famous for painting their bodies with exotic colors and designs. The Romans referred to the Caledonian Kelts of Scotland as Picts, from the Latin past participle *pingere,* "to paint," but Kelts everywhere tattooed and painted their bodies. So did the North American Mound Builders. Their carved stone tablets were used to

Fig. 3.1. Ritual Adena drinking bowl made from the crown of a human skull

impress human flesh with complex, dynamic designs stylistically reminiscent of Keltic expressionism. (As mentioned in chapter 1, the paint residues found on most Adena tablets prove this use.)

Among the most emblematic of symbols shared by the Kelts and the Adena was the swastika. Though associated with numerous cultures around the world and throughout time, a Keltic rendition known in Ireland as *Crosóg Bríde*, or "Brigid's Cross," is identical to that found on Adena artifacts. Still used in rural areas by some Catholic households as protection from fire and evil, it is commonly woven of rushes or, less

Fig. 3.2. Keltic tombstone with a sauvastika (reversed swastika) at the center and a smaller Brigid's Cross near the top

frequently, straw, to form a central square from which four legs radiate outward.

Like all other swastikas, the Irish variant is a symbol of light and regeneration, as affirmed by its traditional creation every February 1, which, in pre-Christian times, was celebrated as Imbolc, the first day of spring, and was dedicated to the vernal goddess, Brigid. Roman church officials usurped the Keltic holiday (i.e., "holy day"), reconsecrating it *Lá Fhéile Bhríde*, or "Brigid's Feast Day," on behalf of Brigid of Kildare, a patron saint of modern Ireland, despite the fact that such a person never existed. (She was instead a Catholic fabrication.)

The swastika was and still is regarded as a sign of good luck by many Native American tribes—most famously, the Hopi—and the symbol appears to have been passed down to them from the Adena, its earliest known users. That their version was nothing less than the Crosóg Bríde illustrates Keltic imprinting on the prehistory of our continent.

Still more hard evidence was found by Fred Kingman in early 1994, while he walked the banks of the Wisconsin River with his metal detector, in search of nineteenth-century artifacts. Getting more than he bargained for, he unearthed a cache of Roman-era coins authenticated by James Scherz, professor of surveying and environmental engineering at the University of Wisconsin, Madison.

Due to its distinctly un-Roman appearance, a single specimen made of a copper alloy stood out from the other sixteen. Unlike the crowned, usually clean-shaven Roman faces surrounded by recognizably imperial details, this one portrayed the bull-necked, Germanic profile of a man with a large, drooping mustache, minus surrounding paraphernalia associated with the Empire. Diodorus Siculus wrote that the Kelts "let the moustache grow until it covers the mouth." If the piece in question was made by the Kelts, it can date only to around 100 BC, during the late phase of an epoch known as La Tene, when the Kelts minted their own coins. This period is significant, because it coincides with another late phase, that of the Adena, whose culture entered its decline at the same time. The Kingman find is not the only such discovery. According to Dr. Gunnar Thompson, a Keltic coin dated to roughly the same era was found in Champaign, Illinois.

The Adena were great weavers, surpassing the plain plaiting or basket weaving of their predecessors to excel in complex twining: techniques including twill; chevron; lattice or complicated bird cage; and over two and under, with a zigzag direction of the warp members in fine strands and the weft members crossing obliquely. Although no more than rare and fragmentary patches have survived the passage of time, enough original fabric still exists to prove that the Mound Builders arrayed themselves in magnificent attire.

The only original source material discovered so far for visual representation of Adena dress is a socketed, ceremonial ax head of stone removed from a typically conical mound near Wilmington, Ohio. On one side is engraved what appears to be a ritual scene of some kind in which a long-haired female figure dressed in a flowing gown makes a libation from a jar held in her left hand, while an alligator rears up before her. Behind the woman, a feline creature confronts a snake. A grid of twenty exact squares containing figures not unlike designs common to other Adena tablets has been inscribed on the left of the other side of the banner stone. To the right, walking away from the grid, is a male figure carrying what seem to be long-handled agricultural or mining tools, one in each hand—appropriately enough, considering the stone's configuration as an ax or mallet head. Surprisingly, the man wears long trousers stitched at the ankles and waist, plus a long-sleeved shirt or jacket with a high-necked collar and tailoring down the front. His attire, entirely unlike anything worn by Plains Indians, is remarkably similar to Keltic dress. The Gauls described by Caesar wore long-sleeved shirts or tunics made of linen and what he called *braccae*—long, woolen trousers. Like the Adena, the Kelts were master weavers, delighting in colorful, complex, expressionistic patterns that bordered on the abstract.

A majority of Adena tablets discovered so far depict stylized raptors, just as birds of prey were the creatures most often represented in Keltic art. In addition, helmets worn by Keltic warriors were often surmounted by representations of hawks or eagles, a style imitated by officers in the Imperial German Army before and during World War I. At least one Keltic helmet was designed in such a way to allow the hinged wings of its eagle to flap menacingly up and down when its wearer ran. We can recall, too, the Adena eagle effigies in Wisconsin and Georgia.

Another beast both the Adena and Kelts revered was the wolf, worshiped as a cult animal in their spiritual lives. Keltic holy men, the druids, believed they could infuse themselves and their initiates with the spirit of the wolf to become invincible in battle. These elite troops were known as the *Ulfheonar*—literally, "werewolves"—who transformed themselves in much the same manner that the later Norse of Scandinavia underwent special training as *berserker,* "were-bears," human warriors with the strength and fury of a bear. Certainly, one of the most remarkable finds ever made in the history of American archaeology was a spatula cut precisely from the upper jaw of a mature wolf. The object was recovered from inside Kentucky's Ayers Mound on Eagle Creek, near New Liberty, in Owen County. Next to the spatula was found the elongated skull of a large man whose incisors and canines of the upper jaw had been removed during his adult years. Some decay had settled in, but soon after went into remission. When excavators compared the neatly rectangular gap in the front teeth of the skull to the spatula, they were surprised to find a perfect fit. From this relationship, they deduced that the wolf-fang spatula had been inserted into the man's mouth at various times during his life, as part of a mask he wore while impersonating the animal or his attempts to meld with it.

By no means anomalous, wolf spatulas and carved jaws have been retrieved from other Adena mounds in Ohio and Kentucky. Doubtless, the earthworks that contained such remains were burials for shamans.

Adena reverence for this cult animal extended beyond elaborate costuming to include various artifacts, such as an effigy pipe with a stem fashioned to resemble a wolf's head (from the Englewood Mound, near Dayton, Ohio). Keltic artists likewise favored the portrayal of wolf

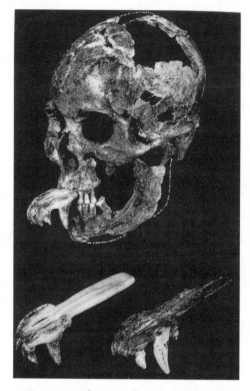

Fig. 3.3. Adena skull with wolf spatula

Above: Fig. 3.4. Restored Keltic carving of a wolf's head

Left: Fig. 3.5. Adena effigy pipe of sitting wolf

heads. An outstanding example is the baked clay mouth of a trumpet, the creature's jaws agape, from the *oppidum* of Numantia, Spain.

Adena shamans dressed not only as werewolves, but also as weredeer. Pairs of antlers fitted to headcaps or full-face wooden masks are more usual finds among the earthworks of the Mound Builders. Keltic art commonly portrayed a man wearing antlers, as most famously represented on the largest known example of European Iron Age silver work: on display at Copenhagen's National Museum of Denmark since 1891, the richly decorated vessel was fished from a peat bog where it had been an offering 2,200 years before near the hamlet of Gundestrup.

With a diameter of 2.26 feet and a height of 1.38 feet, the Gundestrup Cauldron is adorned profusely with the images of ritual activity, mystical symbols, and deities. Prominent among these is

Fig. 3.6. Antler headgear retrieved from an Adena shaman's burial mound in southern Wisconsin, displayed at the Wisconsin Archaeology Museum, Madison

Fig. 3.7. Sketch of human male skull wearing antler headgear found in the late-nineteenth-century excavation of a Keltic burial near Saltzburg, Austria (courtesy of the Voelkerkundemuseum, Vienna, Austria)

Cernunnos, depicted as a horned male figure accompanied by a stag wearing antlers very similar to his own. His name derives from the Gallic *carnon* or *cernon* for "antler" or "horn," and means The Great Horned One. He was the god of ceremonial and spiritual affairs; a shape-shifter who could meld with wild animals and imbibe their magical powers, which he used to help humankind—healing the sick; guiding the spirits of the dead to Paradise; insuring fertility for wives, livestock, and crops; or assisting warriors in battle.

That the North American Mound Builders similarly regarded their horned shamans is suggested by the deer-antler headgear and masks retrieved from Adena earthworks.

Cernunnos was portrayed elsewhere in Keltic art as a mature man with long hair and beard, never without his horns, and sometimes ferociously combined with other animals. Until the mid-eighteenth century, his likeness appeared above the banks of the Mississippi River on its eastern shore near the town of Elsah, Illinois. It was referred to by local Indians as the Piasa, and Father Jacques Marquette, the famous explorer, discovered its representation in a pair of large murals painted high on a limestone bluff. He wrote of his 1673 encounter:

> While skirting some rocks, which by their height and length inspired awe, we saw upon one of them two painted monsters, which at first made us afraid, and upon which the boldest savages dare not long rest their eyes. They are as large as a calf; they have horns on their heads like those of a deer, a horrible look, red eyes, a beard like a tiger's, a face somewhat like a man's, a body covered with scales, and so long a tail that it winds all around the body, passing above the head and going back between the legs, ending in a fish's tail. Green, red, and black are the three colors composing the picture. Moreover, these two monsters are so well painted that we cannot believe that any savage is their author; for good painters in France would find it difficult to reach that place conveniently to paint them.[2]

The mural was destroyed shortly after European firearms became available to resident Indians, who took potshots at it whenever they passed beneath in their canoes. Whatever portions survived such sporadic target practice were obliterated when the cliff face was quarried during the 1920s. A modern restoration at Alton, several miles southeast of Elsah, is not entirely faithful to Father Marquette's eyewitness account. Nothing like the original was ever reported anywhere else throughout Native America, because tribal Indians were not given to creating large-scale murals.

That the Piasa may have been a rendering of Cernunnos is likely when we consider the painting's portrayal of a bearded man (among Indians unable to grow facial hair) who wears deer horns, his body melding with a fish to indicate his association with the Mississippi River. Decisively perhaps, the Piasa's long tail winding "all around the body, passing above the head and going back between the legs" is precisely how the Keltic griffin was depicted in the south of Britain. Eventually, it became the national emblem of Wales. The Mississippi was, moreover, the western boundary of the Adena. In addition, the Mississippi Choctaw told of the Nahullo, an ancient race of red- and yellow-haired, white-skinned giants with tall horns. Could these have been the Kelts' druid-priests, who were known to wear deer-antler headgear while worshipping Cernunnos?

Although nothing of the Mound Builders' long-dead language is known, Algonquian speech, which once stretched from the east coast of North America across Canada to the Rocky Mountains, is peppered with Keltic cognates and loan words. (See appendix 2.) Appropriately, a pocket of Algonquian was centered in the Ohio Valley, the Mound Builders' heartland.

Perhaps the single most persuasive piece of evidence connecting them to the Kelts was found during an excavation of the greatest Adena earthwork, West Virginia's Grave Creek Mound, in 1838. The antiquarians dug out an oval, 1.5-by-2-inch sandstone tablet emblazoned with three lines of a mysterious script above a bird profile. Almost at once,

Fig. 3.8. Replica of the Grave Creek Tablet (photograph by Ida Jane Gallagher)

controversy flared around the artifact, which became the center of a debate concerning accusations of fraud and pleas on behalf of its authenticity.

A leading archaeologist of his day, Ephraim George Squier, condemned it as a planted fake, but was answered by Henry Schoolcraft, who championed the Grave Creek Tablet. Thirty-eight years after its discovery, the man who found it, Peter B. Catlett, stated unequivocally, "it was taken out of the stone arch in a wheelbarrow, and emptied outside. As for anyone placing the inscribed stone there, it could not have been done."[3] He was seconded by another eyewitness, J. E. Wharton, a Wheeling newspaper editor who accompanied the excavators. "Among the dirt was brought out the inscribed stone," he recalled, "and picked up by one of us from the loose dirt. A fraud was impossible. When I first saw it, it was being handled by Dr. Gans [Rudolf Gans, a local physician] with some of the earth still clinging to it."[4]

The Grave Creek Tablet was accepted for analysis by examiners at Washington, D.C.'s renowned Smithsonian Institution, where it disappeared, and has not been seen since. Only plaster copies of the lost original still exist. During most of the twentieth century, the discovery was all but forgotten until the notable British linguist and paleographer Professor David Diringer published *The Alphabet* in 1968. For the first time, its ancient Iberian tables enabled Dr. Barry Fell to attempt a translation of the West Virginia inscription, which he long suspected might have been created in a Keltic language. His suspicion was confirmed when, in 1976, he applied Professor Diringer's data to the three-line text, which read from right to left,

> *The mound raised on high for Tasach. This tile his*
> *queen caused to be made.*[5]

Fifteen years later, author of *The Decipherment of Southwest Iberic* and a veteran cryptographer for the Central Intelligence Agency, Donal Buchanan, brought to bear on the inscription his ancient language expertise and government training. His independent translation closely paralleled Fell's earlier version:

> *Tumulus in honor of Tadach. His wife caused this*
> *engraved tile to be inscribed.*[6]

These linguistic proofs were powerfully supported by another, very similar, West Virginia tablet found during 1931 by a schoolboy, Blaine Wilson, beside a tree stump near Triplett Creek, in Braxton County. He brought the 4⅛ by 3³/₁₆-inch micaceaous sandstone to his teacher, who passed it on to Innis C. Davis, director of the West Virginia Department of Archives, where the object is still stored. Like its Grave Creek counterpart, the Braxton Tablet is inscribed with three rows of South Iberic script, and the two share some vocabulary. They differ only in the Grave Creek Tablet's rectilinear style and the Braxton Tablet's curvilinear style. Returning to Diringer's *Alphabet,* Dr. Fell was able to effect a translation:

> *The memorial of Teth. This tile (his) brother caused to*
> *be made.*[7]

Fig. 3.9. The Braxton Tablet
(photograph by Ida Jane Gallagher)

Long before the Keltiberic identity of the tablets came to light, in 1923, a Kentucky geologist, William G. Burroughs, stumbled upon an inscription in Old Gaelic near Indian Fort Mountain, in Kentucky. Later, according to the Internet website *Timeline,* "A 'No Loitering' sign was engraved on rock at an ancient cemetery near Mill River, Massachusetts, in the Phoenician language called Iberian Punic."

Fifty-two years after the Burroughs' find, a third Keltic-language tablet was found by hiker William Johnson in the Genesee River bed, near Belfast, New York. A dense, granular stone measuring 2 inches by 3 inches, it features two lines of text that Dr. Fell once again recognized as Iberic. This text is translated as:

Confirmation. I have pledged to pay in full.[8]

Writing in the March–April 2008 issue of *Ancient American,* Ida Jane Gallagher observed:

Fig. 3.10. The Genesee Inscription (photograph by Ida Jane Gallagher)

The Genesee River was part of a water route used by American trading parties. The discovery of the Genesee Tablet on a known trading route suggests that native people led foreign traders to America's interior by following the waterways and the Indian paths that connected them. The St. Lawrence River and Great Lakes provided access to America's heartland from the Atlantic Ocean. The Susquehanna River empties into Chesapeake Bay, the Ohio and other tributaries flow into the Mississippi River that terminates in the Gulf of Mexico. Would this explain how Iberians reached Adena territory?

Such a route seems feasible, given the apparent impact on Native America of Kelts from Iberia and other parts of Western Europe they occupied. There was, in fact, a tribe in Portugal who called themselves the Keltiberi, or "Hidden Ones."

But what became of these North American Kelts? How and why did they vanish in the early part of the eighth century after some seventeen hundred years of influence from the shores of the Atlantic Ocean to the banks of the Mississippi River? Folk traditions of the Ottawa, Ojibwa, and Pottawattamie relate that their ancestors formed an alliance to kill the white giants, the *Yam-Ko-Desh*. Long before, these "People of the Prairie" had been "thicker than the leaves on a tree," and were too numerous to oppose. But now, their dwindling population facilitated their extermination. "Long ago, our fathers and our grandfathers killed off the Azgens, a white people from the Eastern Sea," Black Fish, chief of the Shawnees at Chillicothe, told Thomas Bullitt, a representative of Colonial Virginia, in 1773.

William Conner, that investigator of Adena furnaces, concluded in the December 2007 issue of *Ancient American,*

> The story of the Azgens [the Allgens, obviously enough] may reveal those who furnished the economic conditions suitable for the production of iron from the extensive bog ore deposits in the rolling terrain of glaciated south-central Ohio. . . . Among those who received the oral tradition [of the Mound Builders' annihilation] first-hand was George Rogers Clark and two U.S. Army colonels, who heard it repeated at Point Pleasant from Chief Cornstalk. He told of a 'race of white or light-skinned people, originally from the East,' who dwelt in large numbers long ago in the Ohio Valley. Chased by warring Red Men, these ancient white people fled westward to the Falls of the Ohio River near Louisville, Kentucky, where a bloody skirmish took place.[9]

The Indian alliance proved irresistible, and the surviving *Ron-nong-weto-wanca*, or "Fair-skinned Giant Sorcerers," as they were remembered by the Tuscarora, made a last stand below the rapids at Sandy Island. It was here that thousands of human skeletal remains were found by colonists well into the late eighteenth century. But the Falls of the Ohio massacre was only the Keltic Allgens' last stand in a war that raged from the Atlantic coast to the Mississippi River and beyond.

A late-nineteenth-century source entitled "A Prehistoric Cemetery," cited by *Ancient American* writers Ross Hamilton and Patricia Mason, relates:

[T]wo miles from Mandan [at the Dakota Missouri] on the bluffs near the junction of the Hart and Missouri Rivers, says the local newspaper, *The Pioneer,* is an old cemetery of fully 100 acres in extent filled with bones of a giant race. This vast city of the dead lies just east of the Fort Lincoln Road. The ground has the appearance of having been filled with trenches piled full of dead bodies, both man and beast, and covered with several feet of earth.

In many places, mounds from 8 to 10 feet high, and some of them 100 feet or more in length, have been thrown up, and are filled with bones, broken pottery, vases of various bright colored flint, and agates. The pottery is of a dark material, beautifully decorated, delicate in finish, and as light as wood, showing the work of a people skilled in the arts and possessed of a high state of civilization. This has evidently been a grand battlefield where thousands of men have fallen. . . . Five miles above Mandan, on the opposite side of the Missouri, is another vast cemetery as yet unexplored.[10]

A related killing ground was excavated in Ontario, east of Brockville, where "people of robust build" had all died violently, according to a statement released by the Canadian Museum of Civilization. Many had been decapitated, while others still had projectile points lodged in their bones and chest cavities. A prehistoric burial site covering 4 square acres is located near Conneaut, Ohio's Presbyterian church. Similar mass graves were found on the J. H. Porter farm outside the town of Northeast, Pennsylvania; at Cayuga, Ontario; and near Steubenville, Ohio.

Evidence for a genocidal conflict as recalled in Indian lore is profuse, although war was only the final blow for a people already in decline. A number of late Adena burials yielded the skeletons of men and women who were troubled by a variety of genetic deformities. A typical example was excavated from the Robbins Mound, in Boone County, Kentucky, where an Adena adult male had been afflicted with a badly withered left leg. The effigy pipe of a man suffering from dwarfism and goiter described in chapter 1 may also reflect the genetic decline that set in among the Adena. Were they, as so many cogent comparisons suggest, Western European Kelts?

As mentioned earlier, Adena is the modern, archaeological name for a people who called themselves the Alli, Algens, Azgens, or Allewegi. These appear to have been variants of identifiably Keltic names, such as Awena, Angwen, Aylwen, or Alroy. Moreover, these appellations were descriptive of the Adena themselves, because they mean, respectively, "poetic," "handsome," "fair brow," and "red-haired." Southern and central Wisconsin's Winnebago, or Ho Chunk, Indians actually possess an oral tradition of their twin heroes, the brothers Red Hair and Yellow Hair, and their legendary dealings with an ancient race of giants.

The only known European tribe phonetically similar to the Adena, Alli, or Allewegi was the Aige, or "Fire Folk." Because they inhabited the Eastern Mediterranean, the Aige seem less likely to have sailed for North America than their brethren residing in the British Isles or along the continent's Atlantic coastal areas of Normandy or Portugal. Indeed, the Grave Creek, Braxton, and Genesee Tablets all featuring Keltiberi inscriptions demonstrate that members of that tribe occupied parts of West Virginia and New York State more than two thousand years ago.

Revealingly, the names of most Keltic tribes ended in *i,* as did the Alli or Allewegi, suggesting that the Adena people were, in fact, a group of Kelts. Native American references to them as the *Yam-Ko-Desh* or *Ron-nong-weto-wanca* were Indian-language titles or descriptions more than the actual names of these foreigners, as indicated by their respective meanings, the "People of the Prairie" and "Fair-skinned Giant Sorcerers." Following their arrival in North America, the Keltiberi would have reorganized into a new tribe requiring its own designation, especially one that set apart the light-skinned newcomers from their darker hosts. They might have called themselves something like the Aylwen of the Fair Brow or the Red-haired Alroy, long since garbled over two thousand years of Indian oral tradition as the Azgen, Alli, or Allewegi.

Despite a large collection of convincing parallels between ancient America's Allewegi and the European Kelts, however, there are some important discrepancies. The early Adena stone mounds resembling colossal tents, upside-down ice-cream cones, and bread loaves do not show themselves in the Keltic sphere of influence. Perhaps the old stone mounds that appeared so suddenly around 1000 BC and without cultural precedent owed their inspiration to another people.

Nor has one example of the Kelts most iconographic artifact—the *torque*—been found in prehistoric America. The torque was a twisted ornament of precious or semiprecious metal worn around the wrist or neck. Although its precise significance is not understood, its far-flung reverence as a cult object is beyond question. Large numbers of torques were produced by the Kelts for over a thousand years, until their prohibition by the Christian church. Even so, no Mound Builder grave has yielded a single specimen.

Moreover, Keltic warriors were renowned for their silver ornaments and iron and steel weapons, although no such items have been found in any Adena earthworks. Yet a mid-nineteenth-century book *The Wonders of the World* by M. C. Reid describes the excavation of a ceremonial center at Marietta, Ohio, near the confluence of the Muskingum and Ohio Rivers, before it was demolished to make way for farmland. The site's Adena identity was confirmed by the presence on the opposite side of the Muskingum of "quite a number of stone mounds" on the high bluffs, and the skeletal remains, which belonged to man who stood about 6 feet tall in life, and whose "skull was uncommonly thick"— characteristic Allewegi physical traits.

> In removing the earth which composed an ancient mound in one of the streets of Marietta, on the margin of the plain, near the aboriginal fortifications, several curious articles were discovered in the year

1836. They appear to have been buried with the body of the person to whose memory this mound was erected. Lying immediately over, or on the forehead of the body, were found three, large, circular bosses, or ornaments for a sword-belt or a buckler; they are composed of copper overlaid with a thick plate of silver.

But the fronts of them are slightly convex, with a depression, like a cup, in the center, and the measure two and a quarter inches across the face of each. On the reverse side, opposite one is a copper rivet or nail, around which are two separate plates, by which they were fastened to the leather. The two small pieces of the leather were found lying between the plates of one of the bosses. . . . Near the side of the body was found a plate of silver, which appears to have been the upper part of a sword-scabbard. It is six inches in length and two inches in breadth, and weighs one ounce; it has no ornaments or figures, but has three longitudinal ridges, which probably correspond with edges or ridges of the sword. It seems to have been fastened to the scabbard by three or four rivets, the holes of which yet remain in the silver.

The Marietta burial self-evidently belonged to a Keltic warrior. But where was his chief weapon?[11] "No sign of the sword itself was discovered, except the appearance of rust . . ." That, of course, explains why so few iron implements survive from Adean times: they rusted away.

About four miles down the Muskingum from Marietta, another burial mound yielded "some pieces of copper which appear to have been the front part of a helmet. It was originally about eight inches long and four broad, and has marks of being attached to leather. . . . [N]ear Blacksburgh, in Virginia, eighty miles from Marietta, there was found about half of a steel bow, which, when entire, would measure five or six feet; the other part was corroded or broken."

Excavation of a mortuary earthwork outside Chillicothe, Ohio, at an important archaeological site known as Mound City, brought forth a well-crafted copper helmet in the likeness of a bear, with hinged ears and legs attached by rivets that originally allowed these appendages to move, lending the headpiece a lifelike appearance as its wearer attacked the foe. In the ancient world, only the Kelts made articulated military headgear.

Retrieved from a Keltic grave at Ciumesti in Romania was an iron helmet surmounted by a large bronze bird of prey with enameled eyes. Its hinged wings could flap up and down as the warrior rode his horse or ran. The Ciumesti helmet was dated to the Late La Tene Period, circa 200 BC, just when the Hopewell first appeared in the American Midwest. Though the Ohio version was found at a Hopewell site, archaeologists recognize a transference of cultural influences with the Adena, which explains the discovery of some discernibly Allewegi elements—such as stone hill forts and the copper bear helmet—in a Hopewell context. In any case, the contemporaneous manufacture of articulated animal-effigy metal helmets exclusively among the Allewegi and the Kelts defines an authentic connection between the two.

Such comparative evidence is important, because only a tiny fraction of Adena material is available for examination. Far less than 1 percent of its culture survives. Much more has been irretrievably lost, with no possibility of archaeological investigation. Once we understand and appreciate this, the enigma of the stone mounds and missing torques may have been explained in long-vanished evidence, leaving us to complete a picture without enough pieces of the original. It is only natural for human imagination to fill in the open spaces with conjecture.

But were the Adena really civilized? Their Western European fathers were not, according to Roman opinion. Despite the Kelts' invention of soap, the file, the chisel, the handsaw, and the iron plow, along with many other innovations and their high craftsmanship and undoubted seamanship, the outside world abhorred them as painted barbarians riding roughshod across Europe with severed heads bobbling from their saddles, or as people hurling bound and strangled human sacrifices into peat bogs. The Kelts were, after all, a people, never a nation. They were neither state-forming nor militarily cohesive, much less politically united, but instead divided themselves continually into disparate tribes of a related race, culture, and language (though dialectical differences were significant). It nonetheless seems clear that their dynamic expansion from eastern Keltic homelands into Bavaria three thousand years ago carried them irresistibly westward across the vast ocean in their huge, seagoing ships to make landfall on the Atlantic shores of North America.

Simultaneous eruption of the Adena in coastal New York seems to mirror this overseas arrival. The Kelts, in waves of migration over the centuries, moved westward as far as the Mississippi River, but established themselves primarily in the Ohio Valley. Interaction and, increasingly, intermarriage with the indigenous peoples gradually produced a Mound Builder culture, a synthesis of foreign and aboriginal influences. The former dominated from the beginning, reinforced as it was from time to time by fresh waves of Kelts fleeing Roman expansion throughout the ancient Old World.

Over the generations, however, Adena society grew into a cultural hybrid, until, weakened by an irreversible decline in its population and genetic health, its people were overwhelmed by their more numerous, physically healthier enemies. Today, all that remain are some broken bones of the Mound Builders; the gaunt ruins of their grand but failed hill forts; a dwindling collection of their earthworks; fragmentary artifacts; and folk memories preserved by the descendants of their enemies. Thus, the lost civilization of America.

Four

HOPEWELL MASTERS
OF CEREMONY

The Adena had been rulers of the rich Ohio Valley and beyond for eight centuries when foreigners suddenly appeared in their midst. They were as different from the Adena folk as they were from the Plains Indians. Their skulls and facial features were "more gracile" than both, according to archaeologists at Ohio's Moundsville Museum. The newcomers were shorter than the statuesque Allewegi, but robust and vigorous. They were bearers of a singular culture who built unfortified, sometimes gargantuan ceremonial centers enclosing linear and trapezoidal earthworks oriented to a variety of celestial phenomena.

These sprawling sites were linked by embanked causeways and roads engineered with mathematical perfection sometimes over dozens of miles. The Midwestern landscape was abruptly transformed by literally tens of thousands of effigy mounds skillfully formed into the vivid likenesses of birds, panthers, turtles, snakes, lizards, bears, men, and, more perplexingly, creatures supposedly unfamiliar to prehistoric North Americans: oceangoing seals, Bolivian llamas, and Asian elephants. These images may attest to a far-flung commercial network considerably more extensive than mainstream archaeologists are so far willing to concede. To be sure, the strangers imported huge quantities of mica from the Atlantic coast for the production of fine jewelry, which usually assumed animal forms, as did their pipes, precious possessions they took with them to the grave.

What these people, culturally and racially distinct from both the Adena and Plains Indians, called themselves has been lost. Their former existence has been recognized only since the late nineteenth century, when uniquely different remains were found for the first time at the North Fork of Ohio's Paint Creek on the Ross County farm of Colonel M. C. Hopewell. Ever since, these people, who, around 200 BC, appeared fully outfitted with all the richness of their high culture, and just as thoroughly disappeared six hundred years later, have been referred to as the Hopewell.

Despite the passage of sixteen centuries, their singular greatness and impact on North American prehistory is still open to appreciation. For example, to explore the ruins of their immense complex located at Newark, thirty-three miles east of Columbus, Ohio, is to experience one of the grandest miracles of ancient engineering. Its vast network of walls, mounds, and apertures is, according to archaeo-astronomers, humankind's largest observatory in addition to being the greatest earthwork in the world. Newark's Sacred Center enfolds more than 200 square acres, including a double parallel wall running more than six miles long. The Great Circle, with its 14-foot-high embankment enclosing 20 acres, is a gargantuan proof of the Hopewell's extraordinary powers of geometry and surveying.

Archaeologist James D. Middleton, describing this earthwork for *Science* magazine in 1887, observed, "the figure as a whole is very near a true circle. But the most singular fact is presented by the diameters. These, as taken by careful measurements from the quarter stations, are respectively 1,054 and 1,058 feet, the average of which is 1,056 feet, precisely 64 poles or 16 chains."[1] Enclosing 50 acres, the octagonal enclosure to which the Circle Mound is connected is more than twice as large. It is joined by a corridor to another circular wall, the south end of which features a 170-foot-long mound that is 8 feet higher than the embankment and is actually composed of line segments separated

Fig. 4.1. Aerial view of Ohio's sprawling Octagon Earthworks

by regular, measured gaps. Behind each one stands a uniform mound just off center. The purpose of this peculiar arrangement, archaeo-astronomers determined, was to provide accurate fixes for the risings and settings of significant astronomical events.

Ancient Newark comprised a living calendar in which its officiants regulated their existence according to the grand mechanism perpetually swirling above them. The earthworks' chief orientation is lunar, and their most spectacular alignment is a line running straight down the main axis of the Octagon to point at the rising of the moon at its most northerly point during a 18.61-year cycle. On certain days, over a period of about two years during this cycle, the moon rises directly along the Octagon axis. "The ancient architects apparently had a complete or rounded knowledge of cyclical astronomy," Ross Hamilton writes of the Newark earthworks in *Ancient American* magazine, "as the exquisite 18.6-year lunar cycle is expertly represented in an almost faultless perfection."[2]

The Octagon and Great Circle are a single-unit design, 2,898 feet long. As such, they comprise the world's largest astronomical computer, able to determine the eight various maximum and minimum, northern and southern moonsets and moonrises. According to Dr. Bradley T. Lepper, curator of archaeology and archaeological coordinator at the Ohio Historical Society in Columbus, "the walls of the Octagon are like huge gun barrels aimed at astronomical targets."

In fact, a closer analogy for the Newark earthworks may be the spider. Many Native American tribes still venerate Spider Woman as their supreme deity responsible for all Creation, which she continues to spin on her interconnecting web. She is a moon goddess whose pre-Columbian shell engravings, when proportionately superimposed over the Newark earthworks, almost perfectly correspond to each other. Even the circle-cross emblem common to these spider shell engravings lies directly over the parallel walls joining Newark's Great Circle to the Octagon.

It appears, then, that these tremendous landforms represented the Hopewell version of Grandmother Spider, and paid homage to their moon goddess by way of its numerous lunar alignments. Hamilton wondered if "astronomy may be perfectly integrated with geometry, proportion and measure at the expense of neither. Did the ancient Hopewell, even as philosophers and magicians, seek to embody all their science in one, unifying expression of their forgotten religion?"

Fig. 4.2. The Great Circle component of Ohio's Octagon earthworks

No one resided behind the expansive earthworks at Newark. Nor did their impressive ramparts comprise a cemetery or fort. The vast complex was strictly a ceremonial center, the largest outdoor church on earth, where tens of thousands of people gathered for mass rituals dedicated to the recurrence of lunar cycles. Tragically, the ancient center has not survived in its entirety. A major square embankment, many mounds, and large sections of the parallel walls were obliterated in the nineteenth-century expansion of the modern town. But the Great Circle and some of its walls are still preserved as part of a state memorial park. The Octagon has likewise been saved from destruction—although under less dignified circumstances: as a golf course, the Mound Builders Country Club.

The most splendid ceremonies and spectacles at the Newark earthworks must have been on a level of theater comparable to the grandeur of the site itself. They almost certainly involved thousands of people at a time, beginning in one of the enclosures, passing through others via miles of ceremonial double walls, and climaxing in the Great Circle or giant Octagon.

Though the archaeological park at Newark is the largest site of its kind open to the general public, it is dwarfed by a less accessible (due to overgrowth) Hopewell complex straddling two states on both sides of the Ohio River. It is not stylistically different from Newark—although it has no octagonal enclosure, it extends several miles in a contiguous series of earthworks. During the 1840s, archaeologists Ephriam G. Squier and Edwin H. Davis surveyed the Portsmouth, Ohio, complex for the Smithsonian Institution:

> The parallel embankments measure about four feet in height by twenty feet at the base. They run in three lines from the central group, one leading to the southeast, one to the southwest, and one to the northwest, each one of them pointing to important works on the opposite sides of the river. The total length of the parallels is *eight miles,* giving *sixteen miles of embankment* [author's italics].

The group on the Kentucky shore consists of four concentric circles placed at irregular intervals in respect to each other, and cut at right angles by four broad avenues which bear very nearly to the cardinal points.[3]

Despite its larger dimensions, the Portsmouth earthworks do not appear to have been foremost among the Hopewell. Primacy may have gone to Newark, as indicated by a superhighway that connected it to another, entirely different ceremonial center. The road was uniformly 200 feet wide, flanked by clay walls, and complete with circular rest stops as it ran dead straight for 55 miles.

Dr. Lepper, cited earlier for his observation of the Octagon's astronomical properties, was led to the road's discovery during the 1990s, when he chanced upon a neglected manuscript that detailed a survey of the Hopewell highway during the American Civil War that was forgotten soon after peace was declared. A single copy of the 1862 edition by James and Charles Salisbury survived at the American Antiquarian Society in Worcester, Massachusetts. They wrote of this ancient engineering achievement, "These walls proceed south a short distance, thence making one or two slight turns, finally settle to S. 27° W., in which direction we have traced them some six miles over fertile fields, through tangled swamps and across streams, still keeping their undeviating course. The extent of this great, fortified highway, and what other ancient stronghold or place of importance it connects with, is as yet unknown."[4]

Following this lead, Dr. Lepper combined aerial surveys, some made in the 1930s, with ground investigations to identify sections of the road that had fortuitously escaped almost two centuries of agricultural, residential, and industrial development. "Because he had to occasionally deal with landowners unhappy with archaeologists tramping about their property," Hamilton explains, "Lepper was only able to find traces of the road extant in short segments, some of which were barely noticeable."[5] He was thus able to determine that the highway established a direct connection between Newark's Octagon-Great Circle and Mound City, outside Chillicothe.

Aptly described by early surveyors in southern Ohio for its twenty-three earthworks and 13 acres surrounded with a squarish embankment, Mound City, near the Scioto River, is a necropolis—a city of the dead—but no mere cemetery. Rather, the dead are there as part of a sacred site where this life and the afterlife converged. The prehistoric site's pyramids contain the cremated remains of several hundred Hopewell leaders. Their burial mounds were not simple heaps of dirt, but methodically composed structures that still stand after some two millennia.

At the very center of a typical Mound City monument, the Hopewellians raised a circular, hard-clay platform, upon which the cremated remains of a leader, warrior, or shaman were laid, together with potsherds; stone and copper tools; deliberately broken spearpoints of obsidian, flint, or garnet; and shiny pebbles. Smithsonian Institution scientists documented Mound City (although its Hopewellian identity was unrecognized at the time) as long ago as 1848, but the site was requisitioned by the U.S. Army as a training camp during World War I, when many of the ceremonial structures were heedlessly destroyed. The ancient necropolis was rescued from certain oblivion only when it was finally declared a national monument in 1923. Since then, restoration has been proceeding under the auspices of the Ohio Historical Society.

Beginning in the late nineteenth century, Mound City excavators found strange and beautiful objects within its earthworks. Some contained the bones of an extinct mastodon, a creature that vanished from the American plains about ten thousand years ago. Perhaps the Hopewellians preserved from deep antiquity the shamanic paraphernalia of the Ice Age. A so-called "Mound of the Pipes" contained two hundred stone bowls exquisitely carved to represent animals and humans. One of the earthworks was cut open to reveal the entombment of four men laid out on a floor entirely covered by oversized flakes of jewel-like mica. Imported for unknown ceremonial purposes from Georgia, the glittering, pastel wafers were joined by elk and bear teeth, copper ornaments,

Fig. 4.3. Copper representation of a hawk displayed at Ohio's Mound City Museum.

large obsidian points, a cache of five thousand polished mother-of-pearl beads, and toad- and raven-effigy pipes.

Magnificent copper armor was also recovered, including a headdress adorned with three pairs of copper antlers. The workmanship expressed in all these items was of extraordinarily high quality, thereby demonstrating a vast technological difference between the ancient Hopewell and the historic Shawnee, who dominated the Ohio Valley when the French first explored the region during the late seventeenth century. These resident Indians knew nothing of Mound City and made no claims to its precinct. They were, in fact, alien to the large-scale social organization that went into making it.

The number and arrangement of the mounds form a ritual pattern whose precise significance has been lost. Archaeologists cannot identically reconstruct the ceremonial activities that took place at Mound City until sixteen hundred years ago. Even so, the sacred landscape lends itself to interpretation. The squarish perimeter with its rounded corners resembles the outline of a house, including gaps where doors should be at the north and south ends. In post-Hopewell Native American tradition, north is the spirit direction and south is the direction of becoming.

Perhaps ritual enactments began when initiates entered through the northern portal associated with death, participated in shamanist ceremonies among the mortuary mounds, then departed through the southern exit of rebirth. Such an interpretation is suggested by the close proximity of the Scioto River to the northern gap. Along its opposite banks, the residential Hopewell town was located. Crossing a river is a universal human archetype for death. Traveling over the Scioto from their homes to the necropolis might very well have had the same mythic implications as fording the River Styx had for ancient Greeks. Yet leaving Mound City through the southern direction of becoming implies that the ritual that took place within the sacred precinct dealt with death and transfiguration.

The existence of a reincarnation or rebirth cult at work here has been suggested by some of the physical evidence excavated since the late nineteenth century. The so-called Death Mask Mound, largest of the Chillicothe earthworks, contained fragments of a human skull that had been sawed and drilled for use as a mask probably worn by a cultish master-of-ceremonies more than sixteen centuries ago. The same

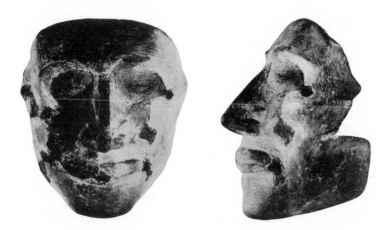

Fig. 4.4. Death mask retrieved from a two-thousand-year-old burial mound near the banks of Wisconsin's Red Cedar River

mound also served as the burial for thirteen adult men accompanied by copper effigies of birds of prey. The bird is another universal symbol for the human soul, and copper or gold is associated with the sun and immortality.

Among the hundreds of skillfully carved stone pipes recovered from the site, most, if not all of those depicting animal forms—for instance, the raven, the serpent, and the bear—clearly personify death and rebirth. Those fashioned to resemble human heads may be portraits of the deceased, at least some of whom were undoubtedly shamans. Among the Hopewell, as among later Native American tribes, tobacco was probably considered the holiest herb: its smoke and the mildly altered states of consciousness it produces were intimately connected with the spirit world. The pipes were not smoked for pleasure alone, but more for purposes of communication with afterlife entities who provided the tribe with guidance and protection.

Indeed, Mound City is a man-made simulacrum of that otherworld. Archaeologists believe the mounds were a visible reminder and demonstration of the power of individuals and families serving as established and perpetual systems of rank distinctions. Though this speculation seems plausible, the overall implication of the site strongly suggests that it was far more than a political cemetery for the privileged dead. Rather, the deceased were part of a communal sense of spiritual empowerment generated within the sacred center. Mound City's connection to Newark is the only known processional way of its kind, although it may not have been prehistoric America's only such engineering feat. "There are other ancient pathways rumored to exist in the Ohio Valley," Hamilton writes, "and efforts are underway to identify them."

In fact, the Hopewell were not our continent's first road builders, although they expanded on the work of their forerunners to create Ohio's longest prehistoric highway. They were preceeded in construction by the Adena, who, along with their numerous other innovations (iron making, mound building, agriculture, and so forth) rank as North America's earliest road builders. In the August 2005 issue,

David Cain told *Ancient American* readers that the West Virginia highway "was twelve miles in length, fourteen inches thick, and nine feet wide, extending from the mouth of the Monongahela River following the east bank to Catawba, Marion County," where he was the county historian. "Constructed from knapped stone, crushed mussel shells, and clay tamped into a hard surface," its Adena provenance was confirmed by associated finds: "Also within about a mile radius on both sides of the river in and near present day Fairmont was discovered extraordinary archaeological sites consisting of stone structures, mussel shell burial mounds, giant human skeletons, and an earthen fort with mound complex. Numerous artifacts ranging from copper bowls and jewelry to finely worked stone weapons and tools were found at these areas."

Strangely, a disaster brought the Adena road to light. As Cain described it,

Local newspaper columnist and historian, E. E. Meredith, related the story of a train wreck on the day before Christmas in 1894 of a locomotive and several coal cars at the Montana coke ovens. Dr. Kramer, an amateur archaeologist from Smithtown, arrived on the scene to help if anyone had been injured. It was then that he made a most interesting discovery. The train, in leaving the tracks, had torn great holes and gashes in the earth. In places, the bedding-slag and top soil had been "skinned off" a space about 40 feet wide and 100 feet long. In this trench-like excavation, about three feet deep, lay revealed a section of the stone and mussel road. . . . Dr. Kramer returned with Fairmont photographer, Israel Foreman, who made prints of the exposed remnant of the ancient construction. Several local residents took their own photographs of the exposed section, but all copies have long since vanished. . . . The section of the prehistoric road uncovered by the wreck was examined by Dr. Kramer and other investigators. They found that the mussel shell mortar had lost its "hold," and it was impossible to remove intact any part of the road much larger than a man's hand. . . . In some places, it was fairly

solid, but mostly it came apart when it was uncovered and subjected
to rain. . . . The road was largely destroyed when grading was done
for the F. M. & P. Railroad. It was reported that the upper section of
the coke ovens at Montana Mines was built on the site of the stone
and mussel road. . . . The last reported sighting of parts of the road
was made in 1959.[6]

So too, the Kelts, whose identification with the Adena was cited in
chapter 3, were remarkable road builders after the fashion of construction revealed in West Virginia.

More certain is the existence of the Hopewell people's most revered
monument. A single, long path leads past a low, egg-shaped mound,
across a broad expanse of green park, to the colossus of ancient Tennessee.
Saul's Mound, the outstanding structure of the so-called Pinson Group,
is not only the tallest earthwork in eastern North America, it is also one
of the most singularly impressive structures from native antiquity. At 72
feet tall, it is second in height only to Illinois' Cahokia. The perfectly
proportioned dome of clay and soil required an estimated 37,200,000
basketloads of earth heaped up by about a thousand workers pulling
ten-hour shifts for nearly three years. Impact on the modern observer

*Fig. 4.5. Representation of Saul's Mound in Tennessee
(illustration by William Wild)*

beholding it for the first time is generated not only because of its massive bulk, but also by the monstrously tall oak trees growing up from its sides, which magnify the mound's height and massiveness. They tower like gargantuan pillars, lending Saul's Mound the aspect of a titan's crown.

The path leads up to and around the south end, where a wooden flight of stairs ascends to a viewing platform at the summit. From there, visitors may best appreciate the greatness of the Mound Builders' achievement. Trails spread in several directions from the broad base of the structure, but the preferable pathway includes a fifteen-minute walk across lovely countryside to the Eastern Citadel. It comprises a squarish, truncated, flat-topped pyramid, about 30 feet across and 12 feet tall, encircled by a ruined embankment. Nature trails lead through a dark forest to a boardwalk and an overlook where visitors may rest while watching the Forked Deer River glide by. It was undoubtedly along this very waterway that the Hopewell came to their sacred complex.

The boardwalk ends at a path with a sign pointing to the Duck's Nest, an unusual depression in a secluded part of the woods atop a slight rise. About 15 feet in diameter and perhaps 4 feet deep, it was used for bonfires of great heat. The trail returning in the direction of Saul's Mound passes another ovoid structure, then moves back toward the visitor's center. Visitors may either drive or walk to the Western Mound Group, which differs markedly from the other features at Pinson.

The path just off the road approaches a beautiful, small lake through a pleasantly wooded area to yet one more egg-shaped structure containing a single burial, that of a middle-aged man, probably one of the site's most prominent personages in life. Surrounding his privileged grave lies a horseshoe shape formed of clay and the cremated remains of at least several human beings. A few paces away are twin earthworks joined at one end, another burial complex of multiple graves, ritually constructed of different-colored layers of clay: red, yellow, and black. Not far from this little necropolis stands Ozier Mound, a 32-foot-tall, truncated pyramid with a sloping entrance ramp leading up its east side, and oriented to the spring solstice sunrise.

Fig. 4.6. The Ozier Mound in Tennessee

Dated to around AD 100, it is the oldest known structure of its kind in North America. Although the structures at Pinson Mounds offer a great deal of variety in shape, size, and configuration, emphasis throughout the site is on regeneration and rebirth, as suggested by the several egg-shaped earthworks and the Ozier pyramid's alignment to the vernal solstice sunrise. Even the dominating Saul's Mound is more ovoid than perfectly circular, and is, moreover, bounded on four sides by a quartet of much smaller structures equidistant from its center. These positions might signify the Four Cardinal Directions, thereby defining the larger structure as an *axis mundi,* or Navel of the World, the midpoint of Creation, the Womb of the Cosmos, from which all life is eternally reborn.

Among the largest of North America's ancient cities, Tennessee's Pinson Mounds complex is also part of the continent's great human mystery. The grandest ceremonial center of the Middle Woodland Period, it was constructed by the Hopewell around AD 1. Thirty mounds, some of enormous dimensions, dominated 1,162 square acres of consecrated ground that drew pilgrims from as far away as Florida and Louisiana.

The area was first surveyed in 1820 by Joel Pinson, after whom the site was named, but no one knows what the site was called in the days of its ancient glory. A religious capital without a resident population, it featured only a few burials. Careful excavations have revealed no signs of war or pestilence, social unrest, or natural disasters. Yet, after four hundred years of construction and ceremonial life, Pinson Mounds was suddenly abandoned, its people lost to the land's unknown past. Nevertheless, they left behind abundant evidence of their genius for large-scale ritualized building. Such interpretation is not baseless speculation, but appears borne out in other structures throughout the Hopewellian sphere of influence.

Seip Mound is outstanding among the dozens of ancient earthworks, which survive in Ohio, because of its impressive bulk. More than 20,000 cubic yards of soil went into its construction. Standing fourteen miles southwest of Chillicothe, the earthwork—20 feet tall, 250 feet long, and 150 feet across—is no mere heap of dirt but a complex organization of alternating levels of earth, gravel, clay, stones, pebbles, and sand. These elements have formed a matrix to hold its shape through twenty centuries of erosional forces.

Originally, the exterior may have been entirely encased in bright red, fire-hardened cap and painted with yellow, geometric designs. Some

Fig. 4.7. Seip Mound in Ohio as it appeared during the early nineteenth century (illustration by William Wild)

pigmented fragments were recovered nearby, suggesting a clay cover. Resembling a colossal egg emerging from the ground, Seip Mound is encircled by a long channel dug around its base, a feature laid out by Hopewellian construction engineers to flood in high water, thereby transforming the earthwork into an artificial island. Some human remains have been excavated from the monument, but they do not appear to have belonged to a necropolis or mass grave. Seip formerly occupied the midpoint in a mound group arranged in a circle behind a low embankment that enclosed almost 100 acres of sacred ground.

Together with its oblate shape, Seip's central position in the original precinct underscores its identity with the Cosmic Egg, the metaphysical source of existence. As such, the mound seems related to another earthwork only twenty miles away. The Great Serpent Mound is the 1,200-foot-long effigy of a snake disgorging an egg from its jaws. Symbolic perhaps of telluric power running in sinuous patterns throughout the Ohio Valley, the Serpent was a visualization of those perceived earth energies as it spat out the Cosmic Egg, the demiurge of Creation. That same theme recurs at Seip, where the egglike mound appears to be disgorged from the bowels of the planet. Encircling Seip with an artificial water course provided an otherworldly barrier officiants had to cross.

Across the Indiana border, above the White River in the eastern part of the state, lies an entirely different but no less spiritually charged ceremonial center. At a place where the ground was too sacred for human habitation, the atypical structures comprise an arena for rituals and mass meetings. Sheltered for twenty centuries in a deep oak forest are weird features shaped like fiddles, figure eights, horseshoes, rectangles, ovals, and cones. Outstanding among them is the Great Circle Mound, a perfectly surveyed ditch with an embankment encompassing a rounded platform structure opening at the south end on a broad ramp. It was 1,200 feet in circumference, 384 feet across, and 9 feet high, and it was formed from 66,900 cubic feet of soil. The precision and perfect proportions of its overall design, to say nothing of its grand

Fig. 4.8. Model of Indiana's Great Circle Mound as it appeared in the first century, at the Bronnenberg Nature Center Museum, Indian Mounds, Indiana

concept, bespeak the surveying technology and sophisticated organizational skills of its builders. A half dozen of their skeletal remains were excavated in the Great Circle Mound fronting the ramp, or Gateway, although the 259-acre site was never a necropolis.

The bodies were surrounded by flint arrowheads, potsherds, copper spear points, and a stone pipe fashioned in the image of a frog. This effigy pipe is of special interest, because tobacco was regarded by the inhabitants as a medium of communication between humans and gods. Prayers rose to heaven on its smoke, and mild narcotics helped in the vision quest for glimpses of the supernatural. The frog itself underscored a connection to the otherworld to which the young men had probably been ritually sacrificed and laid to rest at the ceremonial entrance to the Great Circle Mound. This creature was an archetype known in cultures around the world as the symbol of the soul's purification, transmigration, and regeneration.

Regarding structure, the 10-foot-deep ditch surrounding the Great Circle Mound may once have been filled with water, rendering the central mound an island joined to the "shore" by its gateway ramp.

Another large earthwork, similar in size and configuration, although more of a rounded rectangle and less well preserved, lies exactly one mile northeast of the Great Circle Mound. Until sixteen centuries ago, thousands of people assembled along the ridge of its embankment to observe costumed processions passing through the gateway into the sacred central precinct. For restricted rituals and more esoteric ceremonies, the same embankment served as a concealing wall.

The significance of the fiddleback and horseshoe mounds in the vicinity of the Great Circle Mound is elusive, and no less so are their relationships to one another. Yet there is meaning in those relationships. For example, the distance from the Great Circle Mound's midpoint to that of its companion structure is, as mentioned, precisely one mile. Though it seems ludicrous to suggest the prehistoric Mound Builders used our present system of measurement, the precision of that distance between the two leading features of the area is intriguing. And there are other provocative relationships: the only structures similar to the large mounds in Indiana occur one hundred fifty miles away, in Ohio. Although Indiana's Great Circle Mound does not appear to have any celestial alignments, the gateway of its northern companion is oriented with the spring solstice sunrise, which may have occasioned either the beginning or the conclusion of a ritual that linked both structures.

Ancient earthworks focused entirely on the heavens may still be visited in Minnesota, near the outer limits of Hopewell influence. Overlooking the Mississippi River and the city skyline of St. Paul stand six conical structures arranged in an irregular line and following the ridge of a precipitous cliff from east to west. Formed into graceful domes of earth and clay, each originally contained the body of a young man buried with copper ax heads, needles, and fish bones.

Covered by a mantle of low grass, the site assumes an emerald luster at dusk during summer months. The largest mound has a diameter of 14 feet, 7 inches, with an altitude of 13 feet, 10 inches. It is surrounded by three, slightly smaller mounds, two to the west and one to the east. Standing aloof from this quartet by 25 feet to the southeast is a pair of identically formed mounds. Their irregular arrangement was determined by important astronomical considerations. Each winter solstice, at sunset, a long shadow cast from a tall pole planted at the top of a smaller mound stretched across the flank of the central, largest structure, falling on a similar pole at its summit. Microscopic residue left from the long-disintegrated poles was detected by University of Minnesota archaeologists during the late 1960s.

At sundown on the summer solstice, the other small mound to the north performed the same sky show. The mound to the east cast its shadow on the morning of the winter solstice, while the pair nearest the ridge marked the first day of summer. The young men interred under each of the earthworks were almost certainly ritually sacrificed to the principle of rebirth implicit in the mounds' solar orientations. Copper artifacts found in each burial represented the might of the sun to many Native American tribes. Solar cycles of the longest and shortest days were linked to parallel cycles of life and death.

By endeavoring to fit into that cosmic harmony, the Hopewell put themselves in accord with the rhythm of life itself, a concept made clear at the Minnesota site. Doubtless, that orientation likewise enabled prehistoric peoples to determine planting and harvesting seasons. Yet concurrent with their calendric agricultural functions, the St. Paul mounds comprise a place of solar ritual that affirmed life after death for their celebrants, and helped regulate their society by bringing its members into balance and harmony with the observable cycles of creation. The sun god was commonly perceived as the supreme masculine power. Hence, the six young men sacrificed in the mounds were his mortal symbols. Their ritual deaths were intended to supercharge the site forever after with mystical power. As J. E. Cirlot writes, "the spiritual energy thereby acquired is proportional to the importance of what is lost."[7] Emphasizing the sun's male identity were the phallus-like poles atop each mound.

Hopewell consciousness ranged from the heavens high above to the depths of the earth far below. Descending into one of the world's foremost sacred centers, such as France's Lascaux or Trois Frères, is a spiritual experience of profound intensity. Like them, a Hopewell cavern in Indiana is a place of deep earth power. Its very existence was a guarded secret kept by Native American residents until 1798, when a pioneer, F. I. Bentley, helped a local Wyandotte brave recover from serious injuries received during a hunt. In gratitude, the Indian told Bentley about the holiest place known to his people. Since then, the site, with its more than five miles of subterranean passages, became regionally famous as Wyandotte Cave.

But others predated Wyandotte occupation by many centuries. Radiocarbon tests of an old torch found at the cave's deepest recesses showed that seventeen hundred years ago it lit the cathedral-like interior for some miners or explorers. These Late Hopewellian spelunkers were avid excavators who removed large quantities of epsomite for medicinal purposes, together with chert for tools and weapons. They were not entirely commercial, however. In 1820, state archaeologist Benjamin Adams stumbled upon ancient murals in an obscure chamber, which, in the labyrinth of only partially explored passageways, has not been seen since. If the wall paintings actually exist, they are the sole discovery of their kind ever made.

Expertly crafted, although entirely enigmatic, stone artifacts have been recovered at various levels in the cave. A string run through a pair of holes at their centers produces a mysterious, whirring sound, similar to the *whoosh* generated by a rapidly spinning propeller blade. No one knows what ritual function these ghostly whistles, referred to by archaeologists as bull roarers, might have served. The outstanding natural features of Wyandotte Cave explain, however, why it attracted the Hopewell and human spiritual activity thereafter for so many centuries.

Another such spiritual subterranean world is Monument Mountain inside a cavern known as "Rothrock Cathedral." As geologist Martin Hill writes:

. . . [T]he enormous pile of rock that makes up Monument Mountain in Rothrock Cathedral consists of a breakdown from the upper and lower levels that they may fill passageways of the lowermost level. The breakdown towers to within 31 feet of the ceiling, which is about 135 feet above the passageway entrance to Rothrock Cathedral. Therefore, Monument Mountain (more than 130 feet tall) is both "monument" and "mountain" indeed![8]

The cave hides a feature referred to as the Pillar of the Constitution in the so-called State Chamber. Resembling a fountain frozen into stone, no other cave on earth possesses a larger formation of this kind. Its monumental girth is in excess of 60 feet. Hill describes another feature not shared with most other subterranean sites:

Stalactite (and in some places, stalagmite), called a helictite, can be seen along the trenched corridor between the Pillared Palace and the Crater Room. The origin of helictites remains mysterious, although it is suggested that the grotesquely contorted forms that they assume are the result of random crystal growth of the calcite as it precipitates from ground water rich in calcium carbonate. Wyandotte Cave has one of the best displays of helictites of any cave in the world.[9]

As such, this underground wonder was a place of profound holiness and spirituality for the Hopewell. According to mythologist Clark Mallam, "Water, that underworld and the regenerative forces of creation are synonymous. They embody life, whose powers of renewal and restoration may be accessed through Earth openings and appropriate rituals. This then abounds in the cultural practices, oral traditions and literature of native North Americans."[10]

Simply entering such a subterranean sacred center was to approach what the Hopewell shaman strove to achieve through spiritual experience: moving through an interdimensional reality from this world to the otherworld.

It was on the surface of the earth, however, that the Hopewell indulged their genius in the myriad forms of the effigy mound. From the parking lot of Lizard Mounds archaeological zone, outside West Bend, less than an hour's drive northwest of Milwaukee, a marked trail winds through the woods to each of thirty-one large effigies. Each has been masterfully terra-formed from the earth into vibrant images of birds, reptiles, cats, buffalo, and unidentifiable mythical creatures. About ten thousand such effigies once spread over Wisconsin alone. Only a handful survive, and Lizard Mounds is among the greatest remaining collections in North America. No other group is so well preserved or so diversified in form, and no other exhibits such outstanding examples in the prehistoric art of working on such a large scale.

The figures are expressionistic, though stylized. Nothing about them speaks of the crude, the savage, or the primitive. They are proportional, refined, and graceful, reflecting the ordered minds that conceived, molded, and appreciated them, to say nothing of the skillfully organized system of labor and the level of surveying technology necessary for their creation. A few of the effigies served as tombs. In pits beneath the mounds, the deceased were placed with decorated clay pots,

Fig. 4.9. Lizard Mounds in Wisconsin

bone harpoons, pipes, copper implements, and religious crystals. The precinct was used exclusively for spiritual purposes.

No one ever resided within the sacred area. Settlements were in surrounding villages. The largest effigy of the group is 300 feet long, but the site derives its modern name from a 238-foot-long figure thought to represent a lizard. The figures are not so large that they cannot be identified and discerned at ground level. Seen at high altitude, however, they assume a startling perspective that implies they may be fully appreciated only from the sky.

More than 90 percent of North America's earth effigies were concentrated in what is now Wisconsin, the Badger State. Writing for *Ancient American* magazine, Jan Beaver informs readers that "the largest eagle effigy mound is reported to be on the grounds of the Mendota Mental Health Institute, Dane County, Wisconsin. This mound is almost an exact blueprint of the pattern that can be seen in the soil of Eagle Township. The difference is that the wingspan of the eagle mound at Mendota is about 600 feet, while the Eagle Township effigy is more than twice as great, approximately 1,400 feet."

Yet even this monster was eclipsed in size by other nearby examples. "The giant eagle mound that appears in the soil north of Frank Shadewald's farm (outside Mendota) is about five to seven times larger."[11] In other words, it was between 7,000 and 9,800 feet across. These bioglyphs, the world's largest and perfectly proportionate to their gigantism, prove Hopewell mastery of applied geometry on a supremely colossal scale. Not all effigy mounds were formed into the likenesses of local fauna, however. Among the most persistently controversial aspects of these prehistoric images was the depiction of animals officially beyond the ken of their artists. Nor were the out-of-place figures portrayed in this anomalous rock art the result of modern hoaxers trying to pull something over on gullible scholars.

They were all documented by Theodore Hayes Lewis, an archaeological surveyor who, alone and with little money, made it his life mission to copy accurately any of North America's tens of thousands of ancient effigy mounds before they were mostly obliterated by the advance of agriculture and industry. Beginning in 1881, he covered fifty-four thousand miles, more than ten thousand of them on foot, sometimes foraging through the most forbidding terrain. He was often the first discoverer of the prehistoric geoglyphs, frequently finding them in difficult, remote areas. After fourteen years of meticulously recording thousands of ancient images, Lewis died in obscurity of old age around 1930. Yet his decades-long fieldwork is preserved in dozens of large folders at St. Paul's Minnesota History Center, where the onion-leaf originals were microfiled before they entirely disintegrated with age.

In Dodge County, south-central Wisconsin, Lewis surveyed the 176-foot-long effigy mound of an oceangoing seal whose habitat is restricted to areas above the Arctic Circle. At the north shore of Lake Wingra, in Madison, he found the bioglyph of a Bolivian llama, 127 feet long and 3 feet high. How could a people supposedly confined to the Upper Midwest have been familiar enough with these creatures to portray them with such accuracy? It suggests that Hopewell connections to the outside world were more far-reaching than mainstream archaeologists care to admit. Why an Arctic seal and a Bolivian llama were depicted on the Wisconsin landscape is certainly perplexing, unless their oversized portrayal proclaimed just such distant connections.

More remarkable still, Lewis surveyed no less than six especially unusual effigy mounds in Wisconsin's Rock and Vernon Counties, and Allamakee and Lansing Counties in Iowa: all of them were the unmistakable representations of elephants. In fact, so true to life was their execution that they were self-evidently of the Asian variety (*Elephas maximus*). According to Ho Chunk Indian scholar Larry Johns, nine elephant mounds still exist along the Wisconsin banks of the Mississippi River from Lake Pepin to La Crosse. While they still await rediscovery, on the Iowa side of the Mississippi, patrolled by silent squadrons of soaring eagles, a deep forest conceals some two hundred more easily accessible earthworks of significance. At least twenty-nine of them were formed to resemble animals, some identifiable, others more like beasts from the realm of dreams. Still others were skillfully fashioned into graceful linear mounds and stately cones, their ancient significance no less enigmatic than the vanished people who created them. One or two of the conical features may be more than two thousand years old, but the animal figures appear to have been formed around the turn of the second century. The Iowa Indians occupied the area long after the Hopewellian landscapers disappeared, and though they contributed nothing to the sacred site, they revered the structures and even preserved something of the ceremonies originally associated with them.

Today, Effigy Mounds National Monument comprises 1,475 acres threaded by eleven miles of woodland trails. The earthworks are uniformly 3 to 3.5 feet high. They include representations of lynx, birds, and bears, mostly 90 feet in length. The outstanding exception is 137-foot-long Great Bear Mound. Larger still is a compound or segmented mound resembling a thick, straight line, the largest of its kind in North America at 470 feet in length. But the most important group of geoglyphs takes the form of the so-called Marching Bears. They run in an arc of ten bears apparently led by twin eagles and rounded up by another pair at the end of their line. Abstract linear mounds bring up the rear.

The wooded trail to the bears was originally a logging road, and the abundant oak, maple, and walnut trees fueled paddle-wheel steamboats plying the Father of Waters in the days of Mark Twain. The whole area was formerly infested with rattlesnakes—so much so that a prominent knob of earth near the trail head is still known as Rattlesnake Hill. In 1929, however, a major forest fire was sparked by lightning, and literally herds of serpents fled the blaze. Since then, rattlers are rarely glimpsed among the wildflowers and prairie grasses. Some of the Iowa mounds are burial tumuli, particularly the conical structures.

The bear mounds that are tombs feature the deceased interred at the effigy's head, with copper and flint ritual grave goods in the haunches. Ceremonial fires were lit in the heart area. Most of the bear figures point toward the south, while the bird mounds fly at the southeast. South is the traditional direction of becoming throughout Native American cultures, while the southeast was identified with the rising of the Morning Star, the planet Venus, itself synonymous with the eternal return.

The bear was the powerful symbol of regeneration, because the animal's winter-long hibernation was regarded as a deathlike sleep from which it awoke in springtime to a renewal of life. The creature's "rebirth," combined with Iowa's effigies oriented toward the South—the direction of becoming—clearly define the mounds as representations of a mystery cult with a central belief in an afterlife. That belief is highlighted by the bird figures appearing to lead the bears. Because they are aligned southeasterly with the return of the Morning Star, they emphasize a theme of regeneration.

Birds were also commonly visualized as representations of the human soul. The bird and bear effigies thus dramatized the rebirth of

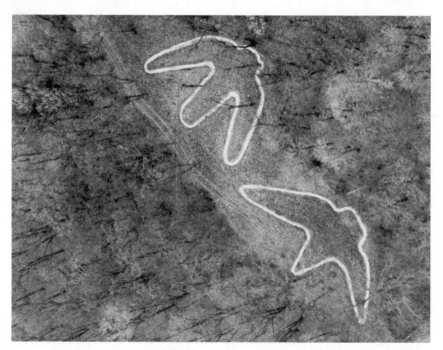

Fig. 4.10. Aerial view of bird geoglyphs at Iowa's Effigy Mounds National Monument

both the body and spirit after death. As such, significance of the interred materials at some of the bear mounds becomes clear. Tools, weapons, and copper are grave goods, symbols of physical existence appropriately buried in that most physical extension of the bear, its limb or haunches. The corpse was laid in the effigy's head, personifying a notion that the skull is the vessel of the soul, while the ritual fire kindled at the figure's heart was the transforming power of death itself, the Phoenix flame of rebirth. These implied metaphysical concepts underlie another, inextricably related level of meaning.

Some observers conclude from the material evidence that the terraglyphs are representations of specific star clusters in the night sky. Indeed, the Algonquian tribes referred to a particular constellation as the Great Bear. Their myth recounted that it was pursued by birds, just as the Iowa bear mounds are tailed by avian effigies. These earthen effigies undoubtedly reflect the Algonquian story. After all, the largest animal bioglyph in the park is known as the Great Bear. It lies near the Little Bear Mound, reflecting, in this proximity, the Western view of the heavens' Ursa Major and Ursa Minor, the Big Bear and Little Bear constellations. This parallel is not only cultural coincidence. "When the first whites came to North America," according to archaeologists Stanley Shepherd and Mack Sanders, "they found that the Algonquian tribes already identified the same stars as the Great Bear that they themselves did. In time, they found that this was true from Nova Scotia westward to Point Barrow and down the Pacific Coast, and even among the Pueblos."

It is far easier to conclude that connections arose from visiting, ancient Old World seafarers, part of whose shared astronomical knowledge was passed down through successive generations of Native Americans, than it is to accept that both pre-Columbian outsiders and Paleo-Indians independent of each other just happened to apply identical names to the same group of stars. The Iowa earthworks' human burials probably cover the remains of shamans, those psychics of long ago who were the spiritual leaders of Hopewell society. Yet these mounds comprised more than a cultic graveyard. In life, the shamans used the geoglyphs for their ceremonial magic, known today as paranormal exercises.

None of the compound linear mounds, however, contained burials. Their function seems elusive, but may lie in the fact that their shamanic designers were also geomancers who divined the special earth energies characteristic of a particular location. They determined which locations were proper for mound building according to the contours of the natural environment and its immanent resonance. They were sensitive to outstanding centers of telluric power, magnetic or otherwise, concentrated at unique places within the landscape. Further, it was the mounds themselves, shaped into the images of vibrant animals, that were visualizations of that power.

The Hopewell shamans believed they could focus and direct earth energies into the effigies through the effigy mounds, regarded as psychic amplifiers. To the geomancer, the precise animal identity of the figures was relatively unimportant, because they represented only the animistic powers of the earth. Their indifference to the correct depiction of species explains why the mounds, with the exception of the bear and bird effigies, are only vaguely recognizable as amorphous land-animal types, with no particular, artistic attention paid to realism. These stylistic bioglyphs served as psychic power foci and points of visual reference during out-of-body exercises that were used as advanced training aids in the schooling of shamanic initiates, as affirmed by enduring Oneida and Obijwa oral traditions. Regular astral projections alone explain the outsized proportions of the effigies, which were clearly sculpted from the landscape to be viewed from above, although nothing in the immediate environment affords a vantage point precipitous enough to observe them from altitude. Nor were such experiences merely psychic stunts, but flights to behold the earth and its man-made designs from an overhead perspective not otherwise available: to see the world as the gods saw it. The chief purpose of these out-of-body transformations was spiritual exercise and empowerment, part of shamanic training. After completing part of his schooling, an initiate was supposed to identify accurately the geoglyphs' otherwise indiscernible configuration. If successful, he was believed to have undertaken his first "flight of the shaman"—the projection of human consciousness outside the body.

Although most Hopewell effigy mounds assumed the images of animals and, to a lesser extent, abstract forms, just two were anthropomorphic. One such survivor is located in Sauk County, near Baraboo, Wisconsin. Originally, it was 80 feet long and 3 feet high. Molded into the northern slope of a hill overlooking declining prairieland, it is the faceless representation of a male figure wearing only a horned helmet. When French immigrants were settling in the town of Baraboo during the early 1830s, resident Sauk Indians still revered the terraglyph as the sacred image of Wakt'cexi, a giant who saved their ancestors by leading them to safety on the eastern shores of Turtle Island—the Sauk name for North America—after a Great Deluge drowned their original lodge place in the Sunrise Sea (the Atlantic Ocean).

Among the Chumash Indians, a tribe that occupied the southern California coast, Dancing Frog was the ceremonial name of Two-Horned

Fig. 4.11. Baraboo's Man Mound in Wisconsin as it appeared during early Hopewell times, circa 100 BC (illustration by William Wild)

Priest, a water spirit associated with the ocean. His magic helmet, like that depicted on the Wisconsin mounds, allowed him to envision the future or look into the past. The Sauk were themselves known by their Algonquian tribal name as the Osakiwug, or People of the Outlet, a reference to their ancestral landfall at Turtle Island as flood survivors. It seems more than ironic, then, that the Man Mound's companion earthwork thirty miles away at La Valle should itself have succumbed to a modern flood, when a Depression-era irrigation project covered it under five fathoms of water.

The Baraboo giant was intended by his creators to be appreciated from a distance and appear proportionate at ground level. Viewed at altitude, the hill figure is distortedly elongated. It seems clear, then, that Hopewell landscapers grasped the principles of applied proportion through foreshortening. After the turn of the twentieth century, construction engineers laying the county's first paved road erased the Man Mound below his knees. Some local residents were outraged by such callous destruction, and they organized a foundation especially for the preservation of what remained of the damaged terraglyph. Today, the Sauk County Man Mound is maintained as a wayside park. A wood observation tower beside the effigy provides visitors with an improved perspective.

The richness of Hopewell culture implies that its social focus was primarily metaphysical and ceremonial. As such, its busy artists and moon-worshipping astronomer-priests were different at heart from the mound-building iron workers and enthusiastic headhunters of the Adena. Yet all evidence suggests that these fundamentally contrary peoples—from their disparate body types to their distinct religious practices—were somehow complementary. Though they never appear to have warred against each other, neither did they engage in wholesale intermixing of either their different cultures or blood. Instead, they seem to have been long-term allies against a common foe, the Plains Indians, who vastly outnumbered them. Not even alliance with the populous Adena, however, could save the Hopewell. Around the turn of the fifth century, they utterly disappeared, as though in a single moment.

The cause is not difficult to surmise. Before the end, many Hopewell fled south to an area between Fort Smith and Hot Springs, Arkansas, where they made a final effort to save themselves at the Aikman Mounds, the last such earthworks ever raised. During the late 1920s, archaeologists from Washington University (St. Louis, Missouri) and the University of Arkansas (Fayetteville) excavated the mounds and their vicinity to unearth thousands upon thousands of human skeletons revealing blunt-force trauma. Many if most of the skulls had been crushed or staved in.

Investigators were led to the area by excavations undertaken thirty years before, nearer Fort Smith, by Professor Edwin Walters, an accredited archaeologist on the staff of the Kansas City, Pittsburg, and Gulf Railway. "It is estimated that there are between two to three thousand remains of warriors to the acre," he reported, "and by simple arithmetical calculations, the strength of the opposing forces has been deduced." In other words, the 30-acre archaeological zone enclosed the skeletons of about one hundred thousand people, ranking it among the greatest massacre sites ever recorded. By way of comparison, the Civil War battle of Gettysburg, which was fought over a much larger area, claimed 7,058 lives.

Six centuries of art and science, together with every man, woman, and child of a gifted people, had vanished forever in a flash of genocidal ferocity.

Five

WHO WERE THE HOPEWELL?

Modern visitors approach the great monument with a sense of increasing awe and wonder. What kind of society, so many centuries ago, could have raised such an enormous and perfectly proportioned structure? Its massive earthen walls slope to form a truncated pyramid or, more properly, a temple mound. Long ago, a steeply gabled, wood-frame, straw-roofed building stood at its top. Within the mound's grass-covered exterior reposed the skeletal remains of a mysterious people, who made their enduring, architectural mark on the landscape, then unaccountably abandoned the vicinity forever.

The nameless dead slept among copper ornaments and weapons, together with amulets and necklaces of skillfully wrought mother-of-pearl. Accompanying them were scant traces of exquisitely woven textiles and more common fragments of fantastically designed pottery, finely engraved bone, and delicately carved shell, all testifying to the high order of intelligence that once prevailed here. Lively petroglyphs deeply etched into a nearby rock face tell something of the artistic and spiritual aspects of the vanished Mound Builders—but this pyramid is not the only one of its kind. Others, some much larger in size and even richer in grave goods, are found along major rivers and down to the seashore.

Though this description might apply to a typical site of North America's ancient Hopewell culture, it just as faithfully portrays an archaeological zone in Watanuki Kannonyama Kofun, Gunma prefecture, Japan. Most experts in American prehistory are unaware that the earthworks they investigate have their overseas counterparts in the Land of the Rising Sun. Remarkably, parallels between those counterparts and earthworks here are both numerous and astonishingly close. Even in mounds that are peculiarly Japanese, points of comparison with monumental construction in pre-Columbian America are unavoidable.

An outstanding example is the massive structure at Shimane-ken, a colossal burial mound curiously shaped to resemble a keyhole. Such unusual structures are known as *zempokoenfun,* or burial tumuli with a rounded rear mound attached to a rectilinear mound at the front. At 1,458 feet long and 28 feet high, it is one of ancient Japan's grandest material achievements. Like some Hopewell sites found near Chillicothe, Ohio, or at Pinson, Tennessee, it was first laid out in courses of flagstone and gravel, then covered over with clay and capped with earth. Unlike anything similarly discovered so far in North America, however, a passageway leads from the eastern-oriented entrance to the innermost recesses of the mound.

Shimane-ken was contemporary with Late Hopewell, circa AD 300. Mound building in Japan began during the middle phases of the Jomon Period (3000 BC–1000 BC), resumed in the Early Yayoi Period (around 400 BC), and culminated during the Kofun Period (AD 250–600). Jomon means "cord mark" and refers to the impressed rope patterns featured on pottery of the period. The name Yayoi derives from the site (Yayoi-chos) near Tokyo, where that culture was first identified. Kofun is a name of the particular burial tumuli associated with the first centuries AD. The end of the Jomon Period coincides with North America's Adena period, when large-scale mound building was going on throughout the Ohio Valley.

Outsized, stone structures, such as southern Indiana's Lewis Mound, appeared in Adena times, just as the Late Jomon Period witnessed the creation of similar stone features at Hokkaido's Kiusu site. Moreover, the reappearance of large earthworks in Japan during the Initial Yayoi

Period coincides with the resumption of American mound building in the Hopewell culture, which came to a close just two hundred years before the end of the Kofun Period.

The greatest building achievement of ancient Japan occurred in the Middle Jomon Period, before 1000 BC, with the creation of a stone-and-soil mound no less than 2,153 feet square. At Kitsu, the largest Yayoi pyramid, surrounded by a complex of lesser earthworks, was 246 feet across on the outside, with an inner diameter of 111.5 feet, and it stood nearly 18 feet high. The 106,000 cubic feet of soil that went into its construction could have been moved by twenty-five laborers in 125 days if each man handled 35 cubic feet per day. These construction details parallel exactly American mound building taking place in the Midwest during Hopewell times at the same moment Kitsu's temple mound was raised. What's more, like their North American counterparts, the Yayoi mounds were primarily burial sites for chieftains and shamans.

Edward Baelz, writing for the Smithsonian Institution in the early

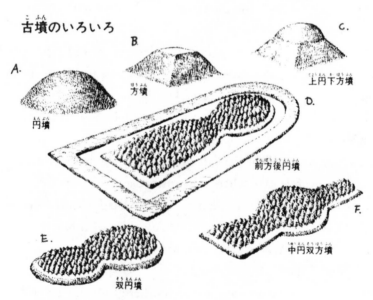

Fig. 5.1. Prehistoric Japan's main types of ceremonial earthworks. Though Kofun Period structures (D, E, and F) are uniquely Japanese, Yayoi examples (A, B, and C) are contemporaneous with and virtually identical to Hopewell mounds. (Courtesy of Ancient American *magazine)*

Fig. 5.2. This model of a fourth-century Hopewell pyramid at Chicago's Field Museum of Natural History closely resembles mounds raised in Japan during the same period.

twentieth century, was among the first archaeologists to describe for American readers a typical Yayoi burial mound known as a *misasagi,* or princely sepulchre: "Around the whole structure runs a large ditch or moat. The orientation of the long dimension is east and west." These fundamental features match exactly Hopewell monuments throughout the Ohio Valley, and most particularly at Mound City, outside Chillicothe. Though Hopewell's Yayoi contemporaries did not construct anything comparable to Ohio's astronomical computer, the immense Octagon Mound, archaeo-astronomy in Japan went back at least to the second millennium BC.

Thirty ancient observatories are scattered from the northernmost tip of Honsu to Fukushima in the south. They are typified by the Manza and Nonakado stone circles, both roughly the same size and about 250 feet apart, outside the small, hot-springs town of Oyu. The 150-foot-wide structures comprise concentric circles of stones from the Akuya River, some four miles east of Oyu. A single monolith stands upright at the center.

Fig. 5.3. One of Japan's Oyu megalithic circles

Although the stone circles have not received the level of attention they deserve, their cursory examination has revealed that they are oriented to various positions of the sun, with particular emphasis on Midsummer Day, still a day of special ceremonial significance in modern Japan. Because insufficient investigation of the monuments' celestial positioning has been carried out, whatever additional orientations they may incorporate have not so far been determined. Researchers, moreover, speculate only that the structures are four thousand years old on virtually no real evidence. In any case, the existence of Honsu's astronomically aligned structures preceding or contemporaneous with the observatory at Newark joins the growing number of commonalities between ancient Japan and Hopewellian North America. Coinciding with Hopewell times, the Yayoi mounds, according to Professor Nobuhiro Yoshida (President of The Japan Petroglyphy Society at Kitakyushi), were all oriented to the setting sun.

The identifiably East Asian elephants portrayed in Hopewell effigy mounds such as those found on the east side of the Mississippi River, from Lake Pepin in the north to the Wisconsin River in the south,

The first meeting of Kelts and Native Americans three thousand years ago, envisioned in this original painting by the late Charles Platt. (Courtesy of *Ancient American* magazine)

Left: A Roman-era coin found in Wisconsin features the likeness of a Keltic tribal chieftain. (Courtesy of *Ancient American* magazine)

Native American spirituality had its ancient European influences, as depicted in Davis R. Wagner's re-creation of a tribal sunrise ceremony: The Keltic solar god, Belenus, appears on a rock, upper left, his four faces representing the different seasons. (Courtesy of *Ancient American* magazine)

Above: Keltic-like stone structure at New Hampshire's Mystery Hill. (Photograph by Brian Sullivan)

Left: A solar orientation at New Hampshire's Mystery Hill. (Photograph by Brian Sullivan)

Pre-Columbian rock art
depicts the *piasu* monster,
rife with Keltic imagery.
Re-creation at Alton, Illinois.

Above: The so-called Beastmaster, a Keltic
shaman wearing antler headgear, sits in
meditative lotus position, as depicted on
Denmark's Gundestrup Cauldron.

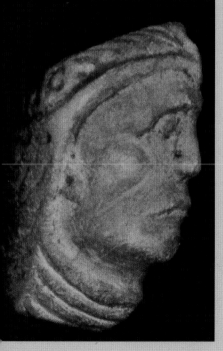

Left: This small stone head from a three-
thousand-year-old burial mound in the
Ohio Valley is among the rare examples
of Adena portrait sculpture.

Above left: The Adena dwarf pipe. (Courtesy of *Ancient American* magazine)

Above right: In this painting by David R. Wagner, Sqannit, matriarch of the Makie wisag, or Little People, administers incense and potions to an ailing member of the Mogoshketomp, as Algonquian myth referred to the Adena, Big People. Keltic themes appear in the star map hung on the wall of Sqannit's beehive stone chamber. (Courtesy of *Ancient American* magazine)

Re-creation of an Adena shaman at the Ohio Museum of Archaeology in Columbus. Ritual use of human skulls was important to both Keltic Europeans and Adena in North America.

Right: A computer re-creation of Ohio's bizarre Fort Hill. By artist Jack Andrews. (Courtesy of *Ancient American* magazine)

Center: Hopewell ceremonial center at Mound City, Chillicothe, Ohio.

Below: Hopewell mounds in St. Paul, Minnesota, were oriented to seasonal celestial phenomena.

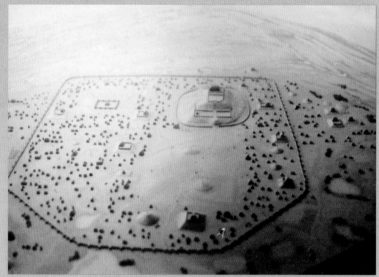

Above: Prehistoric Illinois' colossal Monks Mound, larger at its base than Egypt's Great Pyramid

Left: Monks Mound and ceremonial area surrounded by its wall with palisade. Model on display at the Cahokia Mounds Archaeological Museum, Collinsville, Illinois.

Alabama's Mound State Monument with re-created Mississippian temple at its summit.

The Anasazi solar observatory, Casa Rinconcada, New Mexico.

Above: Ruins of
Chaco Canyon in
New Mexico, once the
power center of the
American Southwest.
(Photograph by
Florence W. McLain)

Left: The cliff dwellings
of Mesa Verde in
Colorado were a last
refuge for the doomed
Anasazi. (Photograph
by Stephen Dempsey)

implies Oriental influences of at least some kind during the Hopewell period. The existence of these bioglyphs has always been and remains a sore spot for mainstream archaeologists, who long ago made up their minds that prehistoric North Americans were entirely ignorant of elephants. The proprietors of official doctrine insist that the effigies do not depict elephants, but must portray something else. What they represent, precisely, is not known—but official archaeologists insist they cannot possibly be elephants, even though they resemble them exactly.

This blinkered dogma was demolished handily more than a hundred years ago by Jared Warner, a writer for *The Smithsonian Report,* together with Henry C. Mercer, prominent in the Bucks County Historical Society of Pennsylvania and author of *Ancient Carpenter's Tools,* still regarded as a standard work on Colonial life, and other works. The seven-story Mercer Museum is today a national landmark located in Doyleston, a Philadelphia suburb. In Warner's 1872 article, he described an earthwork commonly referred to by area residents since pioneer days as the "elephant mound of Patch Grove in Grant County," just below the mouth of the Wisconsin River. The bioglyph measured 135 feet long, 60 feet wide, and 3 feet high. When Mercer personally examined it in 1883, he declared that it unquestionably represented an Asian elephant and nothing else.

The Asian or Asiatic elephant (*Elephas maximus*), sometimes known as the Indian elephant, inhabits primarily large parts of Bangladesh, India, Sri Lanka, Indochina, and Indonesia, where it was and still is venerated as the deity of wisdom, Genesha. Early on, his worship was imported by the Japanese, who called him *Shoden.* This would explain why Asian elephants were repeatedly depicted as effigy mounds in the Upper Midwest during Hopewell times. They featured as bioglyphs because they were religious representations of the god Shoden. All Hopewell effigy mounds were revered as sacred images.

But the portrayal of elephants was not limited to ancient earthworks in North America. Several Hopewell platform pipes were fashioned in the unmistakable shape of the Asiatic elephant. A prime specimen was accidentally found during 1873 by Peter Mare, described by *American Antiquarian* as "an illiterate German farmer," while he planted corn in Louisa County, Iowa. Made of a soft, fragile sandstone, the elephant pipe weighed 5.8 ounces, and was 3.5 inches long, 1.5 inches high, and almost 1 inch thick. Pipes, like effigy mounds, were holy objects.

Many Native American tribes valued cinnabar very highly for both its medicinal and magical properties. The bright scarlet or brick-red iron mercury sulfide belongs to the hexagonal crystal system. In fact, it resembles quartz in symmetry and certain of its optical characteristics. Like quartz, it exhibits birefringence (the resolution or splitting of a light wave into two unequally reflected or transmitted waves), and has the highest refractive power of any mineral. What precisely any of these qualities might have meant to the ancients is unknown. In any case, cinnabar has been recovered from several Hopewell earthworks, just as 66 pounds of it were excavated from a 141-foot wide Late Yayoi temple mound at Tatesuki, Okayama prefecture.

Shell bracelets also played a similar part in both cultures. They were used to establish social rank among the Hopewell. Richard Pearson, a respected authority on ancient Japan, writes of the Yayoi, "Shell bracelets exchanged from Okinawa to Kyushu played an important role in making status distinctions."[1]

In addition, Yayoi mound sites were concentrations of political power in ceremonial centers—the same function served by their North American counterparts.

Nor were Japanese mounds the only construction features comparable to contemporaneous American architecture. The ancient traditional long house (a pole-and-dried-grass shelter built over a ritual firepit; it served as a sweat lodge, ceremonial temple, and council house) is still used by many Native American tribes. A recreated long house may be seen at Seven Pillars, a sacred site in Peru, Indiana. It is identical to structures erected in Japan during the Middle Jomon Period, three thousand years ago. According to Hiroshi Yamashita, a leading Japanese archaeologist, "There are no comparable examples of buildings of similar scale except among the Pacific Northwest hunters and gatherers."

Great quantities of polished shell beads from mounds excavated at the Ryukyus (an island chain trailing southward from Okinawa) might have been found in a dig anywhere throughout the Ohio Valley.

Another similarity: as at most Hopewell sites, large villages clustered around the Japanese pyramids. The burial practices evidenced at Late Jomon and Kofun monuments contrasted sharply with the native Ainu, and defined the Japanese mound builders as a race apart in their own land.

The Yayoi valued hematite, which they sprinkled over their honored dead before internment. This funeral custom involved the same blood-red iron oxide found in trace elements at a number of Hopewell burials. Prehistoric Japanese included clay-fired figurines as funeral gifts, but the statuettes were broken immediately prior to internment, a practice followed identically throughout North America during pre-Columbian times. Particularly revealing, the Japanese mound builders manufactured ritual clay figurines called *dogu*. Holes were drilled through the tops of the dolls' heads and lower jaws; into these were installed feathers. The only people outside Japan to fashion dogu were American Indian tribes of the northwest coast. Of these, the Klamath of northern California and Oregon are especially remarkable. Their Penutian dialect, though incomprehensible to Native Americans of other, unrelated tribes, is partially translatable into the Japanese language. Even today, many tourists from Japan are able to converse with Klamath Indians in their own speech. The modern Japanese language is, in its fundamentals, essentially the same tongue spoken by the Jomon five thousand years ago. This remarkable survival and continuity were established by glittochronologists, linguists who determine time frames for the separation of branches of a family of languages from a parent language.

Dr. Gunnar Thompson reports:

Asian language scholar Don Smithsana believes most of the coastal plains inhabitants used an ancient language called Archaic Japanese.

During World War II, Smithsana observed that Native Americans were able to communicate with Japanese prisoners. He discovered words that were common among North American natives had the same meaning in the ancient language of Japan. Thus, Smithsana used ancient Japanese dictionaries to deduce the meaning of hundreds of Native American terms, such as *kiva, maize*, and *menomonie*.

Smithsana believes the southwestern term *kiva*—meaning "sacred pit house"—was derived from the Archaic Japanese term *kiva*—meaning "place of meditation." According to his theory, the Native American term for "corn'" (*maize*) was derived from the Archaic Japanese *meshi*—meaning "corn porridge." A Great Lakes tribe of Michigan called the Menomonee were so named because they were gatherers of wild rice, called *manoomin*. Smithsana believes their name originally came from the Archaic Japanese *menominee*— meaning "rice gatherers."[2]

International language scholar Nobuhiro Yoshida discovered numerous Japanese words in the daily speech of the Zuni, a tribe residing in western New Mexico. (See appendix 3.) He has been seconded by Nancy Yaw Davis, a Ph.D. anthropologist from the University of Washington. She additionally found that the exceptionally high incidence of a specific kidney disease among the Zuni is also unusually common in Japan. The Zuni "sacred rosette" found on robes and pottery, Davis notes, is strikingly similar to the Japanese Buddhist chrysanthemum symbol of Japan's imperial crest. A Zuni mid-January observance with masked monsters aimed at frightening children into proper behavior is virtually identical to the *Namahage* ceremony in Japan.

She observes:

[S]ome Zuni resemble the Japanese, especially those from the Kyoto region, or relocated Tibetans. Old pictures of the Zuni community, like other pueblos in the Southwest from the late 19th Century, depict Tibetan-like houses in recessed clusters of apartments, many storied, with wooden ladders connecting the rooftops. Zuni women appeared in dresses with a manta at an angle across the right shoulder, also very much in the Tibetan style.[3]

In our discussion of Iowa's Marching Bear Mounds, we noted that the star clusters Ursa Major and Ursa Minor were known as the Big Bear and the Little Bear throughout much of pre-Columbian North America, from the Pacific Northwest across the continent to Nova Scotia. So too, these stellar patterns are known in Japan as Oh-Guma and Ko-Guma—"Big Bear" and "Child Bear," respectively. Though some cultural diffusionists argue that the Indians named these constellations after learning about them from ancient European visitors to North America, the indigenous peoples could have been no less influenced by Japanese arriving in Yayoi or Jomon times.

Nor have Klamath-Japanese comparisons been lost on Japanese archaeologists such as Wanatabe Hitoshi, renowned among Japan's cultural anthropologists, who concludes that the Jomon "way of life was actually closer to that of the Mesolithic peoples, such as the fishing tribes of the Pacific Northwest of North America. Our view of Jomon society may be transformed if we compare the Jomon archaeological record with that of the Pacific Northwest, rather than with the ethnographic record."[4]

Other hard evidence that even would-be debunkers of cultural diffusionism are unable to deny was unearthed during 1975 in Washington State. Excavation at the extreme point of the Olympia Peninsula—known as the Ozette Site—brought to light a well-preserved village that had been completely buried under a cataclysmic mudslide, probably at the close of the fifteenth century. Among the more unusual items, such as otherwise perishable clothing and baskets, archaeologists discovered several lengths of bamboo and almost thirty iron knives featuring blades that had been smelted. The large number of smelted artifacts in a village self-evidently associated with seafaring suggested that the Ozette Site was not the accidental landfall of some hapless Oriental sailors. Rather, the iron knives, together with the presence of bamboo, represent persuasive, physical proof for the presence of prehistoric Japanese culture bearers in North America.

Japanese influences on our continent during antiquity appear to have extended far beyond the native tribes of the northern Pacific coasts, down into southern Mexico, and even to Ecuador. Maya of the Lowland Yucatán traced their ancestry back to a divine cultural hero who arrived from over the sea at a time when the natives reached only low levels of material society. He taught them the arts and sciences, good government, and a religion that involved flower sacrifice instead of human sacrifice. He was accompanied by his consort, his sister, and the couple laid the foundations for Mesoamerican civilization. Their names were Itzamna and Ixchel. Interestingly, Izanami and Izanagi were brother and sister deities who arrived over the sea to create the Japanese islands by catching up pieces of land as though fishing. They bestowed the secrets of rice farming and animal husbandry to the mortals who sprang from the soil and occupy the first place in Japanese mythology. In Maya temple art, Itzamna was portrayed as an aged (i.e., wise) bearded man among men unable to grow facial hair—hence, his implied foreign origins. His and Ixchel's parallels to Izanami and Izanagi, in the details of their myths and the similarities of their names constitute either an incredible set of coincidences, or evidence that both the Maya and the ancient Japanese were visited by the same culture bearer.

The evidence of comparative mythologies was borne out by physical proof beginning two hundred years ago, when construction workers accidentally excavated a number of marble vases at Veracruz. Mexican scholars concluded that the distinctly pear-shaped vessels were identical to Japanese vases from the Late Kofun Period, circa AD 600.

But why would the ancient Japanese trouble themselves by sailing all the way to Middle America? A good answer is the four-letter word for wealth: jade. Highly prized throughout the Orient from deepest antiquity, deposits in China were off-limits to the Japanese, whose islands were not blessed with the precious mineral. Mexico, however, especially

Yucatán, was uncommonly rich in jade mines. Indeed, exquisite necklaces and body ornaments of jade have been found in the early Yayoi site (circa 100 BC) at Yoshitake-takagi, Fukuoka prefecture. Mesoamerica's natural abundance of the blue-green gemstones would have certainly been a strong motivational factor for the ancient Japanese, who already possessed the seafaring capabilities for trans-Pacific voyages to distant, although accessible sources of jade in Yucatán.

The Itzamna-Izanami comparison was dramatically underscored during 1957, when a find was made that shook the archeological establishment to its foundations. The discovery belonged to Emilio Estrada, a businessman from one of Ecuador's more prosperous families and an amateur archaeologist. According to science writer Patrick Huyghe,

> Along the coast of the province of Guayas, he excavated a series of seashell deposits, one of which contained some heavily eroded pottery fragments. The pottery decorations resembled those found on the Peruvian coast and dated back to 2000 BC But further excavations unearthed an even deeper deposit of still better preserved pottery near the fishing village of Valdivia, in southwestern Ecuador. What Estrada found were large, rounded bowls and small, short-necked jars, many of which were polished, and all of which had been highly decorated using a variety of notching, cut-out and stamping techniques.
>
> These finds drew the attention and eventually collaboration of two Smithsonian archaeologists, Betty Meggers and Clifford Evans. Their carbon-14 analysis of charcoal from the cooking fires found in the same level as the pottery yielded an astonishingly old date. The pottery was made about 3600 B.C. The pottery from Valdivia, Ecuador, most resembles the late Early and early Middle period Jomon pottery from the Ataka and Sobata sites in central Kyushu and the Izumi site on the coast of the island.[5]

In support of the Jomon pottery, several figurines resembling dogu dolls were recovered at the Valdivia site.

The substantial number and quality of parallels between the ancient mound builders of Japan and their counterparts in the Americas preclude mere coincidence. If one or two superficial similarities cannot justify conclusions affirming contact between two, widely separated cultures, then the abundance of valid comparisons afforded by the richness of such evidence argues persuasively on behalf of prehistoric contacts.

Already, by the mid-fourth millennium BC, the Neolithic Japanese had become accomplished sailors, as proved by their occupation of the Ryukyu Islands, spread across great distances from the mainland, and the far-flung trading networks they established over prodigious stretches of open water. An example of their maritime proficiency recently came to light with excavation of a seagoing Jomon vessel from the Torihama Shell Mound, Fukui prefecture. Dated to circa 3500 BC, the freighter had an original shipping capacity of 1,100 pounds. With craft such as these, trans-Pacific voyages would not have been denied the ancient Japanese.

An indication of their fascination with long-distance voyages is Okinoshima, an island shrine off the west coast of Kyushu in the Sea of Japan. Honored as the home of the ocean gods, gifts of bronze and pearl from hopeful seafarers piled up along its sacred cliffs and crags for more than five centuries, beginning around AD 375.

Some researchers believe trans-Pacific Japanese preceded even these early voyages by many thousands of years to become the first human settlers in the New World. Remarkably and encouragingly, this conclusion is not the pronouncement of some maverick cultural diffusionist, but the studied opinion of a mainstream scientist. "What was once imponderable now seems entirely conceivable and increasingly likely," Jon Erlandson, an archaeologist at the University of Oregon, told the *Japan Times* in August, 2007. "The oldest form of DNA ever recovered from the New World—around 10,300 years old—is common in type to that found in Japan and Tibet. And similar DNA has been found in American Indians all the way down the west coast of North and South America."

Erlandson believes the Japanese arrived in the New World almost six thousand years earlier, when massive glaciers began retreating from the outer Northwest American coast. He "found evidence indicating that inhabitants of Honshu set out across the North Pacific more than 20,000 years ago to Kozushima, an island in the Izu chain 31 miles south of Tokyo, to collect a type of volcanic glass to make tools."[6]

They journeyed northward from there to the Kuril Islands, then to the Kamchatka Peninsula and on to the shore of the Bering land bridge, and beyond to the New World. The "first people to arrive were probably fishermen who followed a near continuous belt of kelp forests in the coastal waters of the Pacific Rim, from Japan to Alaska and southern California." Erlandson's evidence for Japanese impact on prehistoric America was presented for peer review in the summer 2007 edition of the prestigious *New Scientist* magazine. The following February, his conclusions were affirmed by Dr. Theodore Schurr of the Southwest Foundation for Biomedical Research in San Antonio, Texas, before members of the American Association for the Advancement of Science. Dr. Schurr explained that "power packs" of cells called mitochondria revealed ancestral migration patterns imprinted in the DNA of modern Indians.

The mitochondria traced four major lineages in Native Americans going back more than thirteen centuries to Siberia and northeast Asia, notably in Baikal and Altai-Sayan. But a fifth lineage among Native Americans originates in Europe. The identifying DNA, known as haplogroup X, is found most among Algonquian-speaking groups, such as the Ojibwa. "These data imply that haplogroup X was present in the New World long before Europeans first arrived in the New World," said Dr. Schurr, "before Columbus, or the Vikings, or anybody else"—about thirty thousand years ago.[7] He argued that the Europeans almost certainly arrived by sea, because evidence of haplogroup X has not so far been found in Asia.

DNA studies also demonstrated that the Blackfoot and Iroquois and other tribes from Minnesota, Michigan, Ontario, and Massachusetts are partially descended from neolithic Japanese. These North American tribes found their lineage in the Jomon, who invented pottery manufacturing after 10,000 BC, and who were renowned seafarers. Their pottery dating to at least three thousand years ago had already been recovered along coastal South America in the late twentieth century.

Accumulating DNA research demonstrates that neither first-millennium-BC Kelts nor fourth-century-BC Japanese were the discoverers of North America. Instead, both peoples had been preceded by waves of visitors from Europe and Japan for thousands of years. At least some of these earlier contacts were undoubtedly known to the Keltic and Yayoi mound builders. They did not simply shove off into the unknown, but instead knew where they were going, thanks to generations of transoceanic mariners who made landfall on our continent for the previous twenty-seven thousand years.

Supporting Japan's early links with the sea, the largest Yayoi settlement, a harbor city encompassing nearly 200 acres, was established at Asahi, Aichi prefecture, on the Owari Plain, which stood close to the shoreline two thousand years ago. The area has since silted up, so today, the site is inland. Moreover, a natural, direct highway connected and still connects Japan to the Americas. The Japan current moves in a great, circular motion, making well-provisioned, round-trip expeditions to the Americas entirely feasible.

Striving to prove that such prehistoric voyages were possible, six Japanese investigators sailed from Shimoda, Japan, in 1980, manning a 43-foot replica of the catamarans depicted in Jomon rock art. Christened the *Yasei-go* ("Wild Adventure"), their vessel followed the Pacific currents to arrive in San Francisco after only fifty-one days at sea. From there, they proceeded south through a storm to land in Guayaquil, Ecuador, then on to Valparaiso, Chile, successfully covering more than ten-thousand miles of open water. The *Yasei-go*'s performance established beyond question that such feats of navigation were possible during prehistory. As Dr. Thor Heyerdahl pointed out, to ancient humans, the seas of our planet were not impassable barriers but, on the contrary, beckoning highways.

The mythic impact made by ancient Japanese on the Maya, their enduring linguistic legacy in the speech of the Klamath Indians, and the profusion of Jomon pottery finds in coastal Ecuador do not bespeak unusual, chance contacts in the New World from Japan. A few fishermen accidentally blown off-course across the Pacific would have been quickly and thoroughly assimilated by the natives, without making any impression on the indigenous culture. Yet quite the opposite is true. The evidence suggests that contacts from Jomon Japan were more than infrequent and stamped lasting influences on pre-Columbian American societies.

But what prompted the ancient Japanese to first attempt transoceanic voyages? A natural disaster may provide the answer. In 3550 BC, a major volcanic event occurred on a small island off the coast of Kyushu. Known as *Kikai,* the eruption out-gassed enough ashfall and magmatic debris to render the surrounding territories uninhabitable for at least several years, perhaps decades, thereby displacing regional populations. Appropriately, Kikai's devastating blast and the Jomon pottery found in Ecuador share the same time parameters. It seems, then, that Japanese mariners began visiting the Americas some fifty-five hundred years ago—but only after their Jomon Period reached a certain population density during its Late Middle Phase, around 1000 BC, did the Americas receive numbers sufficient to make a lasting cultural impact. If this is so, then a Japanese presence in the first millennium BC accounts for an otherwise inexplicable aspect of the Alleg, or Adena, people: their linear stone mounds. These characteristic structures were unknown to the Kelts, who appear to have been the progenitors of Adena society and, in fact, the Alleg themselves. Such a monumental style never occurred in Western Europe or anywhere else in the ancient world outside of a thirty-mile-long, twelve-mile-wide collection of islands off the southeast coast of Japan.

During antiquity, the Amakusa islands "were so remote, only a few sea-tribes, known as the Munakata, inhabited them," according to Professor Yoshida. Yet these prehistoric mariners erected stone mounds identical in configuration and dimensions to those found throughout the Adena sphere of influence. Perfectly preserved examples stand near Ryu-toh, or "Dragon Head Mountain," just outside the hamlet of Kuradake-cho. They are joined by lines of much smaller conical mounds just 2.5 feet high, which suggest models of the same design preferred by

Fig. 5.4. A Japanese linear stone mound near Dragon Head Mountain in Japan is identical to structures found in Rock Lake, Wisconsin, and among late-Adena/early-Hopewell sites.

the Allewegi, with special similarity to the stone features encountered by divers at the bottom of Wisconsin's Rock Lake.

Archaeological investigation at Kuradake-cho has been cursory at best, enough to insure official preservation of the pyramidal mounds, but inadequate to determine their precise age or the exact identity of their builders. Yet their enduring, local attribution to a maritime people underscores a singular resemblance to the Adena mounds, thereby making a persuasive argument for ritual Japanese construction influences at work in North America's pre-Columbian Midwest.

The Munakata are enshrined in folk tradition as a semi-legendary people, long extinct, who were renowned for their far-flung sea voyages allegedly undertaken during that nebulous period separating ancestral myth from the uncertain beginnings of Japan's history. If the Munakata did make long-distance voyages to North America, they undoubtedly settled first on the Pacific shores of British Columbia, where their cultural and genetic impact on the Haida and other Northwest coast Indian tribes persists to this day. Some Japanese migrated southward along the

Rocky Mountains, into regions occupied by the Zuni, who still bear distinctive linguistic traces left by contact with the Asiatic foreigners (see appendix 3), who were eventually absorbed into the native population.

Other Munakata wandered farther eastward, settling on the western banks of the Mississippi River. After having been on the move almost constantly through the Dakota Badlands, fending off tribal warfare practically every step of the way, arriving at the Father of Waters must have seemed as though they were entering the Promised Land. The area was not only teeming with abundant game and edible plants, but was also the westernmost boundary of a different people.

A Lenape Indian folk memory preserved by the early-nineteenth-century Moravian missionary John Heckewelder told how "they sent a message to the Allegewi to request permission to settle themselves in their neighborhood. This was refused them, but they obtained leave to pass through the country and seek a settlement farther to the eastward. They accordingly began to cross the Namesi Sipu [Mississippi River] . . ."[8]

The Adena and Lenapee soon after came into conflict with each other when the former grew alarmed at the vast numbers of in-coming Indians, but the story nonetheless illustrates Allewegi willingness to deal rationally with outsiders. The less numerous, less bellicose Munakata were not threatening, and would have been allowed to settle on the western side of the Mississippi, where, in fact, the oldest known stone mounds in North America are found at Camp Lacupolis, on the outskirts of Lake City, and one and a half miles away at Reads Landing, on the river's Minnesota side.

Interestingly, just across the Big Muddy, prominently displayed high atop a bluff on the Wisconsin side at Hagerstown, facing the Japanese settlement, is the colossal, crystal eagle mound. It may have been deliberately laid out by the Allewegi as a very public definition of their territory. In any case, the chronological distribution of stone mound building evolved from west to east, beginning on the Minnesota banks of the Mississippi River, and eventually moving across Wisconsin to archaeological sites such as Butte de Morts and Rock Lake, into Michigan's

Heritage Park and southern Indiana, through the Ohio Valley, and to the Eastern Seaboard, where the last stone mounds were erected in Maryland and New York State as late as 100 BC.

This slow but persistent progression of Kuradake-cho-style burial monuments across the Midwest to the Atlantic coast memorializes gradual Adena acceptance of the gentle Japanese Munakata, referred to by archaeologists as the Hopewell. Heckewelder's Indian informants told him that "for a long period of time, some say hundreds of years, the two nations resided peacefully in this country, and increased very fast." This tradition is borne out by lack of any evidence for conflict between the Adena and Hopewell peoples. Both lived in amicable coexistence—so much so that some scholars believe the latter were an outgrowth of the former.

"The traits shared by Adena and Hopewell," Adena specialist Dragoo observes, "were those already present in late Adena and donated by Adena to the new Hopewell culture which formed after the contact of Adena peoples with the long-headed population which had lived north of the area of Adena occupation."[9] In some Hopewell mounds, Ohio archaeologist Francis Hamilton notes, "the inclusion of broken pottery is similar to the Adena practice of placing broken pottery in the fill of their mounds."[10] To be sure, the Munakata were influenced by the older inhabitants, and adopted some of their material culture, including conical earthworks, resulting in a hybrid no longer exclusively Japanese, but instead unique in prehistoric North America.

The Adena and Hopewell were racially dissimilar. The Adena were tall of stature, big boned, broad shouldered, and fair in complexion. Bilateral eminences formed at the strong jaw hinge of their oversized, heavy skulls, a cranial trait that set them apart from all other ancient Americans. Dragoo points out:

[T]wo outstanding traits have been noted repeatedly for this group. One is the protruding and massive chin often with prominent bilateral protrusions. The second trait is the large size of many of the males and some of the females. A male of six feet was common and some individuals approaching seven feet in height have been found. . . . Not only were these Adena people tall, but also the massiveness of the bones indicates powerfully built individuals. The head was generally big with a large cranial capacity.[11]

In sharp contrast, smaller Hopewell skulls, in the word used on a label showcased at Ohio's Mound City Museum, were "gracile." They were finer featured, their jaws missing any bilateral protrusions. Hopewell skeletons belonged to a people of an entirely dissimilar, more lithe body type of much shorter stature, below 5 feet, 6 inches. Yet both they and the Allewegi were genetically separate from the Plains Indians who surrounded and outnumbered them.

"It should be stated that until now," antiquarian Ross Hamilton tells us, "DNA testing has found no specific match between the Adena–Hopewell and any existing Native American group." In other words, the

Fig. 5.5. This wood figure retrieved from a fourth-century Ohio Valley burial mound indicates strong genetic influences from Japan among the Hopewell.

Adena and Hopewell were two, different races distinct from and unrelated to the Plains Indians, whose lineage stretched back thirteen thousand years to their ancestral homelands in Siberia. That the Adena were Kelts seems abundantly borne out by a wealth of confirming evidence from the Atlantic Seaboard's look-alike stone chambers to Adena iron smelters and Western European body types in pre-Columbian Ohio.

The Hopewell were an altogether different people from the opposite side of the world—the Munakata, seafarers from Japan's Amakusa islands, where stone mounds were raised during the Late Middle phase of the Jomon Period, around 1000 BC. A new, eastward wave of trans-Pacific migration occurred during the initial Yayoi Period, around 200 BC, when identical mound building started simultaneously in Japan and the Ohio Valley. The Hopewell began in the American Midwest at the same time the Yayoi sprouted in the vicinity of Tokyo—because both were Japanese.

For all their racial and cultural differences, Adena and Hopewell overlapped and complemented each other, thanks to their fundamental compatibility. The root of cooperation lay in their combined minority status as civilizers amid a hostile majority of Plains Indians. During this shared period, the Allewegi built stone hill forts to shelter both themselves and their Hopewellian allies against the rising tide of war.

According to Hamilton and *Ancient American* author Patricia Mason, "The accounts of the Allegheny say that they built strong fortifications."[12] Eventually, even these formidable bastions were overrun by outnumbering masses of the enemy. They exterminated the Hopewell people in a paroxysm of mass murder around AD 400. The Adena held out another three centuries, until they, too, were engulfed by extermination.

For the next 200 years, our continent was shrouded under a dark age. It would not be lifted until new torch bearers of an entirely different civilization made their way into the North American heartland from neither east nor west, but from the south.

Six

MISSISSIPPIANS REIGNITE THE TORCH OF CIVILIZATION

With the obliteration of the Hopewell, followed three hundred years later by their Adena allies, the lamp of civilization went out in North America. Over the next two centuries, the abandoned ceremonial centers and monuments of both peoples fell into decay, shunned as haunted places of evil by the victorious tribal warriors and hunter-gatherers whose own ancestors had preceded them by millennia.

Only after the turn of the tenth century did the dark ages fade with the arrival of a very different kind of civilizer. The newcomers showed up in large numbers, settling throughout the Mississippi valley from the Gulf of Mexico to Wisconsin. Hence, the characterization of their society by archaeologists as the Mississippian culture. Its members were serious agriculturists, whose abundant fields of corn were required to feed the dense populations of their cities, such as Cahokia, that megalopolis sprawling on the Illinois side of the Mississippi River. But this city was even greater than described at the opening of our investigation.

On the Missouri side of the river stands St. Louis. Previous to its birth in the late seventeenth century, it was known as Mound City for the profusion of ancient earthworks concentrated in the immediate vicinity. The noted explorer and archaeologist Stephen D. Peet visited the site in 1811, before expansion of the modern city had "destroyed the last vestige of the large group, which could once be seen there, and all the pyramids, cones, 'falling gardens,' terraces and platforms, which once attracted attention, have disappeared."

He counted more than one hundred fifty earthworks, but realized even these formed only part of an even greater urban development:

> There were at the time several large groups of mounds, one situated on the bluffs where St. Louis now stands; another on the bank of the Mississippi River, not far from the present site of East St. Louis; a third on the bottom lands about ten miles below the old village of Cahokia; the fourth about ten miles above the old village. . . . We speak of this because there has been a general impression that the celebrated "Cahokia" mound, or "Monks Mound," is a solitary pyramid, and that it has no connection with any of the works in the vicinity . . . the works of the entire region were all of them of the same class, the majority of them having been truncated pyramids.[1]

Unfortunately, that "general impression that 'Monks Mound' is a solitary pyramid, and that it has no connection with any of the works in the vicinity" prevails today among archaeologists, who continue to underestimate the prehistoric urban center's far vaster extent than the limitations they assign it. After factoring in Mound City and its affiliated, outlying areas, Cahokia's population may have approached two hundred thousand people. Accordingly, their influence was far-reaching. Pottery and stone tools in the Cahokian style have been found as far north as the Silvernail site near Red Wing, Minnesota.

The labor-intensive scope of their metropolitan achievement was apparent even before Cahokia was built. Soil studies reveal that the pre-Cahokia landscape was originally undulating, but later expertly leveled—all four thousand acres of it—by ancient construction engineers. Today's archaeological zone includes sixty-eight mounds, although another forty-one still exist outside the park. Cahokia was the urban hub from which Mississippian culture radiated outward to dominate the North American heartland. An important outpost sprouted in

Fig. 6.1. Reconstructed temple at Angel Mounds in Indiana

what is today the university city of Evansville, at the southernmost end of Indiana. Known as Angel Mounds, the site shared a common solar alignment with its Illinois counterpart. The doorway of Angel's chief temple was oriented to sunrise of the summer solstice, the same fix that occurred at Monks Mound. Cahokia is, in fact, physically linked to Angel Mounds by the Mississippi and Ohio Rivers.

About four thousand residents inhabited the 103-acre settlement, which included eleven earthen platforms surmounted by temples and palaces made of wooden posts and dried grass daubed with white adobe.

The mounds were interspersed with two hundred secular dwellings, some for winter, others for summer. Their walls were decorated with geometric themes colored red, yellow, and blue. Nearby were numerous gardens of corn, beans, pumpkin, gourds, and sunflowers. Pecans were gathered in a grove beside a step pyramid 44 feet high and 4 acres in area. An unusual plaza was sunk like a great bowl into the ground. Within this broad depression ceremonial, athletic, and market activities took place, according to diorama displays at Angel Mounds Museum of Archaeology, in Evansville.

Originally, the site was almost entirely surrounded by a river channel, practically rendering Angel Mounds an island. The site was

Fig. 6.2. The walls of Angel Mounds were composed of posts packed with branches and entirely coated by a thick plaster of ground mollusk shells mixed with clay and water, as shown in this re-created section at the Angel Mounds Archaeology Museum, Evansville, Indiana. The walls of all Mississippian ceremonial cities were identically constructed.

inexplicably abandoned by its leaders and most of its population about 1310. Why they left and where they went remain mysteries still bedeviling scholars' best efforts to understand America's prehistory. The inhabitants left behind no signs of disease, war, social upheaval, crop failures, overfishing or overhunting, earthquakes, or severe weather. For the next one hundred forty years, the site was occupied off and on by diverse, small numbers of primitive wanderers who knew little or nothing of Angel Mounds' former glories. By 1450, the place was deserted.

Among the atypical items recovered by archaeologists was a mastodon's tooth from a shaman's grave and burial urns—circular pots containing the bones of infants covered with pebbles. The most outstanding feature at Angel Mounds is a faithful reconstruction of the large temple building. Unlike Cahokia, little or no human sacrifice took place, and there were no large-scale acts of social violence.

The inhabitants either chose the location for its peculiar features or purposely altered it (formed its earth) to conform to their requirements. In many ancient cultures, water was perceived as a boundary between this world and the next. Consequently, passing over water from mundane existence outside the walls into the otherworld of pyramid mounds constituted an important ritual act in itself. That the inhabitants of Angel Mounds regarded their city as something more than a commercial or political enterprise may also be surmised from the fragments of broken pottery decorated with cultic emblems. Among these are symbols delineating the sacred center, such as the circle cross. In every recovered example, the cross appears midpoint in representations of the sun.

The world is familiar with Chicago, the Windy City of skyscrapers sprawling along the southern shores of Lake Michigan, but few Chicagoans can guess that their "toddlin' town" occupies a site far more remote in human history than they were ever taught in school. In 1673, the first modern Europeans, French explorers Louis Joliet and Jacques Marquette, arrived in the area later occupied by the city of Chicago. All they found at the time was a sparsely inhabited, wildly overgrown region of mudflats that were difficult and often impossible to cross. Not until the close of the nineteenth century, long after the city had arisen, Phoenix-like, from the Great Fire that virtually annihilated it in 1871, did Illinois archaeologists develop serious interest in the area's prehistory.

They were disappointed to discover that much of the region was almost entirely uninhabited until the coming of white trappers, traders, and adventurers only one hundred years before the city was incorporated in 1837. No evidence could be found for more than occasional tribes wandering across northeastern Illinois. As far as the experts could determine, the Chicago area was always a cultural backwater until the eighteenth-century arrival of the French. Their conclusion is largely seconded today by certified archaeologists, who are unaware of discoveries made by Charles Dilg. He single-handedly pushed back the antiquity of Chicago's roots by a thousand years or more, and while his is by no means a household name, Dilg's achievements deserve recognition because they broaden our perspective of northern Illinois' otherwise unsuspected past.

Born in Germany, Charles Augustus Dilg is described by *The Early Chicago Encyclopedia* as "a valuable historian and amateur archaeologist, active in Chicago; wrote a history column and articles for local newspapers, as well as the manuscript, 'Chicago's Archaic History,' now at the Chicago History Museum, containing sketches of historical scenes, Indian mounds, maps of the location of former Indian campsites, pioneer roads and portage routes."[2] Dilg was a child when his parents relocated to Wisconsin for its physical resemblance to their Fatherland. They were among the first settlers in Milwaukee just five years after its incorporation in 1846.

During the Civil War, young Charles served as a member of the 26th Wisconsin Volunteers. After the close of hostilities, he studied geology, but grew more interested in the ancient earthworks of the Midwest. In 1869, Dilg settled in Chicago for the specific purpose of investigating the overlooked possibilities of its ancient foundations. He purchased a small, north-side cottage at Diversy Avenue and May Street, where he lived among his growing collection of local artifacts, and he busied himself handwriting a long catalog of finds. By his fifty-first year, he was known among the general public and professionals alike as an autodidactic expert on regional antiquities.

Dilg's greatest single discovery was of a large pyramid at what was known in the 1890s as Chetenham Beach, where 79th Street terminates at Lake Michigan on the city's south side. During that time, the area was no more than a strand for bathers and not much visited. The structure was covered entirely with sand to resemble a natural dune. Yet Dilg suspected the curiously shaped hill concealed an ancient, man-made feature. He organized a team of youthful neighborhood volunteers to carry off the sand. As his workers shoveled from the top down, they came upon a firm, leveled platform of hardened clay.

Digging more quickly now, the young men revealed a strange building with sloping sides spreading at regular angles to the ground. After a week of daylight shoveling, the edifice was completely cleared of sand, and a great temple mound stood on the shore of Lake Michigan. Press coverage was fulsome, and soon everyone was buzzing with the news of Dilg's discovery.

"I named it *The Chicago Pyramid,*" he told a reporter from *Inter-Ocean,* the city's first newspaper and one of its major dailies. "In height, it is about 45 feet and is some 250 steps or paces around its base. An extensive workshop site adjoins the pyramid mound on the north. In this locality, flint was chipped by the use of fire." He went on to describe "an inclined passageway leading to its top."[3]

Dilg made another impressive find in Chicago when he uncovered an effigy mound in the configuration of a serpent, the sole example known in Illinois and one of only a half dozen such specimens in North America. Bounded by Oakdale, Ellington, and Sheffield Avenues and North Fremont Street, the bioglyph's head pointed due south. The snake was approximately 210 feet long and about 23 feet wide at its widest section, and it was accompanied by three additional mounds: an oblate feature on its head (recalling the supposed "egg" emerging from the jaws of Ohio's Great Serpent Mound); a slightly curved ramp on its west side; and a severely eroded, apparently conical mound at its eastern flank. The northerly tail of the snake effigy turned in a hook. Like the Chicago Pyramid, a large flint workshop lay near the north side of the Oakdale Avenue Serpent Mound.

The find was written up in the *Inter-Ocean* newspaper: "The reporter walked with Mr. Dilg over the course of the Serpent Mound. At the head, the mixture of earth and ashes is to be seen. The ground is literally strewn with flint chips, arrow heads, and other prehistoric relics are discovered when the ground is trenched." While the two monumental earthworks clearly defined ancient Chicago as a ceremonial site,

Dilg found additional material evidence to demonstrate that the area was an important urban center. The same *Inter-Ocean* article reported that "something more than a ton's weight of arrowheads, spades, hammers, axes, and tools unknown elsewhere, all of an excellence that compares favorably with the work of the most advanced of the tribes of the West, have been collected within the corporate limits of Chicago, and nowhere else."[4]

Most of the artifacts were hammerstones identical to those found by the cartload in the Upper Peninsula region of the Great Lakes. It was there that the ancient copper miners excavated a mind-boggling half billion pounds of ore, the last of it from AD 900 to 1300, just when the Chicago Pyramid, as indicated by its Mississippian design, was built and functioned. Could prehistoric Chicago have been somehow connected to that colossal copper mining enterprise? Sitting near the south end of Lake Michigan and fronting important river systems leading directly into the Mississippi, the city's location may have seemed ideal to ancient shippers of the precious metal over great distances across the Midwest. Dilg's similar conclusions were supported and even expanded, as he found clusters of workshops, mostly in flint, within a broad area of the north side.

Surveying their precise locations, he was able to form a general outline of the prehistoric city's parameters:

> Use a pair of scissors to cut out all that part of the map of Chicago lying north of the Chicago River, east of the north branch and following along the lake shore. Then add the map of Evanston (the nearest northern suburb). Cut out nearly the whole of Niles Center (another northern suburb) from the Bowmanville-Niles Center Road (today's Lincoln Avenue) to the north branch. Also cut large slices from the map of the south side in the region of 40th and 79th Streets, and then clip off the southern limits of South Chicago, and you have something like the territory covered by these workshops.[5]

The ancient population center Dilg portrayed belonged to an immense settlement. That the place was overgrown beyond the recognition of archaeologists and was already long evacuated when Joliet and Marquette passed through in the late seventeenth century bespeaks its antiquity. If, as seems likely, the pre-Columbian version of Chicago belonged to the Mississippi culture, it was abandoned for about three hundred fifty years before the two French explorers arrived—time enough for 79th Street's wind-whipped beach to disguise Dilg's Chicago Pyramid as a sand dune.

By then, the metropolis was totally forgotten by the Plains Indians, who sometimes wandered along the lake shore. Yet they did preserve a faint memory of the vanished city's former glory. The name Chicago is usually translated from the language of the Potawatomi as "powerful," as in "powerful smelling" or "stinking," a reference to the wild onions that grew along the banks of the Chicago River. Though the name did indeed translate as "powerful," it actually referred to the area where the onion grew, not to the onions themselves. In other words, "Chicago" actually means "the powerful place" of pyramids, effigy mounds, and workshops of flint and hammerstones.

Prehistoric Chicago fell into obscurity again not long after Dilg found it. As the modern city grew, the workshops were covered by new streets and sidewalks. With housing development on the south side, his Chicago Pyramid was ploughed out of existence. At least part of the Sheffield Avenue Serpent Mound survived behind a fence in a neighborhood backyard until the 1920s, when it, too, vanished forever with the construction of an apartment building. No one carried on Dilg's work, and archaeological opinion after his death at sixty years of age in 1904 fell back into the misconception that nothing much preceded the establishment of modern Chicago. All that remain are a few of his sketches in contemporary newspapers almost illegible with age and his report archived in the Chicago Historical Society.

While Chicago's prehistoric heritage has been all but lost, Oklahoma's foremost Mississippian site achieved state protection. Nevertheless,

Spiro Mounds' modern history began under less than entirely ethical circumstances. The times, after all, were desperate. During the Great Depression, people did things they would have shrunk from even contemplating in better days. The half-dozen men of northeast Oklahoma were armed with picks and shovels, hardly the delicate tools of archaeology later used to investigate the ancient mound they approached on a spring morning in 1934.

Yet these excavators were not researchers after clues to prehistoric America. They were treasure hunters brought up on stories of "Indian gold" allegedly hidden in the oddly shaped earthwork, and they were determined to find it if it existed. In the more prosperous past, no one took such tales seriously, but the hysteria of the early 1930s worked on the overwrought imagination of otherwise sane citizens until they were willing to try anything, no matter how bizarre, that might free them from their ongoing want.

The half-dozen Oklahomans climbed to the top of the 30-foot-high, 300-foot-long structure known as Craig's Mound, after its last private owner. They dug straight down toward what they assumed was the center. After only a few minutes of labor, they began shoveling out pile after pile of shells that were finely engraved with the images of men dressed in unreal costumes, fabulous birds, spiders, serpents, less identifiable monsters, and geometric designs. Often, the incised shells were mixed in with bones and skulls. These were not the treasures sought by the diggers. They tossed together indiscriminately the human remains and delicate artifacts into growing heaps later divvied up and offered for sale as cheap souvenirs to curious tourists at roadside stalls. The gold, the hungry excavators reasoned, had been foreshadowed by these relics and must be deeper inside the mound.

By late afternoon, they had sunk a wide shaft about halfway vertically through the earthwork when one of the excavators' picks at last struck something solid. Furiously bringing their shovels to bear, the men cleared away the dirt to reveal the section of a wooden structure. With whoops of joy, they tore into its peculiar arrangement of planks and logs, which crumbled under their tools like ashes. In seconds, the centuries-old wood disintegrated, while some fragments fell deeper into the interior of the mound. The diggers knew at once that they had struck through the roof of a chamber.

Summoning a flashlight, they peered with mixed apprehension and greed into the silent room, from which arose a musty odor that contributed to the eeriness of their find. One by one, five of the men were let down by ropes into the chamber. The discoverers immediately found themselves in what appeared to be a four-sided corridor extending both east and west for about 100 feet in each of the two directions. Although the floor was tamped-down, compacted dirt, the walls and ceiling were of expertly crafted, palisaded wood. Standing fully erect, they guessed the roof was approximately 7 feet overhead. At the far end of the corridor, toward the east, stood a wall of vertically installed cedar posts that collapsed almost instantly under the blows of a pickax. The fallen wall, more of a partition, revealed a smaller chamber—an oval-shaped vault some 20 by 30 feet, with a cedarwood ceiling about 15 feet high. It and the walls were tapestried with cloth hangings woven together of human hair, animal fur, and bird feathers. At the far end of the chamber stood a tall vat filled with more than one hundred thousand fresh-water pearls beside a cache of engraved conch shells larger than the specimens found earlier in the dig. The pearls were later examined by gemologists, who determined that they were "Oriental"—not in origin, but by classification (i.e., they were of the highest classification).

Nearby stood a stack of copper breastplates beside another stack of shields. But the object that unquestionably identified the premises as a tomb was a raised, clay platform upon which stretched a human skeleton decked out in beaten copper armor. Over the fleshless remains gleamed, in the beams of the diggers' flashlights, the burnished metal breastplate, gauntlets, and greaves of the nameless dead. Riveted together in sections and embossed with lively animal motifs and abstract designs, the armor evidenced a surprisingly high level of workmanship.

Overjoyed at their discovery, the men sold off all their finds piece-meal to private collectors willing to pay top dollar. Most of the artifacts, including all the copper armor, have not been seen since. Only a few hundred of the incised shells were retrieved in time by scholars. After their discovery, rumor had it that the one hundred thousand freshwater pearls, harvested a thousand years earlier and hermetically sealed for their eternal preservation inside the tomb, rapidly decayed into a putrescent, black soup of fetid ooze after exposure to the open air. In any case, whereabouts of the Oriental pearls, like most of the Craig Mound treasure, have never been confirmed.

According to a contemporary newspaper report in the *Oklahoma Star*, the self-styled excavators "made a living for a number of months, selling relics taken from the graves of the prehistoric Indians buried near the surface of the temple-mound."[6] Today, they would have been arrested as tomb robbers.

In the more than seventy years after that disastrous looting of Oklahoma's foremost earthworks, investigators have painstakingly tried to reassemble the scattered clues of the site that has since come to be known as Spiro Mounds. The area is currently a protected state park on the Arkansas River featuring its own museum in the rural community of Spiro. Its 15-acre archaeological zone encompasses a few domed features—outstanding among them, of course, the robbed Craig Mound—all connected by interpretive paths.

At first sight, modern visitors can scarcely imagine what an extraordinary place the rather understated location resembled a thousand years ago. Then, it was a sacred necropolis, or city of the dead, comprising fifteen conical structures, all of them containing numerous human burials. In the Craig Mound alone more than five hundred men and women were interred. The entire mortuary was surrounded by a thin, shallow trench filled with water. Meaningless as a defensive ditch, it symbolically defined the holy precinct as a special place spiritually removed from the mundane world.

What is now known as Spiro Mounds (its original name has been lost to time) was originally regarded as an earthly waystation to the otherworld for departed souls, an occasional home for the ghosts of an individual's ancestors, and an arena for magical rituals conducted by shamans. The earthworks were witnesses to these bizarre activities for five centuries. During all that time, the necropolis was too sacred for permanent occupation. No one ever resided on the other side of its artificial, symbolic stream. Spiro Mounds was a spiritual hub around which a large and prosperous community of perhaps twelve thousand inhabitants revolved. Although the area was occupied on and off by nomadic hunter-gatherers for thousands of years before, civilization suddenly took root there after AD 900, and just as suddenly ceased to exist around 1325.

Aside from their mound-building and artistic gifts, the ancient Oklahomans were remarkable sailors. They were the only pre-Columbian people known to have constructed and navigated three-masted vessels. The sails were made of matting, while hulls may have been two or more dug-out canoes, each about 18 feet long, lashed together to resemble vaguely an outrigger catamaran design, as recreated at Spiro Mounds Museum. In these eminently seaworthy craft, the Spiro sailors operated a trading network that stretched to Michigan's Upper Peninsula (on the Canadian frontier) for copper, and across the Gulf of Mexico to Florida's southernmost tip for conch shells. Oklahoma merchantmen of the thirteenth century left their mark at a famous rock shelter, Wisconsin's Gottschall Site, on their way, most likely, to the abundant copper deposits of the Upper Great Lakes Region.

It was this hunger for vast quantities of the shiny metal, in addition to their maritime abilities, that made them unique among all Mississippian cultures. While the inhabitants of Illinois' Cahokia, Wisconsin's Aztalan and other, related centers certainly valued copper, none appear to have collected it in such abundance. Only a thousand years ago, a boat could have traveled to the Mississippi from northeastern Oklahoma via a now-extinct tributary of the Arkansas River, then northward to the rich copper deposits of Michigan's Upper Peninsula.

Very much less is known about the prehistoric Oklahomans' religious beliefs portrayed, as they apparently are, on Spiro Mound's engraved conch shells. At least one figure from their lost mythology is believed to have survived, however, among the traditions of their suspected, although mixed, descendants: the Wichita Indians. They still tell of Grandmother Spider, who long ago pitied the first humans for their lack of fire with which to warm their huts and cook their food. Descending from heaven on her silken rope, she twirled down to an oceanic island that was blazing with fire ignited by lightning. Waters surrounding the island were too treacherous to cross, so all the Wichita ancestors could do was watch helplessly from shore.

Grandmother Spider carefully alighted on the burning island and picked up a single ember, then reeled herself skyward, swung above the tempestuous waves, and eventually landed at the feet of the startled people. She presented them with the still-burning ember from which they lit fires for hearth and home. Grandmother Spider climbed her strand back to heaven, and she has been revered ever since by a grateful humankind for her Promethean gift.

She appears often in Spiro shell art, sometimes as the benevolent arachnid herself, or, more usually, symbolized by her personal emblem, the hooked cross or swastika. It is depicted as *deosil* (oriented left, in a direction to the apparent course of the sun) when meant to represent her descent to earth, and *withershins* (contrary to that course, oriented right) when meant to represent a return to heaven, as the moon after nightfall. Her deosil representation at Spiro Mounds is more frequent. Grandmother Spider appears to have been, and in fact still is, among the most important and popular deities, with a prominent place in the Craig Mound artifacts and enduring veneration among modern Native Americans.

Far greater than Spiro Mounds, but second in size only to Cahokia itself, was Moundville. Sitting on the Black Warrior River in west-central Alabama, it may have been the religious capital of North America. Biwabiko Paddaquahas, Iron Thunderhorse, the Hereditary Grand Sachem and powwamanitomp (shaman) of the Quinnipiac Thunder

Clan, has published several Native American oral traditions preserving his people's folk memories of Mississippian times, and of Moundsville in particular. The Quinnipiac or Eansketambawg (Original People) belong to the Ojibwa-Anishinaabeg Blackfoot-Niitsítapi of Algonquian-speaking aboriginals who inhabited the Wampanoki, or Dawnland, region that included present-day Connecticut.

Iron Thunderhorse writes of Moundsville during its florescence:

> Four ponds stocked with abundant fish were believed to have emerged from original burial pits which provided the earth for construction of the mounds. Special areas for craftwork and trade, ceremonial temples, a game court, and a sweat lodge used for ritual purification—by warriors, priests and players of the games—contributed to the overall diversity of the central plaza. . . . Approximately 3,000 burials were unearthed at Moundsville, 100 of which—including men, women and children—were associated with exotic grave goods. Among the more common burials, men were found with their tools, children with toys, and one woman was buried with a corncob in her mouth.[7]

The former editor of *Alabama Farmer,* Lyn Chamberlain, stated in *Sacred Sites, A Guidebook to Sacred Centers and Mysterious Places in the U.S.:*

> [O]nce this city of 3,000 residents was the cultural and ceremonial center for an area that stretched from present day Tuscaloosa to Demopolis in South Alabama. Today, Mound State Monument consists of 320 acres and 20 preserved mounds. The Temple Mound, which is the largest, has been restored and wooden steps added. Along with two smaller mounds it is the older part of the site, forming a rough triangle pointing away from the river. Directly behind the Temple Mound is another, wider, lower mound, part of a great circle of smaller mounds surrounding a courtyard.

The entire complex was once surrounded by a palisade of high upright posts. While most of the mounds are domiciliary, upon which people built their homes, some appear to be burial mounds. They hold copper ear-plugs, breast plates and other artifacts associated with the elite class among Mississippian tribes. Structures on these mounds were probably charnel houses with burials made in the floor. Domiciliary mounds also contain burials; burying family members in the floor of the home was a common practice for the period.

Elite status in the community afforded the privilege of living on the earthen mounds. At approximately the end of every generation, the buildings on top of the mound were burned and covered, creating a foundation for new lives. The inhabitants wore ear plugs, bracelets, arm bands of copper, and beads and pendants of shell. Hides and garments of vegetable fiber woven into fabric made simple garments. Body paint was made from bloodroot. Around the neck, many wore gorgets [ornamental stone disks of sandstone, slate or granite].

Society was organized around family groups with rank determined by the power of whatever ancestors an individual might claim. Greenstone from eastern Alabama and Georgia, galena and quartz were all imported. In spite of the reliance on agriculture and trade, Moundville was a warrior society. Pottery and shells were decorated with skulls and bones. During feast periods, people gathered at the Moundville site for games ceremonies and rituals. They worshiped a fire-sun deity, and honored the wind and the rain.

The Moundville residents were part of the Southern Cult rooted in the late prehistoric Mississippian stage, and sometimes called the Southern Death Cult because of its trail of bones and skulls. The cult is thought to be the result of a religious revitalization or complex that swept down the Mississippi Valley and through the deep central South around AD 1200 It was significantly associated with a fire-sun deity and a warrior code, as well as human sacrifice.

The "Southern Death Cult" is an unfortunate term, because it conjures in the minds of many people ghastly images of human sacrifice and bloody appeals to the dark side. Actually, it refers only to funerary artifacts discovered in the mortuary mounds, with no implication of ritual murder. The so-called Death Cult, though headquartered at Moundville, was by no means confined to that prominent site. Followers practiced its elaborate ceremonies throughout the Mississippi valley and the Deep South until the early fourteenth century. Chamberlain continues, "A common art motif is a human male with face always in profile. Arms and legs take a variety of postures that are impossible unless the man is flying. Feathers hang from or are attached to the arms, and he usually has a tail and a birdlike headdress with bands on his wrists, ankles, calves, and upper arms. This is not a god, but a representation of the shaman become a supernatural being."[8]

Keys to unlocking their sacred mysteries are the symbols its practitioners designed in copper sheets and on clay pottery, stone pipes, and tablets. Chief among these was the spiral. It not only appeared on ritual materials, but also the people themselves formed religious processions in a communal spiral, including large numbers of dancers stepping away from a central fire. "An interesting sidelight of these dances," writes University of Nebraska archaeologist Patricia Galloway, "is that the participants warmed their hands near the fire and then rubbed their eyes to give them the power to see snakes."

This gesture perhaps explains the Southern Cult's enigmatic symbol of an open eye in the palm of a hand. The ancient Alabamans believed that the life force turned in a spiral, so that movement in such a pattern would put them in accord with the active powers of the cosmos. Galloway affirms that the spiral "appears to be a generalized or universal force."[9]

The spiral was also identified with the snake who glides between this world and the next, the underworld. He sheds his skin and is the living symbol of regeneration and fertility of the soil for animals and human beings. In imitation of the rattlesnake, Southern Cult shamans used gourds as rattles to call upon sympathetic serpent magic for healing, a theme still alive in the caduceus, a twin snake entwined around a staff: the worldwide emblem of medical science.

The weeping-eye motif displayed throughout the Moundville complex stood for rain from God's omniscient eye, but it simultaneously implied the essential compassion and redeeming beneficence of the cosmos. Victory in struggle was signified by the peregrine falcon, "a swift, aggressive bird whose attack culminates in a war-like blow, instantly killing its victim" according to Iron Thunderhorse.

During rituals, the Moundsville Mississippians partook of a consciousness-altering drug, *Datura stramonium* (jimsonweed). Combined with the music and pageantry of their ceremonies, hallucinogenic affects of jimsonweed undoubtedly made the flashing copper images take on a numinous quality. Chamberlain writes:

> A rattlesnake disk, thought to have been used for religious and war ceremonies, was discovered here. The 12.5 inch circular stone disk is notched at regular intervals and carved with an eye on an open hand. It is surrounded by two knotted rattlesnakes, one facing the same direction as the fingers, the other facing the direction of the wrist. The disk is displayed with the fingers pointing up, and it is often assumed that the eye is etched on the left palm.[10]

This enigmatic artifact appears to have identified its wearer as the owner of his people's most valuable object—the *Ulunsuti* ("Transparent"), a large, clear quartz crystal with a trace of red hematite suspended within it. The hematite signified a drop of sacred blood, while the power stone itself was said to have come from the forehead of an underworld serpent, an apparent parallel to the well-known third eye of psychic vision. The red-flecked mineral encased within the crystal provided whomever possessed it with the power of clairvoyance, prophecy, levitation, and astral projection, but it could turn on its mortal owner if it was not regularly propitiated, or "fed," with fresh sacrifices. No legendary item, several examples of the Ulunsuti have been recovered from the graves of suspected shamans.

Iron Thunderhorse tells of this supremely sacred object's mythical origins in the Tsa-lag-gi, or Cherokee, version:

"Uktena is a great serpent, as large around as a tree-trunk, with horns on its head and a bright, blazing crest, a crystal upon its forehead. This blazing stone glitters like sparks of fire, and is called Ulusunti. Whoever has the Ulusunti is assured success in love, hunting, rain-making, and more. But its greatest use is the life-cycle prophecy. When it is consulted for this purpose, the future is mirrored in the blazing stone and becomes crystal clear as a tree is reflected in the quiet stream below." This traditional lore represents powerful meta-phors; e.g., the great serpent with horns who guards a crystal upon its forehead. The Moundsville Disc serpents have triangular shapes on their foreheads, still further indication that these particular ser-pents must be Uktena.[11]

Although the Alabama mound builders still live in the folk mem-ories of Native Americans, archaeologists must rely almost entirely upon forensic evidence to tell us anything about an altogether differ-ent, if formerly vital Mississippian city in southern Wisconsin between Milwaukee and the state capitol at Madison. Aztalan was home for an aristocratic population of priests, architects, astronomers, and engineers behind three enormous walls. Entirely plastered with a ground mollusk shell–clay mixture in the Cahokian and Angel Mounds' manner, the palisaded ramparts were interspersed with rectangular towers manned by twenty-four hundred warriors. They could respond to a surprise attack by running to the top of the walls from a wide rampart that sloped from the ground. After dark, the entire perimeter was illumi-nated brightly by dozens of large cauldrons mounted atop the outer wall, where they blazed with cane fires.

The fronting landscape was alive with immense effigy mounds in the shapes of lizards, bears, birds, and other animals. Within the triple enclo-sure reared three earthen pyramids, flat-topped structures surmounted by

Fig. 6.3. In southern Wisconsin, behind Aztalan's walls, scaffolding supported archers who fired at an attacking enemy through the rectangular apertures near the top of the rampart.

temple buildings with steeply arched gables. The ceremonial center's foremost earthwork is the Pyramid of the Sun.

Its ascent is most dramatic from the east, where a broad flight of stairs climbs to the top. A large, wooden temple, a tall pole protruding through its grass roof, stood there in the days of ancient occupation. The pole was aligned with another across the Crawfish River, at the summit of Christmas Hill, to sight perfectly each sunrise of the winter solstice, as recreated at Aztalan's Archaeological Museum. It was this life-affirming orientation on the shortest day of the year that underscored the positive principle of the solar cult faith in the eternal return of light and life. The smaller Pyramid of Venus at the other end of the precinct was named after its eight human burials aligned to the appearance of the Morning Star.

Another earthwork in the east, above the banks of the Crawfish River, was oriented to various lunar phases and, as a consequence, dedicated to the moon before the temple mound was plowed out of existence

Fig. 6.4. Aztalan's Pyramid of the Sun

around the turn of the twentieth century. Between this structure and the Pyramid of the Sun lay a shallow, delta-shaped pool for ritual purification practices. Just outside Aztalan's walls, a line of conical mounds was oriented to the positions of certain stars. In a solitary mound removed from the city by about 300 feet, archaeologists found the so-called Beaded Princess: the remains of a young woman wrapped in a fabulous garment composed of twelve hundred polished shells. Another grave held the skeleton of a headless giant.

The city itself was connected at its north end to nearby Rock Lake via a stone aqueduct three miles long. Its waters conceal the Aztalaners' cemetery, which was inundated over time by a river that gradually emptied itself into the valley—and the river became Rock Lake. Volcanolike family vaults, inverted sundials like upended ice-cream cones, and elongated linear stone mounds lie at various depths from 12 to 60 feet beneath the surface. Sonar readouts have also identified on the bottom the effigy mounds of a turtle, a headless man, and a dragonlike creature, together with the remains of a small village site. Aztalan itself possessed only a dozen burials: the Beaded Princess, a decapitated man, a pair of boys, and the eight people interred in the Pyramid of Venus. At the precise midpoint of the ceremonial district were buried an inverted pair of adult, human skulls, one facing east and the other west. A population of perhaps two thousand elite confined themselves to the northern part of the site, where they raised squash and corn. Archaeological excavation beginning in the 1930s revealed that most residents dwelled behind high walls on the other side of the river.

Altogether, the ten thousand or so inhabitants were primarily farmers who traded their produce with local Indians in exchange for fresh meat, and who cooked their meals in convection earth ovens. Domestic construction consisted of single-family homes positioned against harsh winds from the northwest, and featured beds made of deerskin. Today, the archaeological park's 21 acres represent less than half of the original city, whose walls extended inland across both sides of the Crawfish River. Excavators have mostly neglected the eastern section, which is one and a half times larger.

The choice of location was determined by Upper Michigan's copper mines, some two hundred fifty airline miles distant. Aztalan lies just below the hard-snow line, and therefore is as close as possible to the mines during winter. Prehistoric miners freighted their ingots southward down the navigable waterways that directly connected to Aztalan. In confirmation of this connection, archaeologists found a central storage area at the site where large quantities of copper had stained the matted floor on which they sat more than seven centuries ago.

Early-twentieth-century excavation of one of the many thousands of ancient graves that formerly surrounded the shoreline of Rock Lake before they were mostly obliterated by housing developers contained the remains of a man buried with his mining hammer. He and his fellow miners dug out the Lake Superior metal and transported it in raw form to Aztalan. From there, it was processed for shipment to the Cahokian megalopolis and elsewhere throughout the Mississippian culture.

As well as serving as a clearinghouse for the copper trade, Aztalan was an observatory—that is, its section west of the Crawfish River. Astronomical information poured constantly into the city, day and night, by way of its numerous stellar, solar, and lunar alignments, providing farmers with the timetables they needed for optimum planting and harvesting. Celestial data additionally regulated all aspects of ritual life, from marriages and coronations to fertility ceremonies and human sacrifice. Since the founding of Aztalan around AD 1100, its people prospered and expanded their direct influence on cave painters at the Gottschall rock shelter in southwestern Wisconsin; further south to Oklahoma, where they left some of their commercial goods at Spiro Mounds; and southeastward through northern Illinois in search of "milkstone" admirably suited for agricultural work. During its heyday, the pyramidal city received imports from as far afield as the West Indies, which sent a unique type of conch shell for religious rites.

To all outward appearances, Aztalan was at the zenith of its cultural and commercial splendor by 1320, when it burst into flames. A mighty conflagration completely incinerated its walls and everything they had protected for the previous two hundred years. Crops, homes, and monuments were bathed in a vast cauldron of fire reflecting itself in the Crawfish River. Thereafter, the charred location was abandoned by the former inhabitants and shunned by successive generations of tribal Indians. During the first state-sponsored archaeological study of the long-dead ceremonial city, investigators recovered tons of carbonized ash and much of the site's outer wall, which had been burned to the ground.

Aztalan's self-immolation heralded the simultaneous collapse of Mississippian culture all across the North American heartland. Three centuries later, Spanish conquerors, French fur traders, and English explorers stumbled upon the overgrown temple mounds, neglected garden beds, and other decaying remnants of an unknown civilization that had obviously died out long before. The newcomers were amazed by the extent and sophistication of the bizarre ruins—and investigators have been trying to unravel their mystery ever since.

Seven

WHO WERE THE MISSISSIPPIANS?

The great mystery of the Maya, is: Why did their civilization suddenly shut down? And what became of them? These questions have bedeviled archaeologists since the nineteenth century, and remained unanswered even with the late-twentieth-century translation of Mayan hieroglyphs. After more than a thousand years of building city-states across Yucatán, the Maya abandoned them, never to return. Yet they left behind no evidence of plague, famine, or war to explain their disappearance.

To be sure, the collapse of their agricultural system resulted in widespread hunger, even starvation, and the once idyllic image of the Maya as humane astronomer-priests more interested in celestial matters than murderous militarists bent on subjugation was dispelled when their temple inscriptions were translated. These inscriptions do indeed reveal a race of genius mathematicians, colorful artists, and urban builders— but with a darker streak of intercity struggle and human sacrifice. Some scholars conclude that this disappointing penchant for bloodshed eventually rendered civilized existence impossible.

The translations, however, also show that military campaigning was part and parcel of the Maya world for the length and breadth of its history. They reveal that Maya society was in a virtually constant state of war punctuated by episodes of treaty-brokered armistices during which opposing sides contracted new alliances and rearmed themselves for renewed conflict. Conquests undertaken at the close of the Maya era were neither more nor less bloody nor far-flung than those waged since its beginning.

True, Yucatán experienced bouts of mass-starvation due to agrarian practices overstretched by burgeoning urban pressures, but these, too, were endemic to Maya agriculture from the start. In fact, crop production throughout Middle America was bountiful at the time civilization there winked out. Neither incessant warfare nor failed crops can explain adequately why a vast population that spread across the entire Yucatán Peninsula and beyond, north into Mexico and south into Central America, abruptly and simultaneously ceased to function, if only because the Maya never exercised any central authority over these extensive areas.

Shortly before AD 900, their cities everywhere were abandoned in concert, as though some kind of a call or order went out to terminate society. When an entire culture suddenly ceases to be, the comprehensive, decisive event invariably leaves behind clear, abundant evidence of its overwhelming impact. The collapse of civilization in the Indus Valley graphically appears in the mass graves of its people slaughtered by invading hordes. The fall of Homer's Ilios is clearly outlined in the stratum of burned material at Hissarlik's Troy VIIb level, on the Aegean coast of Turkey. The nuclear scars left by USAAF bombers at Hiroshima and Nagasaki will still be clearly visible for centuries to come. Yet nothing of the kind appears anywhere within the Mayas' former sphere of influence. Even their preserved remains show no extraordinary indications of disease, famine, or warfare.

As their way of life evidenced little or no sign of development, progress, or change from first day to last, so nothing suggests social decline leading to a fall, or any event horizon that definitively brought their history to an abrupt close. Why, then, did they shut down their still-prosperous cities and abandon their country after more than a millennium of unrelieved greatness? Only one cause can account for Maya mass-evacuation, in unison, of every city-state across the Yucatán and beyond.

First, however, to grasp its identity and universal power, something of the Mayas' origins and mentality must be understood. Mainstream scholars believe the Maya arose during a Formative Period around 200 BC, followed by population increase and social coalescence in an Early Classic Period. Ceremonial cities and pyramid-building sprouted with a Classic Period, reaching their florescence before AD 900, in a Late Classic Period. Professional archaeologists are unable to explain exactly why simple hunter-gatherers, after uncounted millennia of preliterate existence, suddenly decided to become hieroglyph-literate, pyramid-building Maya astronomers and mathematicians.

Researchers can guess only that third-century-BC tribes may have reached a certain population density from which organized society possibly emerged as a matter of course. This baseless assumption is a hard pill for any rational person to swallow, and it smacks of eighteenth-century scholars who believed mice formed from corner cobwebs. More important, it ignores the Mayas' obvious inheritance from their Olmec predecessors. While the earlier Olmec culture differed stylistically from the Maya, material and chronological connections are nonetheless obvious.

Olmec culture went extinct around 400 BC, and while its epoch predates the Mayas' Formative Period by two hundred years, the archaeologists themselves appear to have miscalculated. In 1978, they were shocked to learn that the Mayas' largest ceremonial city was built centuries before such complexes were supposed to have arisen. Located in the north of the modern department of El Petén, in Guatemala, *El Mirador,* "The Look-Out," flourished from about the tenth century BC, reaching its height from the third century BC to the second century AD, with a peak population of perhaps eighty thousand people.

None of this, according to the experts, was supposed to have appeared until Classic, even Late Classic Times, many hundreds of years later. El Mirador covers some ten square miles and features a large, low, artificial platform topped with a set of three step pyramids. One, nicknamed *El Tigre,* stands 180 feet high. But its companion, *La Danta,* is taller by fifty feet, making it the tallest structure the Maya ever built—this allegedly from the first day of their history, if not before. The sprawling platform on which it was perched is a base covering 74,000 square feet of ground.

Most of the structures at El Mirador were originally faced with beautifully cut stone covered by large, stucco murals depicting the gods and goddesses of the Maya, all fully fleshed out in the otherworldly identities familiar to mythologists. Dating the site prior to the presumed origin of Maya civilization are the remains of a wall that perhaps enclosed the entire location. The stones that went into its construction were reused from even earlier structures. El Mirador sits at the center of a series of ancient *sacbeob,* or raised stone pedestrian causeways, one stretching to another Maya ceremonial center at Nakbe, almost ten miles away.

El Mirador's age substantially overlaps the last few centuries of Olmec times, and its already advanced, even matchless construction affirm that the Maya not only inherited that earlier culture, but also were, in fact, latter-day Olmecs, who carried on and developed the civilizing mission that their predecessors began. El Mirador is little known to the outside world, perhaps because its mere existence threatens to overturn the neat chronologies established by mainstream archaeologists. Indeed, the Maya themselves had nothing whatsoever to do with such academic timetables.

As universally acknowledged mathematicians of unparalleled greatness, Maya understanding of Mesoamerican beginnings is certainly worth more than the scientific guesswork of modern scholars. These people were, in fact, very exact—as they were in all things mathematical—concerning the precise moment of their coming into the world. In short, they believed their civilization was born on August 12, 3113 BC. Though archaeologists dismiss this date as impossibly contrary to modern understanding of Maya chronology, it coincides remarkably well with Olmec origins around 3000 BC.

Until the 1950s, the Olmec were believed to go back no earlier than

twenty-five hundred years ago. With the advent of radiocarbon techniques, however, a period circa 1200 BC became more acceptable, until
improved testing pushed it back another three centuries. Most recently,
research at the Olmec site of Jalapa revealed a late-fourth-millennium-
BC date, as confirmed by Dr. Pablo Bush-Romero, head of the National
Archaeology Department for the Mexican government. It seems, then,
that the Maya were an outgrowth of Olmec culture, as they themselves
suggest in their national birthday of 3113 BC.

Like their Olmec predecessors, they worshiped numerous deities.
But one mythic figure dominated their vast pantheon of gods and goddesses, nature spirits, and chthonic demons. The Mayas' supreme being
was the god of time, *Hunab Ku,* the "Sole God." They made no statues of him, no temple carvings or codex illustrations, because he was
without visible form. They realized that this mythic personification of
time created everything throughout the universe, destroyed everything,
and restored everything in new form. Further, Hunab Ku made his will
known in the progress of celestial movement. Hence, the Mayas' preoccupation with astronomy. Through attentive, accurate observation of
the sky, they learned what the Sole God expected of them. By putting
themselves in accord with his celestial commandments, as expressed in
the progress of the heavenly bodies, they fulfilled his plan for humankind. That was the spiritual basis for designing the Mayan calendar. It
came absolutely to rule their lives, and was consulted in all matters of
state, as well as personal affairs. Marriages were contracted, children
conceived, food eaten, burials conducted, wars waged, journeys undertaken, professions assigned, kings crowned, captives sacrificed—every
human activity, high or low, was religiously regulated under the tyranny
of time. The lives not only of the Mayas, but also of the high cultures
that preceded and followed them, were absolutely overshadowed by this
temporal god.

The later Aztecs inherited his will in the form of the *Tonalpohualli,*
a ritual calendar astrologers, known as *Tonalonamatl* used to plot the
horoscopes of each member of the empire. The *Tonalpouque* were yet

other priests who determined good and evil days. Merchants, sailors, traders, and couriers could not begin their travels until the Tonalpouque had discovered the proper "One Serpent," or "Fortunate Day." As the calendar had brought Mesoamerican civilization into existence at the end of the fourth millennium BC, so it would bring down the curtain on the high culture of the Mayas at the proper moment. Their ritual almanac was an abstract mechanism of intermeshing cycles strictly coinciding with the celestial patterns they observed. As the final Long Count ground to a halt, it signaled the end every Maya must obey.

That moment arrived with the last gasp of the ninth century, when its universal recognition signaled a simultaneous evacuation of all ceremonial centers, including El Mirador. Most Maya henceforward melded into the cultures of other peoples, losing forever their former identity and scientific greatness. A relative few traveled north, where they built the famous, shining structures of Chichén Itzá and Tulum.

Another contingent pushed beyond Yucatán and into the Gulf of Mexico, voyaging far up the Mississippi River into what is today known as western Illinois. There, across from Missouri's Gateway to the West—the modern city of St. Louis—another, far older metropolis arose near the east bank of the Big Muddy. Although conventional scholars are loath to admit it, they cannot deny Cahokia's unmistakably Maya features. If Monks Mound had been discovered in Yucatán instead of Illinois, they would have found it indistinguishable from any of the other step pyramids raised by Mesoamerican construction engineers.

True, none of the Maya temple platforms were made of earth, but ancient architects were no different from their modern counterparts in that both were/are forced to build with the materials at hand; the area chosen for Cahokia has no limestone for quarrying. Even so, most archaeologists argue that any superficial parallels between Cahokia and Maya Civilization were just circumstantial, and they point out that no written records, unlike the abundant, inscribed stele of the literate Mayas, have ever been found in the vicinity of Monks Mound. With a discovery around the turn of the last century, however, skeptics of

Maya culture-bearers in the Mississippi valley found their conclusion challenged.

In March 1998, Illinois archaeologists organized a project to stabilize the west side of Monks Mound. They were drilling for the installation of horizontal pipes to drain water that had accumulated within the structure, causing part of it to slump during the previous twelve years. About 40 feet below the top of the second terrace, the drill was transecting some 60 feet above the ground when it struck a stone obstruction a little more than 140 feet into the earthwork. After burrowing through some 32 feet of cobbled stone, the bit broke and the drill was removed. Referring to the mysterious obstruction, Cahokia's public relations director William Iseminger said, "It should not be there. No stone has ever been found in other mounds here or other Mississippian mounds that we are aware of at this time. It might have been some kind of a ceremonial platform, or something else. We just do not know."[1]

If the internal obstruction does indeed prove to be a stone ceremonial platform or wall, Cahokia's identity as a neo-Maya site is substantially enhanced. Some investigators suggest that before leaving Yucatán, the Mayas may have disassembled one of their most sacred temples and transported it piece by piece along the Atlantic shores of Mexico, up the Mississippi River, to Cahokia. There, it was reassembled and finally buried under Monks Mound. Such a scenario is not as far-fetched as critics believe, because the Maya did indeed cover older ceremonial buildings under later, larger structures, piling layer upon layer of temple buildings over time. Unfortunately, Director Iseminger and his colleagues have said little publicly about the stone discovery inside Monks Mound since its discovery more than ten years ago. Repeated inquiries after what if any research has been done to ascertain the precise nature of the obstruction are invariably met with official silence. If finally verified as a stone temple, it would go far to prove that Cahokia was founded by the Maya, particularly if, as might be expected, the stone structure is covered with hieroglyphic inscriptions.

Such a spectacular find is not necessary, however, to build a strong case for Mesoamerican influences in prehistoric Illinois. Just beyond Monks Mound, Woodhenge represented an astronomical expertise unique in the American Midwest and wholly unlike Plains Indian cosmology, but identical to the high science achieved by the Maya. None of these observations are new.

Speaking of Cahokia after a visit in 1810, Henry M. Brackenridge told Thomas Jefferson, "I concluded that a populous city had once existed here, similar to those of Mexico described by the first conqueror Hernán Cortés."[2] The ex-president, together with Brackenridge—a government official who traveled extensively throughout Mexico and South America—were the founders of scientific archaeology in the United States.

The ceremonial center of Cahokia was laid out in a diamond-shaped pattern approximately a mile from end to end, while the entire capital was originally five miles across, east to west. In 1973, archaeologist Joyce Marcus, explained to *Science* magazine readers how the Lowland Classic Maya territorial organization was organized into hexagonal patterns, with capitals at the center surrounded by secondary and tertiary

Fig. 7.1. Model of Woodhenge at the Illinois Historical Society, Collinsville. Although only forty-six vertical posts are represented, the observatory originally featured forty-eight, a multiple of the cosmic numeral twelve, to accommodate the months of the year, and perhaps even a Mississippian version of the houses of the zodiac.

settlements that formed a diamond shape. No other two cultures on earth built their cities in a prearranged diamond pattern, a fact that powerfully underscores Cahokia's Mesoamerican roots.

Just what Cahokia's prehistoric inhabitants called their city is unknown, so scholars refer to it after a local, unrelated clan of Illiniwek that the first French explorers encountered in the 1600s. These Cahokia themselves were attacked soon after by other regional tribes—so ferociously, in fact, that none survived. The Winnebago (aka Ho Chunk) preserve some oral traditions of the pyramidal city they remember as *Towakana,* or "Snakeskin." A reference to regeneration or rebirth, the name implies a people or culture that died and was reborn—as a snake sheds its old skin for a new one—signifying perhaps the collapse of Maya civilization in Yucatán and its revival in Illinois. As though to clinch a connection with southerly origins, Cahokia arose suddenly, without precedent, around AD 900, the same moment the Mayas abandoned their civilization in Yucatán.

It seems clear they reestablished it in our country according to the will of Hunab Ku, their chief deity. Evidence of the Mayas' impact on Mississippian culture was not confined to Cahokia. In her examination of Alabama's Moundsville, Lyn Chamberlain observes:

> Many of the motifs and symbolic representations recovered here are similar to those found throughout the Yucatán and Central America. The mounds themselves suggest the pyramidal shape of Mesoamerican structures. Many motifs are classic Mississippian, such as the rattlesnakes, woodpeckers or predatory birds and eagle warriors. Others are Pan-American, such as the long-nosed god masks, reminiscent of Yacatecuhtli, god of Aztec traders. The feathered serpent, a universal symbol of the union of heaven and earth, appears here, along with raptorial birds and rattlesnakes with residual wings.[3]

Don W. Dragoo, the Carnegie Museum archaeologist cited in chapters 1 and 2 for his expertise in Adena affairs, wrote of Ohio's

Quadranau Mound, "Within the larger enclosure are four elevated squares or truncated pyramids of earth, which, from their resemblance to similar erections in Mexico and Central America, merit a particular notice."[4]

More than earthworks told of Mayas crossing the Rio Grande. Jim Iler reported in *Ancient American* magazine:

> During 1921, an uneducated farmer in rural Oklahoma was digging for Indian relics by probing a low, grassy mound with a metal rod. He soon detected a "hollow" spot, and dug into an apparent pit. What he found was more than a few arrowheads. After hours of laborious digging, Mack Tussinger unearthed some 3,500 pieces of exquisitely chipped flints. Their design and manufacture were of a radically superior quality not found above the Rio Grande River.

Researchers never imagined that such extraordinary artifacts existed within the borders of the United States. The site of their discovery eventually became known as the Rhoades Mound. Amazed at his find, Tussinger removed all the pieces and reburied them near his home in several, smaller caches. For some years, he kept the secret to himself, but with the onset of the Depression and a general worsening of economic conditions, he furtively began selling a few pieces to support his large family. By 1936, the bulk of his find had been sold off, and several large blades were given as toys to his six children.

Iler continues,

> The previous year, Tussinger guided members of the Oklahoma Archaeological Society to the Rhoades Mound. Together with anthropologists from the University of Oklahoma, they carefully examined the site, and found several more "eccentric flints," at least one of which was still embedded in the undisturbed soil. These flints were virtually identical to the Tussinger pieces.

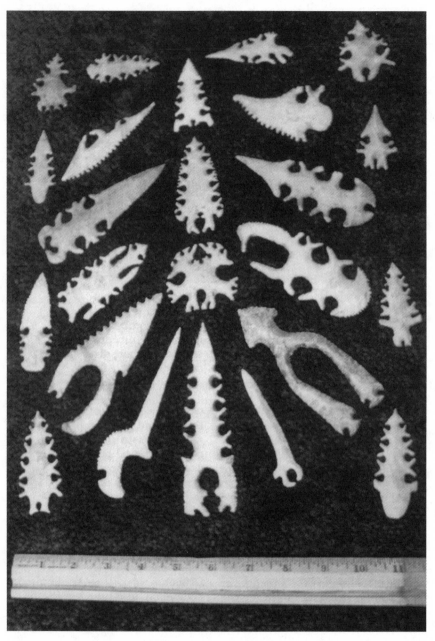

Fig. 7.2. Elaborate, finely crafted, identifiably Maya flints dug out of the Oklahoma soil.

The location was accessed as the site for a multiple burial typical of the kind found among the Mayas of Lower Yucatán.

In a 1939 article for *American Antiquity,* archaeologists Forrest E. Clemens and Alfred Reed said of the Tussinger objects, "[T]he general pattern and type of workmanship recalls the so-called 'eccentric flints' of British Honduras and Guatemala."[5]

According to Iler,

Forty years after Rhoades Mound was opened, during the summer of 1961, Mr. Carl Murray of Joplin, Missouri, found a cache of 107 eccentric flints in the same county [Delaware] where Tussinger made his discovery. Murray's affidavit details the circumstances of his excavation, while some of the blades he recovered are significantly similar to those found by Tussinger. Other eccentric flints have been found in Oklahoma by surface hunters, and a prominent collector claims that eleven blades were discovered in the vicinity of Spiro Mounds.[6]

Some feel the evidence, such as that found in Rhoades Mound, leaves little doubt of the Mesoamericans presence here, or their influence, at least, on Mississippian cultures. As early as October, 1938, an article in *Science Newsletter* reported that "astonishing discoveries made in excavating Indian mounds and village sites in Oklahoma show influence by Maya cultural patterns."[7]

Cahokia's Wisconsin outpost likewise suggested Mesoamerican themes. As long ago as 1870, Stephen D. Peet, a prominent antiquarian and organizer of the Ohio Archaeological Association, pointed out significant similarities between Aztalan and the Post-Classic Maya ceremonial city of Tulum on the coast of Yucatán. Indeed, both were surrounded by a rectangular wall with squarish watchtowers, which was completely covered by a white limestone plaster. The Yucatán enclosure featured a plaza, ritual area, trapezoidal pyramids, and a secluded residential section—the same elements at the Wisconsin site. Both were open to water on the east, and both were commercial centers at the hub of extensive trading networks connected by river routes. They even shared an important cultural common denominator in astronomically oriented structures.

In his comprehensive and well-known *Guide to Ancient Maya Ruins,* Bruce C. Hunter observes, "The time of the summer and winter solstices and the vernal and autumnal equinoxes determined the work patterns and religious events" at Tulum.[8] So too, Aztalan was outstanding for its solar, lunar, and stellar alignments, particularly those focused on the solstices. Tulum's wall possessed another singular feature duplicated only at Aztalan: an interior walkway that connected all the watchtowers. Is it more than coincidental that Aztalan was founded in AD 1100 at the same time Tulum was abandoned?

It would seem, then, that Hunab Ku, the Maya's god of time, decreed an across-the-board closure of their Mesoamerican cities through the priestly interpretation of his sacred calendar. Though their universal abandonment spelled the end of the Maya era in Mexico and Central America, it simultaneously sparked its rebirth as the Mississippian culture north of the Rio Grande River. The sudden growth of Maya-like urban centers, replete with obvious influences from the Lower Yucatán, in the American Southwest and Midwest can be understood only as the result of a mass migration from the high civilization of tenth-century Mesoamerica.

The same ritual calendar that had ordered withdrawal from Tulum, Copan, Tikal, and Uxmal together with all of Middle America's other shining cities, and instructed its inhabitants to resettle throughout the Mississippi valley, demanded that the neo-Maya ceremonial centers of Cahokia, Moundsville, Spiro, and the rest be likewise forsaken at the close of another temporal cycle.

Aztalan was not the only Mississippian metropolis abandoned and incinerated by its own inhabitants. A 1923 issue of *Science* magazine describes the "charred and blackened remains" of a great prehistoric city "destroyed by fire long before the advent of the white man, but formerly covering an area of 500 acres, and defended by a palisaded wall and breastworks more than a mile in length." Located at a bend in the Harpeth River near Kingston Springs, about twelve miles east of Nashville, the site was professionally excavated by W. E. Myer, a "special archaeologist" for the Smithsonian Institution. He found temple mounds, plastered walls with squarish guard towers, and numerous other remains that clearly identified them as Late Mississippian.

Science continues:

> On one bend of the river is a great hill which was artificially shaped by the ancient builders from bottom to top. Three wide terraces were built at various levels along this hill, and its original summit was cut away until a level plaza about one thousand feet in length and five hundred in breadth had been formed. On this level plaza, they had erected a large mound. Around the edge of the plaza and the terraces, other mounds had been formed.[9]

Although the entire, vast complex had been burned from end to end, Myer found no indication of struggle; nothing suggesting an enemy attack or conquest. He concluded that the complex was incinerated by the inhabitants themselves when they abandoned it around 1320. Although not all Mississippian cities were similarly torched, they were evacuated in the early fourteenth century.

Where their former residents went is uncertain. Ho Chunk Indian oral tradition relates that the Aztalaners migrated into the south. At the same time, Aztec civilization sprouted in the Valley of Mexico, where its priests claimed their fathers had come from the north. Were the Aztecs the Mississippians, just as the Mississippians were originally the Maya? In any case, mass migration from south to north and back into the south again appears to have been cyclically undertaken by the peoples of Mesoamerica. Natural catastrophes, wars, or economic distress did not randomly spark these great mass movements of whole populations. They were set in motion instead by the god of time, the Sole God, whose inviolable command was expressed in his sacred calendar. When, around AD 900, he commanded the Maya to abandon en masse the city-states they had occupied for the previous thirteen centuries, some migrated into the far north. From the seeds of their venerable culture planted in the Mississippi valley a new civilization blossomed and prospered, until it, too, was forced to heed the commands of Hunab Ku, and allowed to decline into obscurity.

Eight

THE SORCERERS OF
CHACO CANYON

The last North American civilization before our own began 1,900,393,485,400 miles away, or sixty-three hundred light-years ago. At that time, an entire star detonated in the Crab Nebula of the constellation Taurus, emitting instantaneously as much energy as the sun does in its ten-billion-year lifetime, or more energy than one hundred thousand suns combined, momentarily outshining its own galaxy.

Traveling at 1,930 parsecs, light from the stellar explosion reached earth on July 4, AD 1054, when Chinese astronomers recorded what they saw in documents of the Royal Observatory at Peking: "During the first year of the period *Chihha,* the fifth moon, the day *Chi-chou,* a great star appeared approximately several inches southeast of *T'ien-Kuan* [Zeta Tauri]. Pointed rays shot out from all sides. The color was reddish-white. After more than a year, it gradually became invisible."[1]

The Chinese reported that the supernova was six times brighter than Venus, as brilliant as a full moon, and could be seen in broad daylight for twenty-three days. It finally faded from view on April 17, 1056, after having been visible to the naked eye for six hundred fifty-three days. Similar observations appeared in Japanese, Arabic, and Italian accounts. More than six centuries later, in 1731, John Bevis discovered the Crab Nebula through his telescope, but the Englishman was only an amateur, so credit went to a professional French astronomer during

1758, when the nebula was "officially" identified by Charles Messier. It is still recognized by his twenty-first-century colleagues as "Messier 1."

Not until 1928, however, did Edwin Hubble—after whom the famous telescope, among other astronomical achievements, was named—determine that the Crab Nebula was a remnant of the "guest star" documented by Chinese astronomers in the mid-eleventh century. Its dramatic appearance coincided with the equally sudden florescence of a sophisticated, vibrant civilization in the American Southwest known as the Anasazi, thereby affirming that ancient and universal principle of perennial mysticism: "As Above, So Below." Perhaps to no other people did this dictum apply more thoroughly; the spiritual powers they invoked really did seem to draw the otherworld into their earthly existence.

Their so-called classical phase was ushered in by a period geophysicists refer to as the Medieval Climate Optimum, when global temperatures were two degrees warmer than they were centuries before or than they have been since. Just eight years after the Crab Nebula explosion faded from view, lava eruptions spewing from Sunset Crater just north of Flagstaff devastated 800 square miles of Arizona, engulfing human settlements between the Jemez Mountains and Bandalier. A volcanic eruption of such magnitude in that state was unprecedented. Beginning after AD 1100 and continuing sporadically over the next two hundred years, clouds of volcanic ash and torrents of molten rock inundated a large area near Flagstaff, snuffing out all life in much of the Wupatki Basin. During Sunset Crater's last, eleventh-century gasp in 1066, the skies were once more illuminated by an unfamiliar visitor: this time, Halley's Comet, in all its terrifying magnificence. Yet another supernova, though not as spectacular as the 1059 incident, appeared in the heavens on August 4, 1181. What modern astronomers call 3C58 was a star that blew up in the constellation Cassiopeia.

It is impossible to know how the Anasazi interpreted this series of extraordinary natural events that was compressed within a relatively short space of time, encompassing less than two hundred years. It appears, however, that such occurrences figured crucially into the ultimate fate of this mysterious people. They documented the Crab Nebula detonation in a surviving cliff painting, or pictoglyph, near Penasco Blanco, that shows a large star and crescent moon with a handprint; archaeo-astronomers believe the supernova's first appearance coincided with the final quarter of the moon. Contemporary civilizers in the Southwest, the Hohokam, used pottery art to memorialize not only 1059's stellar explosion, but also the arrival of Halley's Comet one hundred seven years later.

This running series of celestial, climatological, and volcanic episodes found their proper setting within a correspondingly bizarre landscape—the Four Corners region where Utah, New Mexico, Arizona, and Colorado meet. It enfolds the Petrified Forest, still inadequately explained by geologists; the Grand Canyon; the Painted Desert; and the Superstition Mountains, more a ragged set of volcanic extrusions than actual mountains, rated the most forbidding terrain on the planet by professional hikers, and shunned as gateways to hell by most local Indians. Only a coven of Apache medicine men still practice black magic there in secret caves, perhaps at a peak known as Geronimo's Head or near Weaver's Needle in Needle Canyon. Other sorcerers make a pilgrimage to the Tres Hermanas Hills, not far north of Columbus, New Mexico, which conceal an extensive subterranean network. Winding through a trio of conical peaks, the caves' deepest, darkest sections are surprisingly illuminated by a nimbus of faint, purple-red-green light. Radiant salts responsible for this eerie phenomenon were collected by Anasazi mystics for the persuasive performance of their arcane rituals.

These same shamans also traveled to the San Pedro Mountains and the Cerrillos mining district about fifteen miles northeast of Santa Fe for lodestones, the magnetic properties of which made possible some of the religious magic used to impress the faithful. It was as though the high strangeness of the heavens was in competition with especially bizarre features on the world below. Into the Southwest arena where this uncanny interplay between Father Sky and Mother Earth was taking place, the Anasazi made the desert bloom with civilization at the turn of the eleventh century. Theirs was more a cultural surge of several distinct if congenial cultures, rather than creation of something from nothing. The Anasazi had been poking into the American Southwest for hundreds of years before, but pursued nothing on the scale of urbanization that drew them into the lives of numerous other peoples around AD 1000.

Prior to that common florescence, these disparate, compatible societies had been hardly more than outposts, colonial extensions of outside cultures materially superior to the meager Desert Archaic populations that sparsely occupied the region. These indigenous groups were not settled pastoralists, but hunter-gatherers—more hunters than gatherers—indistinguishable from and no more advanced than their Ice Age ancestors who had crossed over the Bering Sea land bridge into Alaska from their Siberian homelands some eight millennia before. Until the arrival of the Anasazi, they had not progressed beyond a troglodyte existence, holed up in places such as New Mexico's Atlatl Cave. Their numbers began to grow, however, as they were increasingly attracted to the largesse in food supplies generated by Anasazi agricultural methods.

Bumper crops were afforded by exceptionally heavy and regular amounts of rainfall, which made prosperous dry-land farming—so dependent for water on precipitation, not ground sources. Maize production became widespread and successful, leading to the bioengineering of whole new strains, including a variety still harvested today and known as "Hopi blue corn." The early-tenth-century birth of civilization throughout the American Southwest in large measure came about due to the coincidental moisture of the period, when wealth and power were primarily measured in crops.

As some indication of their sudden rise to prominence, the Anasazi set themselves up in Chaco Canyon, New Mexico, where they established the navel of their empire. They created edifices of superb masonry known as "Great Houses," lofty affairs sometimes rising as high as five stories, all according to a formalized floor plan. These monumental structures spread across the canyon floor in a leveled area two miles wide by nine miles long. The largest complexes stood at the canyon center, although some were placed on the tops of mesas or in washes and drainage sections to take advantage of rainfall.

Archaeologists have identified fourteen Great Houses, every one of them well-planned and meticulously executed with vast sections or wings. Literally hundreds of finely plastered, high-ceilinged rooms were organized into suites, with the largest in front. One sunken, ceremonial pit known as a *kiva* corresponded, on the average, to every twenty-nine rooms. The kivas were geometrically elegant features of plastered dry stone sunk usually 12 to 15 feet into the ground. A bench was fashioned around the inside of the wall, with a small hole called a *sipapu,* Hopi for "navel," at the very center.

Access was available via a descending ladder. Ritual activity inside the kiva concerned mostly the emergence ceremony, a kind of reenactment that affirmed for its participants the immortality of the human soul based on a unifying pan-American folk myth of the Great Flood

Fig. 8.1. An Anasazi kiva near the edge of a cave high in the cliffs of New Mexico's Bandelier National Monument

that destroyed a former age. As it abated, the waters drained down into the sipapu to create an underground lake or sea from which survivors reemerged into a new era. Hence, the practice of dousing kiva initiates with water when they climbed out on the ladder.

A few Pueblo peoples who still claim at least partial descent from the Anasazi, such as the Tewa, continue to celebrate their old religion in a kiva, which they refer to as the *te'i,* or "place of the cottonwood tree." Climbing its bough, so the Deluge story goes, the ancestral flood survivors emerged from the waters sucked into the bowels of the earth through the sipapu, which the Tewa call *p'okwi koji,* or "the lake roof pole." Modern re-enactors believe they can access the same kind of immortality, because the te'i is nothing less than the Tree of Life itself.

Strangely, only about 16 percent of all investigated kivas contain a sipapu or p'okwi koji. No one knows precisely how many subterranean temples were used by the Anasazi. Around the summit of Yellowjacket Canyon alone four hundred of them have been excavated. At 81 feet in diameter, the largest kiva, southwestern Colorado's Ackmen, forms a perfect circle of dry stonework.

The Great Houses themselves arose in core-and-veneer walls of dressed flat sandstone blocks. These were coated with a matrix of clay and mortar, then covered in layers of mud decorated with distinctive patterns of surfacing stones. The complexes were extensively preplanned and tastefully landscaped, suggesting they may not have been urban communities for thousands of Anasazi elite, as archaeologists originally suspected, but ceremonial centers on holy ground visited only during religious occasions. This interpretation is supported by what appear to be residential areas in and around Chaco Canyon. It is possible, however, that these presumed "neighborhoods" might have belonged to lower-class inhabitants whose betters occupied the great houses. In any case, within one hundred years, the Chaco Canyon culture expanded to include seventy or more outlying towns and trading posts, directly controlling twenty-five thousand square miles of territory throughout the San Juan Basin.

Grandest of all the Anasazi houses is Pueblo Bonito, the "Beautiful Village." It rises in five tiers or stories above 2 acres at the foot of Chaco Canyon's northern rim. In pristine condition, Pueblo Bonito covers three times the square footage of the White House in Washington, D.C., is as large as the Roman Coliseum, and contains eight hundred spacious rooms. During January 1941, a large section of the nearby canyon collapsed on the building, destroying parts of the rear and several rooms. Walls were originally 3 feet thick to support a ceiling weighing 90 tons. A wall flanked on either side by a large kiva divided the site into equal halves surrounded by more than thirty, smaller kivas that spilled over into a large, central courtyard.

The immense structure was certainly capable of enclosing several thousand inhabitants at a time, but no significant trash middens indicating a residential status have been found in the immediate vicinity. More likely, the entire site was not some pre-Columbian apartment building, but rather the Anasazis' foremost ritual center, an identity underscored by the presence of so many kivas. It and other, related great houses were curiously D-shaped, part of a sacred architectural canon long ago lost with its builders and worshippers.

Chaco Canyon is filled with more than three thousand rooms of various sizes. Pueblo Bonito's nearby but smaller counterpart required 29,135 man-hours of labor to erect. Chetro Ketl alone absorbed approximately fifty million stone blocks, plus wood from more than five thousand trees. Altogether, building these great houses required nine hundred million stones and a quarter of a million coniferous trees—and their felling and transportation was no easy affair. After having exhausted local stands by the mid-eleventh century, ponderosa pine, spruce, and fir that went into construction came from mountain ranges up to seventy miles away.

How this immense haul to Chaco Canyon was undertaken is a mystery, because not one of the easily damaged trees bears a single scratch or mar. Some archaeologists speculate they must have been carried by hand over such formidable distances before being carved into wood beams 15 feet long, 9 inches wide, and 600 pounds each. They guess that the timber may have been moved over an extensive road system the planners laid out for this and other purposes. At the maximum extent of their influence, Anasazi settlements were connected by six road systems accurately surveyed and skillfully engineered over ninety-five thousand square miles.

The longest surviving example, the Great North Road, stretches sixty miles from the San Juan River to Pueblo Alto, the "High Village," so called because of the eighty-nine-room structure's position atop a high mesa. It was here that turquoise-processing industries and chert tool production were located, so distribution of these important commodities throughout the empire was vital to its success. In one great house alone, a pair of richly dressed, adult, human skeletons lay on a bed of fifty-six thousand pieces of turquoise surrounded by other precious grave goods. Anasazi priests buried turquoise in the construction of every kiva, perhaps to connect somehow with the lake of floodwaters believed to lay far below.

Breaking into a sealed niche at Casa Rinconcada, the canyon's best-known kiva, archaeologists removed a turquoise necklace that was 17 feet long. The roads used to move turquoise and other goods were not crude trails, but depressed and scraped beds of *caliche,* a hardened deposit of calcium carbonate, also known as hardpan. It acts as a natural cement, bonding gravel, sand, silt, and clay, and is still used today in the manufacture of Portland cement. With an average width of 30 feet, Anasazi roads were clearly defined along their edges by earthen berms or rock walls. More extraordinary, the roads ran in unerringly straight lines for mile after mile, oblivious to any obstacles in their way. Even natural obstructions, such as boulders—instead of being removed or simply skirted by a few feet—were provided with steps, while steep cliffs were overcome by stairways cut into the living rock.

One of the longest and most bizarre thoroughfares begins at the middle of Chaco's central complex, around which the sun and moon revolve in various alignments. From this solar-lunar axis, two roads, each 30 feet wide, stretch in a pair of unerringly straight lines for thirty-five miles across the open desert, unrelieved by resources or structures of any kind, until they terminate at the badlands. Here, broad steps have been carved into a wall at the edge of the canyon to fall down its steepest precipice. Below are many thousands of pieces of deliberately broken pottery, possibly fragments of funeral urns that originally contained cremation ashes or offerings to the spirits of the departed at this lifeless place—quite literally, the end of the road.

The double route allowed for pilgrimages back and forth to the dry lip of the badlands—the dead place—from the central complex, its navel, the origin of life at Chaco, around which the sun and moon dance forever. In following such a ceremonial path, pilgrims participated in a cosmic life-death-rebirth cyle that affirmed the phenomenally transient, fundamentally eternal nature of existence. Walking a seventy-mile-long round-trip through the worst of the New Mexico desert was undertaken not alone, but in large numbers provided with support groups—food suppliers, water bearers, medical personnel, and guards. Traveling along this sacred highway, participants proceeded in prayer and meditation as a means of melding with the experience.

Timing for these events was undoubtedly determined by various celestial cycles tied with particular meaning to each ritual activity. The roads were part and even an expression of this institutionalized order, but the Anasazi were also operators of an information superhighway unmatched until the advent of the Internet. Signaling posts were set up at regular intervals along the entire network. During daylight hours, data was flashed from one relay station to the next in code by polished obsidian mirrors. From dusk until dawn, their places were taken by bonfires able to pass on an equivalent amount of news. According to Tom Windes, an archaeologist who researched the canyon for thirty years, "You could flash messages in minutes across the whole Chaco world. It even looks like a dual-route system in some places, so if one went down, you would have another line to back it up."[2]

Anasazi roads were not only commercial or communications enterprises, but primarily facilitated deliberate spiritual functions that reemerged after seven hundred years when Chaco Canyon was remapped in 2000. Information from thirty-year-old, plane-table maps of the archaeological zone were fed into high-powered computers for analysis, with results far beyond anything the operators expected. The monitors began lighting up with, as archaeologist Craig Childs explained, "a master plan of alignments that had never before been recognized."[3]

He was told by Richard Friedman, one of the geodetic-computer researchers, "Nothing is out of place here, nothing arbitrary . . . everything has some sort of relationship to something else."[4] Kivas, great houses, rivers, and rocks had all been deliberately aligned with one another—often over dozens of miles—and combined in a complex network outlined partially by the roads. Interconnections spread outward from Chaco, which sat at the center of a web embracing this sacred landscape. For example, a line from the north portal of Casa Rinconcada—"House of Corners," the canyon's best-known kiva—runs through Pueblo Alto's front gate, then proceeds straight through buttes as though they did not

Fig. 8.2. Inside Casa Rinconcada in New Mexico

exist to another great house twenty miles away. Major Anasazi centers at Chaco Canyon, Solomon Ruins, and Aztec Ruins to the north, plus Casas Grandes in the south were aligned with absolute precision along a meridian more than three hundred seventy-five miles long.

Linear connections between ancient buildings, or between man-made structures and selected natural features, were discovered by the amateur archaeologist Alfred Watkins in 1921, when he noticed direct relations between ancient sites across the south English countryside that were sometimes many miles apart. He referred to these directional relationships as "ley lines," after the phrase "lay of the land," and concluded they belonged to an "Old, Straight Track" walked by traveling merchants, religious pilgrims, and ceremonial processions from one sacred site to another during prehistory.

Beginning thirty years after his death in 1935, his ley lines were misappropriated by New Age enthusiasts, who equated or confused them with energy lines of telluric current from within the earth and who believed they were capable of awakening mystical powers in properly receptive humans. "Watkins never attributed any supernatural significance to leys," John Bruno Hare points out in his introduction to *Early British Trackways, Moats, Mounds, Camps and Sites*. "He believed that they were simply pathways that had been used for trade or ceremonial purposes, very ancient in origin, possibly dating back to the Neolithic, certainly pre-Roman . . . he would be a bit disappointed with some of the fringe aspects of ley lines today."[5]

The same spatial interrelationships apparently applied to the sight lines (and often out-of-sight lines) connecting the great houses of Chaco Canyon. Every ruin there is similarly oriented to another location—usually man-made, but sometimes natural—especially if a rock or mountain can be made to align with astronomical phenomena. Casa Rinconada itself incorporates a north-south alignment within forty-five arc-seconds or a three-quarter degree, while the error in its east-west orientation is only eight arc-seconds. The alignment is dramatized on mornings of the winter and summer solstices, when sunlight entering an opening of the kiva falls upon a niche—seventh in an irregularly spaced series of niches cut into the inside wall. This seventh niche to the left of the T-shaped main entrance frames the sun in its narrow, window-like feature. Whether or not the niches of Casa Rinconada originally contained statues or representations of solar deities is unknown. If they did hold such statues, they would have been gloriously illuminated by sunbeams on their feast days. While the south entrance features a sunrise alignment, the north opens on the North Star, or Pole Star.

Some researchers argue that the site's astronomical alignments are entirely accidental because the structure was once covered by a vast roof of wood that would have blocked out sunlight. Here too, however, the timbers were arranged in a precise east-west configuration, implying a deliberate orientation to center the building directionally. Others suggest Casa Rinconada may have been designed originally as the open-air structure we see today before some shift in metaphysical perspective from the sky to the earth, or more serious religious change added a roof. We do know that in order to make Casa Rinconada's precision alignments possible, the perfectly level platform upon which it sits was terraformed

Fig. 8.3. Solar-oriented aperture at Casa Rinconcada

from the canyon rock floor prior to construction. Such an extraordinarily careful undertaking would not have been made unless designers had demanded it, probably for purposes of astronomical orientation.

Not far from Casa Rinconada, a band of sunlight passes between a pair of rock slabs—deliberately set in place?—to intersect the center of a spiral every spring and fall equinox at Tse Diyil, better known as Fajada Butte. The dramatic effect of this bright beam moving slowly over an otherwise unilluminated petroglyph has been likened to a sun dagger stabbing through the shadows, symbolically killing darkness (death) with light (life). A larger spiral nearby is perfectly bracketed by twin sun daggers during the winter solstice. On Tse Diyil's east side, a shadow falls perfectly lengthwise across the petroglyph of a snake on noon of the vernal and autumnal equinox, just as another sun dagger spikes the center of a double spiral's left lobe.

Thirteen examples of solar rock art occur at three sites at Fajada Butte, the 405-foot-high core of a long-vanished mountain standing sentinel at the south entrance to Chaco Canyon. According to the woman who discovered the first sun dagger spirals in 1977, Anna Sofaer, they "are unique among known archaeo-astronomical sites in several respects":

(a) [T]hey use the changing altitude of late morning and midday sun to indicate the solstices and equinoxes, (b) they record solar noon on rock art, and (c) most especially, they combine recording of both the season and noon in the same markings. The markings at one site are the only known ones in the New World that combine recordings of the extremes and mid-positions of the moon and the sun. The use of the features and topography of a prominent landmass to create these complex and varied markings on carved petroglyphs is also unique in our current knowledge of prehistoric astronomy.[6]

Although the astronomical orientation of Chaco markings and alignments incorporate utilitarian calendric information, they do so with a redundancy and accuracy far beyond the practical requirements of time-keeping devices. For example, precise noon markings high on a steep butte serve no apparent useful purpose, nor do the markings of the lunar standstill cycle. The accurate alignments that define the major axes of the central ceremonial structures of the canyon are similarly abstract; for example, the east-west alignments could not have been used to determine (or have been determined by) equinox sunrise/sunset because of the locally elevated horizons. Similarly, the North Road was built elaborately and accurately in a direction that serves no apparent utilitarian purpose. Rather, what may be seen in the alignments and markings is the geometric expression of astronomical concepts and of the culture's cosmology.

As Childs observes, "each Great House lies on an axis pointing to particular celestial events." Sunbeams entering through apertures in a pair of buildings at Cajon Canyon, a small group of Anasazi ruins, form luminous disks against opposite walls marked with time placement symbols corresponding to the annual solar cycle, thereby allowing room occupants to follow the progress of the sun. Chaco Canyon, too, runs along a lunar sight line, an astronomical significance that is reason enough for Anasazi planners to have chosen the location. Doubtless, its fortuitous orientation facilitated alignment from man-made structures to a number of natural features in the immediate environment.

Typical is a sandstone pueblo of fifty rooms atop a mesa 1,000 feet above the valley floor. Chimney Rock defines precisely an 18.6-year cycle when the moon appears directly between a pair of natural, stony towers at its most northerly point in the sky. The same observatory sighted alignments during the full moon after sunset on the winter solstice; during a half-moon rise in the following vernal equinox; during a new moon rise around the summer solstice; and during another half-moon rise at the autumnal equinox—an outstanding number of significant alignments taking place at a single site.

Fajada Butte rock art repeats the 18.6-year cycle in a special manner: during the southerly minimum extreme of the moon's rising, now a *lunar* dagger pierces a spiral at its center. Crossing 9.4 turns in the spiral, 9.4 years later, the dagger reappears at the northerly maximum extreme to slice the petroglyph's outer edge. In doing so, it duplicates the position of a sun dagger stabbing another Fajada Butte spiral at the winter solstice. The turns in the lunar spiral correspond to the precise number of years oscillating with the 18.6-year cycle. Its great length precludes any practical value in terms of agriculture, but seven buildings at Chaco were constructed in alignment with the moon's extreme maximum and minimum positions, as dramatized by the Fajada Butte spiral. The moon rises at its minimum extreme above the main wall of Pueblo Pintado, setting exactly six months later in perfect alignment with Chetro Ketl at the far end of the canyon.

Beyond it, in southeastern Colorado, there still stand seldom visited stone complexes, as remote as they are inexplicable. Located atop high cliffs or promontories overlooking the Apishapa River are several complexes of paired circles, sometimes in ellipses or concentric configurations. Their sandstone slabs, 8 or 10 inches thick, show severe weathering, and are precisely laid out in fitted walls rising no more than 30 inches above the ground. Natural rock faces in the immediate vicinity are crowded with petroglyphs, implying formerly intense activity here or the site's importance. The first collection is separated from the second by more than a mile into the enormous Apishapa Canyon, while the third and largest composed of significantly larger stones is about four miles distant.

Surrounded by a rectangular wall with an opening toward the west, a 60-foot-long row of six circles are arranged side by side in three sets. At the exact center of each circle stood a single stone pillar, four of which are still upright. Additional complexes probably exist in the canyon and further east toward the equally forbidding Timpas River area. Why such configurations were placed in these far-removed and difficult settings is unknown, although the apparent astronomical qualities of at least the third set, with its standing monoliths, implies celestial purposes.

In any case, Anasazi observatories were not built to generate mere calendars or almanacs given over entirely to agricultural practices.

Neither was planting and harvesting in this part of the world connected to regular, seasonal schedules, but influenced instead by the vagaries of drought or frost. No, the unnecessarily redundant heavenly orientations were not agrarian almanacs, but designed to put society in accord with the cycles of the universe; to tie every individual into a grand order, an organizing whole of humans and nature. The Anasazi strove to exist in harmony with this living cosmology through the applied axiom of "As Above, So Below," as articulated at places such as Pueblo Bonito, where its sun-directed wall at noon left no shadow, creating a passing—though daily—bond between earth and sky.

To transform the natural and man-made chaos of life, astronomer-priests sought to call down the orderliness of the heavens by bringing their sacred architecture and ceremonial behavior into alignment with the periodic harmony of the heavens. As such, Chaco Canyon was an arena for the ceremonial reenactment of a spiritual worldview through the mass participation of its followers. It was a place where people visited, but did not reside. The absence of trash middens, plus all but a handful of hearths inside more than three thousand rooms lacking any ventilation, serve to define the great houses as spaces for holy rituals, not mundane apartment complexes for some elite class. Abundant alignments between themselves and the sky were designed to draw participants into a living mechanism for the transference of cosmic order from above onto the world's chaos below.

Ceremonies replicating the sky's repetitive patterns aimed at establishing the same kind of peaceful regularity in human and natural affairs, thereby creating a heaven on earth. There was, however, an exoteric political side to the abundant ley lines and celestial alignments. They constantly preached the necessity of order—cosmic and public—associated with the conquest of light over darkness (chaos and fear). The Anasazi were light worshippers, as personified in their emblem, the T-shaped doorways and windows of their great houses. These portals were open not only to the sun, but to the moon, as well, and, at least at Casa Rinconada, to the Pole Star.

All these grand structures nevertheless belonged to the architecture of dominance. Being unlivable, their exterior purpose was to impress, awe, and engender a sense of collective centeredness through Anasazi order. A sun dagger at Fajada Butte stabs the center of a solar spiral at midday on midyear's day, while, at the same moment below, the main wall of Pueblo Bonito, standing at the midpoint of Chaco Canyon, exactly divides the seasons of the year. The wall totally absorbs its shadow at the precise moment of high noon, as though the monument itself caused darkness to evaporate.

Another Fajada Butte petroglyph depicts an arrow pointing from the great house to the noonday sun. Observers of these repetitive phenomena are reminded over and over again that they stand in the middle of time, a timeless moment of triumphant light, just where they should be and what they must continually strive to attain. The propaganda campaign is omnipresent and round the clock, a constant re-indoctrination to embrace universal order. For their attempted integration of heaven and earth, the Anasazi had to use and pacify the diverse, native masses who formed their labor force and comprised the majority population. As such, the most comprehensive measure of authority lay in controlling the minds and behavior of all those outside the ruling families. Given their minority status, there were no other political alternatives.

On an engineering scale to match their genius as subtle statesmen, the Anasazi built a spectacularly huge dam in New Mexico's Animas Valley. Discovered in July 1892, during federal efforts to define the state boundary line with neighboring Arizona, government surveyors measured the dam at five and a half miles across. At a juncture where its course changed direction they found an artificial breach that had once allowed drainage. If this feature was still operable, the engineers determined, it could have formed "a reservoir with an average length of five miles and a width of one-quarter mile," according to a contemporary report in *American Anthropologist* magazine. "The maximum depth would be about twenty feet, and the mean depth about ten feet." They estimated that the entire structure, which had "the appearance of great age," was built from 8 million to 10 million cubic yards of material, which made the dam seem "almost impossible that it could have been the work of human hands."[7]

Another large-scale water management project was built near Tsin Kletzin, a compound less than three miles south of Pueblo Alto, on the other side of Chaco Canyon. Residents at the "Place of Charcoal" obtained their domestic water from the Weritos Dam, a massive earthen structure operated by retaining in a reservoir any storm water runoff. Its engineers achieved related marvels on the surface of the earth and beneath it. They extracted quartzite "by the hundreds of thousands, if not by millions of tons," according to a *Science* magazine article in 1898.

Four years earlier, during July, archaeologists stumbled upon prehistoric quarries about one hundred twenty-five miles north of Cheyenne, in east-central Wyoming, outside the known fringe of Anasazi control— but not much beyond it. The diggings occurred across the full length of a prominent bluff five or six miles long, where nineteen openings were examined. Expedition member Wilbur C. Knight described a "work of great surface extent where exposed blocks of quartzite have been dug up." Shallow pits only 2 or 3 feet deep were nonetheless "quite extensive." Deeper shafts had been sunk 15 or 20 feet, and a single tunnel was discovered nearby.

Refuge mounds and an abundance of primitive, unusually oversized implements testified to an ample labor force engaged in excavating prodigious amounts of material. Stone hammers and mauls did not originate locally, but had been brought from neighboring mountains twenty miles away. Additional tools included spear points, axes, scrapers, and even anvils—all evidence of a large, serious industry organized during pre-Columbian times. Knight was particularly impressed by "the vast amount of work done" and the unusual cleanliness of the site. "The absence of chip heaps leads one to suppose that the quarrymen carried the quartzite away to manufacture."[8] He contrasted the large-scale, systematic diggings with irregular, far less ambitious jasper and agate mines occasionally excavated by historic Indians, whose tools, in any case, were neither as diversified nor as numerous as the implements left behind by the Wyoming quarrymen.

Anasazi greatness was expressed not only in such colossal undertakings. Naturally, a majority of its smaller-scale, more perishable, far less significant details have been lost, just as most such items disappear with the collapse of any civilization. But in rare instances where these cultural minutiae survive, they may throw more light on their former owners and operators than a statue or monument. A case in point was the discovery, as recently as 1997, of a human jaw bone from Colorado's Rio Blanco County. Still in place, a canine tooth had been neatly bored by an obsidian drill to remove decay, which, under microscopic scrutiny, left telltale striations on the surface enamel. Dated to before AD 1200, the tooth had been treated by a form of dentistry centuries ahead of its time.

Anasazi pottery was no less beyond the crude workmanship that previously typified cultures in the American Southwest. Designs were geometric and strictly standardized, perhaps less for artistic reasons than because each type of vessel could be identified, sometimes with instructions or directions for its bearer. An early Chaco Canyon black-on-white ceramic pitcher depicts what may be stylized representations of a metropolitan grid, plus four-storied structures that could represent the great houses themselves. A later black-on-white-on-red vessel displays very similar structures and a possible city layout. The bottom of an early-fourteenth-century polychrome bowl is illustrated with a curving swirl flowing into a zigzag pattern, implying a river controlled by irrigation canals. These interpretations are entirely speculative, however, because the Anasazi left behind no evidence of ever having resorted to a written language.

Nor is there at least some suggestion that they employed any form of numerical notation, deficiencies that seem impossibly at odds with this people's ability to survey two hundred fifty known miles of roads, plus astronomical and geodetic alignments over literally thousands of square miles. The Anasazi were, in fact, remarkable for what they did *not* have. Though the desert's arid condition preserved much of their material culture, from the beginning of its florescence around AD 1000 until the heart of the Four Corners Region was abruptly abandoned one hundred forty years later, there is no indication that they relied upon standing armies. Nothing in the way of weapons, equipment, or organization characterizes the early Anasazi. Their complexes of great houses did not hide behind defensive walls. There were no fortifications, arsenals, or military headquarters; no generals or chains of command; no slaves, prisons, or poverty. Even evidence for statecraft is largely absent in the form of identifiable palaces or private courts, though there must have been some authority powerful enough to command the extensive labor and organize its forms that filled Chaco Canyon and beyond.

The Anasazi were probably ruled by the elders of extended families interested in agricultural wealth and religious ceremonialism. Although they themselves formed elite councils, the regionalized affluence resulting from their organizational success created an open society available to anyone who wanted to work for it. Not surprisingly, when word spread beyond the Four Corners of the bountiful sorcerers who transformed an immemorially inhospitable wasteland into a desert paradise, tribal peoples from throughout the Southwest migrated into Chaco Canyon. The elders had their labor force.

Simple hunter-gatherers unchanged since the last Ice Age could comprehend the Anasazi only as sorcerers who commanded the forces of nature. This impression had been enhanced fortuitously by a simultaneous increase in rain. Judging from Chaco's florescence at the time, its leaders succeeded in putting a proper spin on the extraordinary celestial and geological phenomena of the era, such as the appearance of two different supernovas or Halley's Comet and other comets, to convince anxious native populations that these events were conjured and manipulated by astronomer-priests as demonstrations of their cosmic power. Even the massive volcanism that devastated part of the Southwest could have been turned to reinforce popular perceptions of Anasazi sorcery.

The Crab Nebula's brilliant display beginning in AD 1059, when the canyon floor and all its bizarre structures glowed phosphorescent scarlet each night in the radiant supernova, presented unique opportunities for imaginative public relations.

Successful as they may have been in awing and psychologically subduing the masses of "ancestral puebloans," such propaganda trickery could some day backfire in the worst possible way—if the all-powerful magicians were ever confronted by a dire situation over which they failed to exert obvious domination. Then the illusion would stand unveiled for the deception it had always been to spark the wrath of suddenly enlightened victims. Part of Chaco Canyon's surviving legacy is the persistent Indian memory of the Anasazi as "evil wizards" who misused their supernatural control over nature and society. It was this perception that would eventually reveal that the high culture of the great houses was more fragile than their astronomer-priests may have suspected.

Nine

LIQUID GOLD

The Anasazi were not alone when they made their entry onto the stage of American prehistory. They were accompanied by another distinct and complementary people who occupied a large area south of Chaco Canyon in Arizona. Relations between the Anasazi and the Hohokam were close, going back for many generations before both folk blossomed together around the turn of the eleventh century. Yet, for all their centuries of mutual respect and cooperation, and though they shared the same ethnic origins, they were different from each other and not interrelated by family ties. As a separate group, the Hohokam were close, long-standing allies of the Anasazi, with whom they were to share the common cause of civilization—and a common fate.

What most distinguished the two peoples from each other was their fundamentally different approach to agriculture. The Anasazi were dry-land farmers who relied on precipitation stored in the soil and upon dams, such as their Animas Valley project, to reservoir water. The system worked well, because, beginning around AD 1000, the Chaco Canyon area enjoyed unusually sufficient rainfall. Not so in southern Arizona, where desert conditions prevailed, and the Hohokam were forced to apply their irrigation skills to survive. They arrived as sophisticated hydraulic engineers, and at once recognized the potential for greatness promised by the Middle Gila River and Lower Salt River. Drainage areas offered a permanent flow of clean water that itself supported a dozen species of fish life, including shellfish, while marshy sections along the banks were havens for game and fowl.

Here, in the middle of the desert, there was water, if managed properly, for a whole people to drink, cultivate land, and mature crops on a monumental scale. From this Edenic environment, the Hohokam founding fathers began building a thousand miles of canals, long enough—if formed single file—to run from their base below Tucson and Phoenix to the Canadian border. Their enterprise was not a simple matter of scratching out some ditches in the earth, but instead entailed the construction of hundreds of ridges uniformly raised above ground level in 10-foot high embankments and organized on a preplanned grid.

While Richard B. Woodbury, writing in *American Antiquity*, doubts all of them were floored in a thick, calcareous coat of caliche, "there seems to be little doubt that at least part of a large canal was carefully lined to render it practically watertight, even though the cost in labor must have been enormous." The north canal to which he alludes extended for nine miles; a southern example is shorter by two miles. Woodbury observes, "Both canals are comparable in length to some of the modern canals in use today [1960]."[1]

Since then, the longest so far identified extends twenty miles, and many more that are longer than twelve miles have come to light. They were part of regularly spaced watercourses occasionally grooved or rifled at particular sections to speed flow where desired. At their junction with a river, the main canals grow progressively smaller toward their terminus, thereby increasing flow velocity to counter evaporation and seepage. This control was additionally important in maintaining a constant water rate. If the rate was too high, it eroded the canal; too low and it permitted soil particles to silt up the watercourse.

Spillage into dipping pools allowed local removal or ran through channels to farming areas, making possible a twice-annual growing season, together with a profusion and diversity of crops—including at least two different types of corn—where nothing had grown before. According to archaeological evidence gathered during the mid-1960s,

some 1,773 acres of tillable land on the lowest terrace of the main population center were thus irrigated, but this figure is a fraction of the full
extent served. One watercourse alone, referred to by archaeologists as
"Canal System Two," was capable of irrigating more than 10,000 acres.
To build it, approximately 2,624,000 cubic feet of soil were removed,
with an additional 1,312,000 removed during later reconstruction. The
canals were about 80 feet wide and 20 feet deep, impossible to ford,
so they were regularly crossed with foot-traffic bridges that were high
enough to allow for passage underneath of balsawood rafts that used
the watercourses for traveling swiftly throughout Hohokam territory.

So efficient was this superhighway for the transportation and rapid
distribution of people and goods that it may solve the mystery of those
quarter-million trees logged by the Anasazi. Undamaged timber for
their great houses from the distant Pinal Mountains appears to have
been more credibly achieved via floating on canals than via carrying
more than fifty miles of roads by teams of careful porters. As some measure of the expertise that went into designing one of the foremost public works projects ever undertaken in pre-Columbian America, Arizona
authors John P. Andrews and Todd W. Bostick indicate that "most
Hohokam canals were constructed with different gradients, depending
on the canal's location within the system and its distance from the river.
Canal gradients within Canal System Two, for example, varied from 4.8
feet per mile to 1.2 feet per mile."[2]

In planning their massive waterworks, Hokokam engineers designed
them to conform to the irregularities of terrain, and accounting for
every dip and rise. "They developed a sophisticated knowledge of the
flow of water through channels," observes Arizona historian Jerry B.
Howard, "and developed a series of techniques for delivering water to
the surface of the fields." Among the most vital of those techniques was
the installation of a weir—a dam partially extended into a river—at a
45-degree angle to the flow of water, thereby forcing it into the main
canal. There, a head gate regulated the entering flow, which passed
into distribution canals. Through these it moved to the fields, where

tapons, or diversion gates, regulated water amounts. Closing the tapon would cause the water to back up and rise, producing a head of water. Finally, small, lateral canals released water directly onto the fields. So immense was this ancient enterprise, that its full extent will never be known. According to Andrews and Bostick, "Many modern canals in the Phoenix metropolitan area are located in the same place as the prehistoric Hohokam canals."[3]

In fact, virtually all of the Hohokam canals have been obliterated by urban development and modern farming. At least two large, prehistoric canals are still preserved at Park of the Four Waters, located in the southern portion of the Pueblo Grande Museum and Archaeological Park. "Because of its strategic location," Andrews and Bostick point out, "Pueblo Grande would have been very important to other villages using the canals along the same system."

The Big Town (Pueblo Grande) was situated at the headwaters that controlled water distribution for most Hohokam villages on the north side of the Salt River. As an indication of the site's importance, an earthwork at Pueblo Grande contains 50,000 cubic feet of soil and stone, making it the largest of its kind along Canal System Two. Many other similar, if less monumental, mounds were set up at important junctures throughout the network as organizational offices and observation posts to supervise operations. They served as local water management headquarters, surrounded by high walls, less for defense (at least in the early days), than to delineate the administrative precinct. Other pueblos at Mesa Grande, Plaza Tempe, and Tres Pueblos featured platform mounds at the heads of major systems where the flow of water in main canals was controlled, yearly repairs to the weirs and headgates were coordinated, and all local necessities were provided.

The canals demanded constant maintenance to keep them operating at maximum efficiency against breakages, silting, weed growth, rodent activity, and flash flooding, which could cause serious damages. Additional mounds placed along the canals at regular, three-mile intervals were secondary centers for the regulation of less extensive districts.

Erecting this formidable project was no small task, particularly for a preindustrial people. "Having no draft animals," write Andrews and Bostwick, "the Hohokam had to dig by hand through the hard, sun-baked soil using large, wedge-shaped stone hoes, stone axes, and digging sticks. The excavated dirt probably was then removed in baskets and used to build embankments along the sides of the canals." The waterways took not years, but generations to construct, yet they were never finished, because Hohokam population continued to expand with productivity generated by the waterworks. Thus, a peak population of fifty thousand inhabitants was directly supplied with fresh water.

Yet the canals were only part of Hohokam food industry that involved other massive projects. In 1926, archaeologists from New York City's Museum of the American Indian, the Heye Foundation, found a whole series of prehistoric salt mines about six miles from a ruined pueblo undergoing excavation in southern Nevada. More than 300 feet from the opening, they discovered several spacious vaulted chambers littered with refuse, together with hundreds of stone hammers and picks. The complex consisted of an entire hill or "peak" of rock salt that had been internally excavated by the Hohokam into an upper chamber connected by a shaft to a lower, larger chamber above a main passageway granting access to the outside. A water channel for flushing out debris ran in an opposite direction from the passageway. Archaeologists were first puzzled by unfamiliar markings chiseled into the walls of the mine.

Upon closer examination, a team member told *Science* magazine, they observed "that the circles had been carved into the salt with stone picks, grooved around and around, deeper and deeper, until a raised, circular block had been broken out with the stone hammer to be taken home by the miner."[4] A final tally of salt removed by this process from the Nevada site was made more difficult to determine after additional quarries came to light, but the total amount was undoubtedly immense. Salt was invaluable for preservation of the superabundant produce generated by Hohokam farming.

The resulting agricultural wealth spawned pueblos through-out Arizona. They were connected to an expanding commercial web actively trading with contemporary mound builders of the Mississippi valley, most notably in the form of ceramic containers, and as far south as the Valley of Mexico. The Alleg hooked cross, originally the Keltic sun wheel symbol, was introduced along trade routes from distant Ohio, where the Adena culture coincided with that of the Hohokam for a thousand years prior to the Hohokam's eleventh-century florescence. Swastika variants, including the identifiable Crosóg Bríde, or "Brigid's Cross," dominate Hohokam pottery, and were subsequently incorporated by virtually every pueblo or tribal people of the Southwest into modern times. To the Hopi and other regional tribes, the swastika represents the *meha* flower signifying human mass migrations and the four great forces of nature—earth, wind, fire, and water—working together as a single, universal energy through the Four Cardinal Directions.

The hub of the Hohokam network—their first and largest settlement—was Snaketown, located on the north side of the Lower Gila River, less than twenty-five miles southeast of what would much later become the modern city of Phoenix. Contrary to alarming imagery generated by its name, the site was not an outstanding congregation for serpents, and few were ever met there during archaeological digs. Known to area Pima Indians as *Skoaquick,* "Place of Snakes" referenced the Hohokam themselves as wise sorcerers and water witches. Snakes signified spiritual energies, water (particularly from underground sources), and the power of regeneration, as exemplified by the creature's ability to slough off its old, dead skin for a new one.

Like the canals, Skoaquick was laid out on a square-grid system of about seven thousand adobe houses on 207 acres for approximately twelve thousand inhabitants. Their residential areas comprised clusters of homes opening on a common, open-air courtyard. Some featured raised, wooden floors on stone spikes marked to standardized measurement, and spacious rooms were often workshops for various arts-and-crafts activities, particularly weaving, and jewelry-making from stone, bone, and shell. Clear quartz crystal, green and red quartz, specular hematite, muscovite, amethyst, malachite, azureite, chrysocolla, rhodochrosite, and opal were favored minerals.

The Hohokam undertook extensive turquoise mining operations in Arizona at Mohave County, seventy-five miles from Snaketown, and Cochise County, twenty miles east of Tombstone on the eastern flank of the Dragoon Mountains; and in New Mexico in the Burro Mountains outside Silver City and, most particularly, at Las Cerrillos near Santa Fe. As such, they substantially augmented their already affluent water management by becoming the most important suppliers of turquoise throughout all pre-Columbian America—for cultures from northeast Mexico's Toltec priests to tribal chiefs in Chile.

The Hohokam also invented acid etching hundreds of years before the technique was independently rediscovered by Renaissance armorers in Europe. Seashells from the Gulf of California were adorned with pitch by the Snaketown artist, then were placed in a bath of weak, acetic acid. Scraping off the pitch revealed the designs. Emil W. Haury, the foremost authority on this creative people, marvels, "The invention of etching enabled the Hohokam to create some remarkable works of art."[5]

They were also advanced metalsmiths. Small, silver bells found under Snaketown perplexed investigators, who until then assumed Hohokam furnaces were incapable of reaching the 2,006 degrees Fahrenheit necessary to melt silver. The discovery threw into question the provenance of similar copper and bronze bells assumed to have been traded from the Valley of Mexico. In fact, archaeologists already knew that Hohokam ovens were large affairs for baking communal bread and capable of producing higher temperatures.

Pottery for everyday and ceremonial purposes flourished. As might be expected, water symbols commonly adorned Hohokam vessels of all shapes and sizes: these crawled with the images of frogs, ducks, birds, and fish. This preoccupation with water generated a salubrious effect on the Hohokam.

Snaketown became extraordinary for its tidiness. More than sixty middens for the collection and separation of trash have been identified. Refuge landfill was formed into attractive mounds and a pair of open-air courts for the performance of ritual ballgames. The Mesoamerican-inspired sport caught on, fostering hundreds of similar playing fields throughout the Hohokam sphere.

Already abundant water resources at Snaketown were supplemented by deep wells. In searching for that elusive definition of *civilization*, we find that at least one of its major traits is unquestionably public water management. Every high culture—from those of the Indus Valley to that of the United States—has been distinguished by the will and genius of its creators to achieve the proper distribution of fresh water. Such organization is impossible without social cooperation, which is itself the kernel of civilization. The two mutually arise from each other. Hence, water management is not only fundamental to the early construction and existence of a high culture, but also generates the common spirit that typifies and motivates it. Thus deeply involved in applying this primary resource, a people's close relationship with water naturally generates a standard of civic hygiene higher than others less able to use it for one reason or another.

The Roman custom of bathing at least three times daily amounted to a prophylactic measure that saved the Empire from most disease outbreaks that ravaged the rest of the contemporary non-Roman world. Thus some of the Eternal City's most glorious architecture was lavished on its public baths. After they were closed as sinful places by bishops of the church triumphant, the West was overwhelmed by a Dark Ages best remembered for pandemics that pushed Europe toward extinction. We may conclude, then, that the public organization of water by particular peoples who value it characterizes them as "civilized." As such, a society ascends or declines between high culture and base savagery as the appreciation of its members for general hygiene rises or falls. Well-run civilizations are clean. Those in decline are not. If this is so, then the Hohokam were eminently civilized.

Their hygienic instinct expressed itself even in standard burial methods: Snaketown had at least eight crematoria. Ashes of the dead were placed in shallow graves, sometimes in pottery containers, along with clay figurines of dogs and nude men and women. More than a thousand of these figures have been retrieved, and doubtless many thousands more were originally added to the remains. Fine workmanship seems concentrated on the human torso. These tiny effigies probably represented the deceased accompanied by a spirit guide to the next world, just as the originally dog-headed Anubis led souls of Egyptian dead to the afterlife. In fact, dogs joined their human masters in the Hohokam crematoria. Tiny deer effigies were likewise mass-produced as mortuary symbols of revitalization: shedding antlers precedes the growth of a new rack, suggesting regeneration. Bears were also depicted for their death-like hibernation from which they emerge in the spring, just as insect cycles signified life-death-rebirth patterns for the Hohokam.

Pottery designs were primarily geometric—spirals, single or linked, represent an apparently standardized form as symbols of eternal life. Among the Anasazi, spirals signified the movement of the sun, which was likewise associated with life itself. Such repeated emphasis throughout funeral art indicates a belief in the survival of death, as affirmed by the observable processes of nature to continually rejuvenate itself.

Despite Snaketown's ceremonial figurines and two ritual ball courts, the site appears to have been given over mostly to economic and administrative concerns. A far more substantial indication of Hohokam spirituality is found thirty miles down the Lower Gila River from Snaketown, near Coolidge. Casa Grande is a modern name given to the sparse ruins of a once monumental structure erected at the start of the Southwest florescence of the Hohokam one thousand years ago. Originally a rectangular, three-story building of caliche and adobe, it contains five contiguous room tiers. Four rise two stories to enclose a three-storied tier.

This unusual arrangement was dictated by the Big House's function as a temple for accurate observation and ritual veneration of the sun and

Fig. 9.1. This modern Pima Indian bowl perpetuates ancient Anasazi and Hohokam symbols of the moon (signified by the central sauvastika) connected to and encircled by solar swastikas. Artifact at the National Museum of the American Indian, New York City.

moon. The entire edifice known as Casa Grande had been sited with level perfection upon a single-story platform to allow these alignments, most of which occurred at precisely positioned windows or apertures in the second-story western wall and third-story walls. Observations were made at various doorjambs. According to R. D. Hicks, III, in *Sky and Telescope* magazine, "Sightings were not reckoned from an imaginary center-point of the lunar disk, but rather were referred to the first sighting of the limb."[6]

Known alignments at Casa Grande include moonset at minimum northerly, minimum southerly, and maximum northerly declinations; sunset of the summer and winter solstices; and sunset at the vernal and autumnal equinox. Archaeologists suspect the temple originally featured additional alignments—potentially many more—but the site is too ruinous for further determinations.

The golden age of prehistory in the American Southwest lasted about one hundred-thirty years. During decades of toil and prosperity, the formerly uninhabitable Four Corners area and its outlying regions, suddenly glittering with a miraculous civilization, attracted upwards of a quarter million people. Most of them, however, were neither Anasazi nor Hohokam. Chaco Canyon had been inundated early on with diverse populations of indigenous peoples who comprised the immense labor forces that actually made places like Pueblo Bonito or the Animas Valley dam. These disparate ethnic groups, with common roots in the postglacial Clovis aboriginals who existed ten thousand years earlier, were unrelated to the talented outsiders who worshipped their own ancestors and presumed to institute a high culture in the desert.

Their civilization was, as we have learned, founded on and sustained by water management. As long as the master agriculturists were blessed with uncommonly high precipitation, as they were throughout the eleventh century and well into the twelfth, their dry-land farming flourished to sustain abundantly the swelling numbers of previously nomadic hunter-gatherers who now regarded the alien civilizers as divine masters of nature. As Arthur C. Clarke famously observed, "a sufficiently high level of technology is indistinguishable from magic."[7]

Consequently, as rainfall declined, the illusion began to fade. The masses who had for six generations revered their beneficent overlords as living deities were unsure now if the old sorcerers had either lost control of the weather to superior, as yet unseen spirits or, as devils now, were unjustly punishing mere mortals. There is nothing more hated than a failed god—and as burgeoning resentment was exacerbated by steadily declining productivity, food grew less abundant. People began hoarding. The next, inevitable consequence was civil unrest. Adverse meteorological conditions were not dispelled by prayers and rituals. Instead, increasingly arid conditions slid into a full-scale drought.

Violence rampaged like burning lava flows through Chaco Canyon, incinerating the great houses and massacring their despised elitists. Upheaval spread across the region with wholesale arson and mass murder. As the entire fabric of civilized life was tearing apart, no one knew where or how to stop it from completely unraveling. Not a few tribes, but bands of marauders by the thousands were closing off the far-spreading network of roads even into Hohokam territory, where Snaketown was burned. Its survivors fled along those routes still open to them, joining their allies under siege in the north.

Unprepared for so catastrophic a turn of events, the Anasazi concluded that the experiment on the Colorado Plateau had come to an end and was no longer tenable. An emergency convocation was held to determine some course of action that must involve the immediate future of both communities. Because negotiation with mobs was not possible, evacuation was the only available option. They determined that a free-for-all stampede must inevitably result in virtual annihilation, allowing the brigands to pick off their victims piecemeal. With safety in numbers, the sole alternative was mass emigration.

An entire population moving as a single organism would be too much even for stone ax–wielding gangs. Moreover, the periphery of such an amoebic migration afforded some measure of numerically significant defense. Serious attrition was to be expected in such a large-scale, desperate undertaking. Yet if it succeeded in evacuating the Four Corners area across the Sonora Desert, the refugees could find protection in northern Mexico at the huge and thriving commercial center of Paquimé. The trek was four hundred miles due south, and would require every ounce of organizational skill the Anasazi possessed, but salvation beckoned.

Not everyone was convinced. Skeptics argued that an expatriation of overwhelmingly unmilitary individuals would be broken up and devoured like a herd of sheep by ravenous wolves. The dissenters cautioned a less risky strategy: retreat to aerie locations such as Mesa Verde, where they could live free from fear in unassailable cliff dwellings, simultaneously protecting farmers working the land below. Any coming attack might be observed far in advance, thereby allowing everyone to reach safe quarters in time. As backup, stone towers of refuge in the fields could afford immediate protection. Besides, no one believed the drought could last forever. Once it had passed, things would return to normal.

Childs recounts a Zuni Indian version of events in which the emergency convocation was held south of Antelope Mesa, not far from the Colorado River. Here, in the Painted Desert, the issue would be decided by a pair of eggs. Most chose an ordinary-looking example. Far fewer picked a more colorful specimen. From the former sprang a parrot, which told them to go south. As soon as a raven emerged from the second egg, those who had chosen it knew they were to remain behind, because the bird made its home in the Four Corners area.

In this oral tradition, myth has been verified by material evidence, when construction engineers excavating late-twentieth-century trenches for a gas pipeline in the desert south of Antelope Mesa inadvertently dug up the ruins of numerous kivas. Alerted to the unexpected find, archaeologists uncovered the remains of a previously unknown great house surrounded by a populous settlement. Zuni folk memory preserved an accurate description of the mass meeting to determine an entire people's course of action. The majority heeded the parrot's advice, and a prehistoric exodus of twenty thousand men, women, and children moved with grim determination off the Colorado Plateau.

Those relatively few who stayed behind repaired to the northern San Juan basin, where they built white palaces in capacious, naturally formed recesses high up sheer canyon walls. Places like Wetherhill Mesa, Montezuma's Castle, Tonto, Betatakin Ruin, Spruce Tree House, and Canyon de Chelly were America's first gated communities. They lasted no more than forty years. The deluge of violence drowning the Southwest in blood surged not far below, licking at their high foundations.

An extensive network of stone towers made available as places of refuge for farmers caught out in their fields was transformed into individual torture chambers. More than a thousand *torreones,* as Spanish travelers much later called them, were scattered across southwestern Colorado and southeastern Utah, with the greatest concentration in

Fig. 9.2. Cliff dwellings at Canyon de Chelly in Arizona

northern New Mexico. Here, throughout the Gallina Valley, some five hundred towers guarded a thirty-five-by-fifty-mile area, although total distribution encompassed tens of thousands of square miles. Some towers were circular, but a majority were rectangular or square with rounded corners, and most were hastily if well made of irregularly shaped and sized sandstone blocks fitted neatly in a matrix of adobe and mortar. Rooms were plastered; floors and ceilings featured heavy, wood beams.

The two-story structures rose in 38-foot-high walls averaging 2 feet thick, beginning at 6 feet thick on bases between 15 and 26 feet. Crowning the summit was a parapet cut with slit windows for defending archers. Surviving examples of these castlelike structures may be seen to best advantage at Hovenweep National Monument, in Utah, where they were situated atop gigantic boulders, overlooked the edges of mesas, and watched from the rims of canyons. Around Mesa Verde, they formed an early-warning system and bulwark for the cliff dwellers. In the McElmo Canyon area, towers stood guard over the pueblos and at the canyon entrance.

Clearly, the Anasazi put much faith in this last-ditch strategy of point defense. Yet it was misplaced. According to encyclopedist William R. Corliss:

> [T]he towers were methodically picked off one by one, and their defenders ruthlessly murdered down to the last man, woman and child. Most towers were also burnt, perhaps during the assault, but also possibly to erase as completely as possible the traces of a detested culture. The latter inference is quite reasonable, because each tower excavated showed signs of an almost maniacal assault. Skulls were split open. One woman warrior fell with sixteen arrows in her body.[8]

In his archaeological investigation of a pit house adjacent to one of the Gallina towers, *Natural History* magazine's Charles B. Gallenkamp found a pile of ten skeletons: "The victims had apparently been thrown into the pit together and fired upon at close range. The fingers and toes of several skeletons were roughly severed in a way that suggested torture before death. The bones were badly splintered by stones hurled down upon the writhing pile, and part of the flaming roof timbers had collapsed upon them."[9]

Such horrific scenes took place at each tower site, revealing, as Corliss concludes, "the depth of hatred one people can feel towards another." Their screams echoed off canyon walls to the last of the cliff dwellers, who were forever safe in unassailable niches from hordes of homicidal maniacs—but who were not safe from endless siege. The invaders had come to stay, and the last defenders, utterly cut off from the outside world, passed into the slow death of starvation, a dubious alternative to the relatively quicker, though hardly less unthinkable fate of being burned alive or some related atrocity. The foreheads, cheekbones, and jaws of skulls littered in profusion around Mesa Verde still carry deep ridges made when faces were scraped off from living heads, commonly encountered indications that someone sought to obliterate the Anasazi. Nearby, limb bones were smashed open with stone hammers for the removal of tasty marrow. In Marcos Canyon, Colorado, archaeologist Timothy White uncovered, according to a 1997 article in *Science* magazine, "the findings of a feast in which seventeen adults and twelve children had their heads cut off, roasted, and broken open on rock anvils. Their long bones were broken—he believes for marrow— and their vertebral bodies were missing, perhaps crushed and boiled for oil. Finally, their bones were dumped, like animal bones."[10]

Already, by 1970, about five hundred cannibalized skeletal remains had been collected from more than forty Anasazi locations, such as Chaco Canyon's Penasco Blanco Great House. Since then, virtually every excavation of this high culture's major and minor sites during their final years amounts to a crime scene. "The archaeological record from the 13th Century around the Four Corners reads like a war crimes indictment," observes Childs. "Infants and children burned alive, skeletons marred by butchery, entire villages left with bodies unburied."

Below Sleeping Ute Mountain, part of a small range in the southwestern corner of Colorado, workers had dug into only about 5 percent of Castle Rock Pueblo when they came upon the incomplete remains of forty-one bodies in a state of violent confusion. A right leg, the bones still articulated, was found in its own room. In another chamber more than three hundred feet away, most of the same man's mutilated skeleton, including his face-defleshed skull, still lay upon the floor. Ground up finger and toe bones among the sacked towers of the Gallina Valley appear to have joined the removal of faces as favored treatment for Anasazi victims, because evidence of an identical technique was uncovered at Castle Rock Pueblo. DNA testing of human feces there proved that someone who dropped them in the early thirteenth century had consumed the body parts of four different men.

Ute Indian myth appears to recall the carnage at Castle Rock Pueblo, because it tells of a "great warrior god" who fell asleep there after slaughtering "the Evil Ones"—in Navajo, the same Ancient Enemies, or Anasazi. At some point before such deplorable events overwhelmed them, the cliff dwellers must have regretted their decision to hole up in the northern San Juan basin while most of their kinsmen emigrated en masse to Mexico. According to Childs, "at least forty thousand people living in parts of southern New Mexico and southern Arizona simply vanished from the archaeological record."

What became of those who chose the raven's egg is evident in burned or abandoned ruins filled with their broken and cannibalized bones. The destiny of the Anasazi who fled this holocaust gave them a new lease on survival. That the goal of their epic trek was finally reached in northern Mexico seems clear, given the contemporary and sudden florescence at Paquimé, which blossomed with an influx of prosperous émigrés. Little more than one hundred years later, however, this prosperous and vibrant commercial and ceremonial center was overwhelmed by the same hurricane of hatred that had raged across the Four Corners region. "For months afterward," according to Childs, "the area must have reeked of death, corpses blackening in the sun."[11]

He picked up a refugee trail through the northern Sierra Madre mountains into another canyon region, where yet one more attempt was made at pulling things together. It did not work this time. Too much slaughter and forced migration had eroded their numbers and diluted their social cohesion. Countless potsherds and burial mounds at Barranca del Cobre testify to the final dissolution of a people. Their mixed, living descendants inhabiting the canyonlands are the Raramuri, "those who walk well," a descriptive name that echoes ancestors who completed, long ago, an epic march from a lost high culture. Lacking the dynamic imperialism of Aztec empire builders getting started in the Valley of Mexico, final generations of threadbare survivors lived out their lives relatively secure from the hate-crazed forces that had pursued them relentlessly for centuries.

As the last Anasazi and Hohokam went to sleep forever in the shadow of the Sierra Madre mountains, the winds back home blew through Chaco Canyon, burying its deserted, crumbling great houses under piling layers of oblivion. The network of roads was obscured.

Places such as Casa Grande, in the end transformed from temples for worship of the heavens to banquet halls for cannibal feasts, virtually disintegrated. A thousand miles of canals no longer brought fresh water to fifty thousand inhabitants, but instead flowed with their blood and was choked by their corpses until most traces of their engineering marvel vanished under the sands.

Barrens that had been made to bloom became a proper desert by 1928, when the 580-foot-wide Coolidge Dam was completed. Though this project made possible the irrigation of 100,000 acres on one side of the Gila River, the area of Snaketown was rendered more desolate than ever before, as the land instantly shriveled up, parched, and died. Throughout the previous six hundred years, time and nature had reduced the ruins of civilization in the American Southwest to crumbling fragments scattered across an arid wasteland. The American anthropologist Professor U. Francis Duff was moved to write of them after the turn of the twentieth century: "Out of the brooding and ineffable silence which hangs over these places of the dead comes no voice."

Ten

WHO WERE THE
LOST OTHERS?

A people's identity is revealed by its origins.

The prevailing belief among American archaeologists has long held that the builders at Chaco Canyon were regional Indians who, over many centuries, gradually coalesced into a larger, more sophisticated culture. Given enough time, such things are supposed to occur. Today, of the Southwest's thirty-five thousand pueblo natives divided into about twenty tribes, only some, such as the Hopi, Apache, and Zuni, are believed to be descended from the Anasazi. Yet, this name applied to the eleventh-century builders at Chaco Canyon has always proved troubling and become an increasing embarrassment for scholars doubling as diplomats among various Southwest tribal groups that are uncomfortable with it. Anasazi is Navajo for "Ancient Enemy."

The name is rejected by the Hopi as an appellation for their ancestors, because the Navajo, regarded as Johnny-come-latelies, did not even exist in the Four Corners region during any of the periods under discussion. During 1540, the explorer Francisco Vasquez de Coronado reported that the western Apache area—Navajo country—was uninhabited. Forty years later, other Spaniards were there sharing corn with Navajo farmers. This slender time span defines the arrival of the Navajo in the American Southwest, as additionally confirmed by the earliest Navajo site near La Plata, New Mexico, tree-ring-dated to 1541, just a year after Coronado's visit. The name "Navajo" derives from *Navahu,* or "fields beside an arroyo," as the Spaniards heard the Indians refer to themselves.

The former almost got it right by the 1670s, when they began using the name *Dinétah* for a Navajo-occupied area about sixty miles west of the Rio Chama valley. These Indians were (and still are) the *Diné,* Athabascan "people" from Pacific Coastal Alaska to British Columbia. Even today, tribal members of the Diné inhabiting Great Slave Lake in the Northwest Territories are able to converse in the language of their Navajo cousins who left Canada five hundred years ago. Named for the Slavey Indians, Great Slave Lake, at 2,015 feet, is the deepest in North America.

No less deep are Hopi objections to the use of the Diné name for their own ancestors, because the name Anasazi applies to the Ancient Enemies of tribes other than the Navajo, who were not around at the time of troubles, and so could not have been implicated in the nastiness of the period. The implied insult contradicts claims of descent from Chaco Canyon civilizers, who, the Navajo suggest, were actually exterminated by the Hopi and other tribes then inhabiting the Four Corners region. These insinuations are hurtful because the Hopi know they are at least partially true.

For their part, the Hopi regard themselves as a gathering of many peoples representing tribes from distant areas and epochs, including the eleventh-century civilizers, whom the Hopi referred to as either the *Hisatsinom*—a generic term for "ancestors"—or perhaps, more specifically, as the *Pavatsinom,* an enigmatic variant of "the old ones," instead of Anasazi. The Hisatsinom or Pavatsinom were surviving cliff dwellers, the last of the Hohokam and Chaco Canyon culture bearers, mostly young women taken as wives by the victors into whose own lineage dissolved the newly introduced genetic heritage of a liquidated people.

Hopi descent from the lost Pavatsinom-Anasazi is strongly suggested by the existence of Orayvi, better known to outsiders as "Old Oraibi," a settlement in northeastern Arizona perched on the edge of Third Mesa. This dusty pueblo is the oldest continuously inhabited community in the United States, founded around AD 1150, and it therefore dates to that pivotal epoch at the zenith of Chaco Canyon's greatness and the onset of its destruction.

As a bastion of Hopi mysticism, Christian attempts at conversion there were doomed to fail. A government census at Old Oraibi around the turn of the twentieth century revealed that more than eight hundred residents were approached by a Mennonite minister, H. R. Voth, who built his church nearby in 1901. Its incineration by lightning forty years later was regarded by the imposed-upon Indians as heaven's welcome judgment, and no further attempts were made to proselytize them.

In Old Oraibi and its related villages, ceremonies are still governed by the lunar calendar, recalling alignments to the moon at temples such as Casa Grande, while communal life is bound to the growing cycle of corn, introduced by the Anasazi. The appellation "Hopi" is almost a nickname for *Hopituh Shi-nu-mu*, the "Peaceful People," from a concept rooted in reverence and respect for all things—the importance of being at peace with them and living in accordance with the nonviolent instructions of Maasaw, the "Creator or Caretaker of the Earth." This tribal ethic is in sharp contrast to the ancestral pueblo peoples' murderous fury displayed from the mid-twelfth to early fourteenth centuries. Perhaps they gradually became the Hopituh Shi-nu-mu from a developing sense of collective guilt for atrocities committed against the murdered relatives of their captured Pavatsinom wives and mixed offspring.

There is also a fundamentally telling distinction separating the Chaco Canyon "wizards" from modern Pueblo Indians. The latter popularly associate their ancestral origins with the north, not in terms of mundane geography, but in an esoteric, metaphysical sense. For the Anasazi, however, north was the realm of death. Their Great North Road departs from light-affirming structures, stretching in a straight line for thirty-five miles across the open desert to terminate at the badlands, where pots were ritually broken to honor the dead. None of the great houses or related structures, for all their abundance of astronomical orientation, feature northerly alignments, save only Casa Rinconcada's northern entrance fixed on the Pole Star. Such a primary divergence of belief between the Anasazi and modern Pueblo Indians suggests that the basic, cosmological outlooks of these two peoples were dissimilar.

While partially descended from the Old Ones, Hopi are not entirely identifiable with the lost Anasazi, who really were, after all, their Ancient Enemies (though now distantly related). Even now, many Indians never visit places such as Pueblo Bonito or Mesa Verde, and they refuse ever to do so. One thousand years ago, astronomer-priests carved rock art precisely aligned to solar cycles at Fajada Butte, a holy place venerated by worshippers from all around the Four Corners region. How the same location is regarded today may be gleaned from the words of an anonymous Navajo:

> No one is allowed on top of the butte nor even allowed to lean against its sides. A long time ago, they used to say that there was a lady who lived on top of the butte called *She Who Dries You Out*. She would go to a nearby canyon and fill her jug with water. Then she would take her jug of water back to the top of Fajada Butte. To get to the top of the butte, she would take a trail leading to the top of the butte on one of its sides.
>
> The lady was considered beautiful. She would come down off the butte and mingle with the people. Then she would take a man back up to the top of the butte with her. Next morning, her beauty would be gone, and she'd be an old woman. The man who she came back with would be tied up. When he asked for water, she wouldn't give him water. Instead, she'd urinate into a bowl for him, telling him to drink it. Soon the man would get thin, then die.[1]

"She Who Dries You Out" was the *yei,* or lady vampire, Asdzaa Nadleehe, "Changing Woman." This demonization of Fajada Butte transformed it in the minds of non-Anasazi peoples from a sacred observatory of eternal life-giving light to a forbidden rock haunted by an evil presence that caused death.

Often, in conversation with Four Corners Indians (Navajo excepted), they are proud to acknowledge Chaco Canyon as the achievement of *"our* people." Yet, at the same time they speak of that achievement, the identification of its builders commonly morphs into *"those* people." Whether subconsciously or not, this shift usually occurs when they begin referring to the Lost Others as "sorcerers" who exercised magical powers over nature, abusing its forces to dominate society, and therefore, by implication, deserving of the fate that overtook them in the end. This was most likely the aboriginal response to the technologically sophisticated Anasazis' failure to dispel the catastrophic drought of the times. Because they were the masters of earth and sky, surely, out of pure malice, they sought to punish humankind with disastrous climate change—so the thinking has been.

If, as mainstream archaeologists tell us, some Indians of the American Southwest are descendants of an original ancestral pueblo people that laid out prehistoric Arizona's colossal canal system, filled Chaco Canyon with great houses, and connected these immense structures to highly sophisticated geodetic and celestial alignments, why are these civilized achievements absent from every tribe in the region? The archaeological discoveries made by modern field researchers were as surprising to university-trained scholars as to the Hopi, Zuni, or Apache, who could contribute nothing more than oral traditions about powerful sorcerers. The Indians have not constructed monumental architecture, engaged in applied astronomy, or completed massive public works projects. We must conclude, then, that either their culture has backslid from its former greatness or that the tribal peoples of the American Southwest are not descendants of the Lost Others after all. Because this alternative seems unpleasant, however, it is not considered.

Today's Hopi are more likely descended from the Mogollon, a people halfway—geographically, as well as culturally—between the Hohokam and the Anasazi. Their actual name having been long forgotten, archaeologists have classified them after the Mogollon Mountains, where they arrived as Mexican farmers to displace the resident Desert Archaic inhabitants. Before the Anasazi or Hohokam arrived, they dwelled in clusters of dirt-covered pit houses dug into the ground. Unrelated to either people, the Mogollon adapted elements of each into their simpler, more introverted, less materially rich culture.

Yet members of a subset known as the Mimbres branch did atypically engage in outside trade, and they crafted the finest Mogollon pottery, indicative of a richer ceremonial life. They got on well with the Arizona and Chaco Canyon civilizers, learning enough from them to build larger and better houses, but they were driven from their namesake mountains by Apache ancestors after Snaketown was burned. Some remained behind even after that disaster, but most made common cause with the cliff-dwelling Anasazi and Hohokam, and they suffered much the same fate. More Mogollon survived to disappear through assimilation with the Hopi, and were the real Hisatsinom.

Inhabiting a remote region of western New Mexico, the Zuni are less troubled by such contradictions. They live by irrigated agriculture as a deeply traditional people most interested in the faithful performance of religious events. Many ceremonial cycles celebrate various stages in individual as well as communal life from birth through death. Every four years, the Zuni make a barefoot pilgrimage to Kachina Village, a 12,482-acre sacred arena, for their four-day observance of the summer solstice.

To them, four is a sacred numeral signifying the Cardinal Directions in time as well as space. Zuni worship the sun as the supreme being, so much so that their conception of "daylight" and "life" are expressed by the same word. They revere corn as a holy crop, and are master silversmiths. These cultural characteristics clearly delineate Zuni inheritance from the long-dead Hohokam, who were said to "carry the waters, bringing new soil," according to mythic tradition recorded by the late-nineteenth-century ethnologist Frank H. Cushing. He learned that the Zuni also preserved an ancestral memory of meeting with another people who lived in "great towns built in the heights": the Anasazi as cliff dwellers.

The Zuni fought them until only a few survivors, their faces black-ened with smoke, were pulled from ruins charred by the flames of war. Known henceforward as the *Kwinikwakwe,* or "Black People," they were assimilated into the Zuni tribe. The same myth describes both the cliff dwellers and Hohokam as foreigners who were "wild of tongue"— that is, they spoke a different language. The name of the Hohokam derives from *hokam,* Pima for something "all used up" applied to a folk that died out long ago. How the ancient Arizona irrigationists actu-ally referred to themselves was lost with their extinction, but there can be no doubt that they and their co-civilizers in the north represented unique peoples.

Despite heavy emphasis that mainstream archaeologists place today on mere cultural variations shared by a common population of ances-tral pueblo peoples, the Anasazi and Hohokam were essentially differ-ent from the aboriginals in whose midst they built civilization. Childs states:

> Based on physical remains, these people were physically distinct from one another. . . . The two, innermost tombs of Pueblo Bonito may have contained two separate ethnic groups with genetic ties to different parts of the Colorado Plateau. . . . Some people who were physically taller than others were buried near others who were shorter and more heavyset; some with high, peaked foreheads were buried close to others with more rounded faces.[2]

Zuni elders still remember these long-dead foreigners as the Lost Others—unrelated strangers. Dissecting the Navajo name for them reveals that *Ana'i* means "enemy alien." In a *Saturday Evening Post* arti-cle about human remains found at Utah's stone towers of refuge, author Frank Hibben writes, "It seems obvious that the Gallina people were not ordinary Pueblo Indians."[3] He was seconded by *Natural History*'s Charles Gallenkamp, who reports that the tower victims "were taller and leaner than the stocky Pueblos."[4]

According to Emil Haury, the Hohokam "preferred to live at arm's length from their tribal neighbors, and from each other."[5] To maintain their group unity and separateness from all the indigenous populations surrounding them, the Anasazi were avid ancestor worshippers, and, Childs notes, "kept rigid systems of lineage." The basis for this sense of exclusivity becomes clear in the naturally mummified remains of Anasazi at Grand Gulch, in southeast Utah. Ninety miles east of Mesa Verde and far more inaccessible, its ruins have been continuously abandoned since the last of their conquerors painted the yellow-green portrait of a skinned head at one end of a hidden alcove appropriately known now as Green Mask Spring. Less-easily-found rock art unfolds in a 30-foot-long panel depicting human figures standing beneath a shower of comets, perhaps a memorial to the appearance of Halley's Comet in AD 1066.

Grand Gulch was more illuminating for its several dozen mummies, all of which were shipped east to New York City's Museum of the American Indian during the early twentieth century. Centuries of undisturbed aridity resulted in their remarkably lifelike condition, and thereby revealed a surprising diversity of human types. Some were indistinguishable from Indians residing today in the Four Corners region—but a majority were entirely different. Their broad shoulders, long limbs, and slender torsos, so opposite the squat, robust Pueblo Indians, were contrasted most dramatically by their discernibly Caucasoid skulls with well-preserved facial features and abundant fine, red hair.

This anomalous people must be the tall, red-haired Evil Ones recounted in tribal tales of a great warrior god who fell asleep in the Ute Mountains after having killed the foreigners at Castle Rock Pueblo. Hopi traditions of *Pahána,* the "Lost White Brother," refer to a period long ago when his fair-haired folk lived in common greatness with their ancestors. Some tragedy put an end to their co-prosperity, and Pahána's people left the Four Corners region. Generation after generation, the Hopi anticipated his return, in vain.

Their story echoes the Anasazi experience from its florescence at

Chaco Canyon to its violent demise and the mass emigration of its residents. These Ute and Hopi myths are by no means unique. The Apache, Isleta, Jicarilla, Keresan, Maricopa, Mohave, Taos, Yuma, and probably every Indian tribe in the Southwest keep their own versions of red-haired "giants" who dominated the world long ago. The Grand Gulch mummies are among the only biological evidence for this lost race, because the Anasazi and Hohokam cremated their dead. From the fortuitous preservation of a few, representative specimens must be extrapolated the previous existence of an entire people described in an identical fashion throughout native oral tradition.

But who might they have been, and from where could they have possibly come? Emil Haury half believed in Western Mexico origins: "Parallels in culture elements are demonstrable, but absolute identities are more difficult to establish." He pointed to Snaketown figures of a reclining man with a bowl over his navel (like Maya *chacmools,* statues in the round depicting the same posture); mirror backs; earplugs; macaws; platform mounds; and ceremonial ball courts, with their solid, rubber balls—all obvious Mesoamerican imports. In addition, some Hohokam pottery decorations are identical to contemporary Toltec motifs, and the so-called Van Liere Site figurine from a Hohokam cremation depicts someone squatting with elbows extended, like the famous Olmec "Wrestler" statuette.

These comparisons were not, however, strongly enforced by physical proofs for a Mesoamerican presence in the American Southwest. Haury knew that the combined imports his archaeology team collected were "barely enough to make it worth a trader's time and effort to pack it northward over an arduous trail." That effort would have been still less worth the trouble if, as seems probable in the light of Hohokam silverworking, even the several hundred copper bells found at Snaketown were locally manufactured. Haury had to admit that "the evidence we do have does not support the idea of large-scale importations by the *pochtecas*" (traveling merchants from the Valley of Mexico).

Socially organized irrigation projects were undertaken in Mesoamerica prior to the Hohokam, but nothing on the magnitude of ancient Arizona's canal network, which was, in any case, of an entirely different, far more advanced design and function. No indications of any kind suggest that water management skills passed from Mexico into the American Southwest (nor from north to south). Limited commercial goods and some associated concepts from beyond most likely drifted across the American Southwest through a gradual process of cultural condensation via the far-traveling Mimbres traders, whose Mogollon population did, after all, overlap the Rio Grande River far into Mexico.

Yet the imported items and ideas were superficial influences—more at Snaketown than anywhere else—that marginally effected, but did not stamp or sustain the Anasazi and Hohokam. These high cultures were never outposts or cultural or commercial extensions of Mesoamerica, which is primarily demonstrated by a total dissimilarity between their monumental building styles. Nothing like Pueblo Bonito was ever seen in Mexico, and nothing like Tula, the Toltec capital, ever occurred at the Colorado Plateau. Still, Haury could not shake his suspicion that Hohokam "elements can only be attributed to a southern source where they were not only earlier, but also more developed."

If the actual name of the Lost Others was known, a philological link might be established with their origins. A tenuous connection does indeed lead to Mesoamerica through the Tohono O'odham—aptly named "People of the Desert"—via their residency in the Sonora wilderness. Their extinct ancestors, known as the *Sobaipuri,* were contemporary with the Hohokam, remembered as the *Siwan,* a name foreign to the Tohono O'odham. Was this how the redoubtable canal builders actually referred to themselves?

Siwan is pronounced almost identically to *Shiwanni,* the Zuni term for "rain (water) priest," a comparison made all the more remarkable because, being a linguistic isolate, the Zuni tongue is wholly unrelated to the Tohono O'odham's Pima language—as it is to all other tongues spoken by Pueblo Indians. The prehistoric Guatemalans believed they originated from Seven Caves, Wuqub' Siwan, as described in the *Popl Vuh,* or Council Book, a collection of Maya myths rooted in preclassic times around 200 BC and earlier. Unfortunately, comparison between the Tohono O'odham Siwan and Zuni Shiwanni and the *Popol Vuh*'s Wuqub' Siwan seems little more than coincidentally philiological, unsupported as it is by any substantial commonality between the Maya and Anasazi-Hohokam.

Siwan does, however, open a number of intriguing possibilities in Sipán, site of one of South American archaeology's most spectacular discoveries, near the coast of northern Peru, in the middle of the Lambayeque valley. It was here during 1987 that an ancient mausoleum was found in undisturbed condition. Filled with gold and silver necklaces, pectorals, ear- and noserings, helmets, armor, and bracelets, the royal burial included more than four hundred precious jewels and eleven hundred fifty examples of funerary pottery. The find led to four other rich burials in the immediate vicinity. "These are the richest tombs ever excavated in the Western Hemisphere," remarked Christopher Donnan, an anthropology professor at the University of California.[6] They belonged to the Moche, South America's first imperialists, who, long before the rise of the Incas, attempted to subdue and organize the Andean region into an imperial state. Although the Moche civilization collapsed thirteen hundred years ago, the language of its builders was still spoken in isolated villages until the beginning of the nineteenth century.

Thanks to this remarkable linguistic continuity, and with the assistance of a Spanish friar's Moche dictionary, compiled around 1600, *Sipan* has been translated as "House or Place (*pan*) of the Moon (*si*)." Its phonetic resemblance to the Tohono O'odham Siwan is but the first in a rich set of dramatic, revealing parallels between the American Southwest and South America during prehistory.

"Extraordinary irrigation systems allowed the Moche to tap into rivers and run water canals through a dry, coastal valley where rain was rare," according to *Ancient American* reporter Mary A. Dempsey.[7]

Michael E. Moseley, a reliable authority on pre-Inca archaeology, agrees: "In Lambayeque, enormous irrigation works supported the largest of coastal populations."[8] Dempsey writes that Moche "metallurgy skills were more advanced than those of subsequent craftsmen."

They were also a maritime people whose pyramid walls and pottery are replete with images of the balsa freighters they plied up and down the Pacific coast as far north as Ecuador for a very specific type of marine treasure. *Spondylus princeps* are large mollusks favored particularly in the manufacture of luxury items and as material for crafting the highest quality service for state ceremonies or sacred rituals. So prized was its shell that trade in *Spondylus princeps* actually developed into a kind of monetary exchange that generated cultural and economic enrichment.

As the Andean progenitors of canal building, metallurgy, seafaring, and shell harvesting, the Moche set precedents for what was to come. Their Peruvian homogony was extensive, with the founding of numerous and enormous cities, mostly along the northern coasts. These immense urban centers of commerce, manufacturing, political administration, and religion spread out farther still in surrounding agricultural settlements. Everything—from pyramids and palaces to shops and farmhouses—was made of sundried mud brick reinforced with wooden beams. The ubiquitous employment of this medium did not result in drab population centers, but, on the contrary, allowed builders to mold and paint the easily malleable surfaces into relief friezes for a vibrant metropolitan environment. The exterior and interior spaces of virtually every structure—and certainly every government and ceremonial building—were alive with boldly colorful imagery signifying spiritual, natural, commercial, and political themes. Adobe construction is ideally suited to the fringe of the Peruvian Desert, where rain occurs less frequently than anywhere else on the planet, but it is particularly vulnerable to major climate change.

Some time between AD 562 and 594, a meteorological phenomenon all-too-well-known today unleashed a deluge on the Moche empire. An

El Niño event of cataclysmic proportions "washed massive loads of sediment into the sea," according to Moseley. "The sea deposited it as sand along the beach, which strong, daily winds off the ocean blew inland as massive dunes that buried fields and cities." At the capital of Huaca del Sol,

> . . . flood waters inundated the city with such power and force that sections of the urban landscape were completely stripped away, removing several layers of deposit. Surrounding fields and irrigation systems were similarly stripped and damaged. . . . Potable water and sanitation systems would have broken down, disease and pestilence broken out, and infant mortality soared. Famine would have been acute, as irrigation systems were washed out, taking years to repair . . . [T]he nation confronted severe food shortages for many years.[9]

Huaca del Sol was abandoned and completely buried under the rising sands, but it was only one of virtually every city the Moche built. When they began begging for assistance from tribal neighbors, everyone knew their imperial days were done. The resulting political vacuum was filled immediately, however, by a people waiting in the wings for just such an opportunity. The Huari are the least remembered, most important people in South American prehistory. They built the cultural foundations of ancient Peru, perfected everything that had come before them, and later passed it on to the Incas, who, for all their own undeniable contributions at statecraft, nevertheless took the credit. The latter's relationship to their predecessors was not unlike that of the Romans to the Greeks: ambitious conquerors commandeered the superior achievements of a higher culture for their own expansionist agendas of wealth and power.

Not to be confused with a modern, wholly unrelated ethnic group and language known as Wari', driven by numerically superior enemies, "the Huari had moved up from the coastal valley foothills," into the central and north-central Peruvian highlands, according to Andean mythologist Paul Steele. From this refuge, their numbers and influence grew over successive generations throughout the region near Lima and across the intermontane valleys of Ancash, Cajamarca, and Cajatambo. They were among Peru's primeval populations, and considered themselves the founding fathers of Andean civilization, the builders of its most important cities. Pachacamac, South America's leading oracle center; Cuzco, before the Incas made it their capital; and Bolivia's renowned Tiahuanaco, near Lake Titicaca, were all attributed to the Huari. Their claim is not hard to accept, given the ruins of massive urban centers near the town of Quinua, the Warivilca ("Primieval Holiness" in Quechua) Sanctuary, and Pikillaqta—"Flea Town"—capital of the Huari.

Their name encapsulates identity and origins. It derives from Huiracocha, their original teacher, who is less well known than the much later Inca *Viracocha*, revered throughout the Andes as the Creator of Life and instructor in the civilized arts. "Sea Foam" referred simultaneously to his transoceanic arrival in the company of several "brothers" (i.e., a tribal migration) and the whiteness of their skin. They were also remembered as bearded giants, in contrast to the smaller, beardless natives of Peru. It was from these mariners that the Huari claimed direct descent, and they knew themselves as *Huiracochas*, or "Sea Foam People," from their distant homeland, Pacaritambo, a *huagaiusa*, or "holy city," lost in the Pacific Ocean. In the so-called *Idolatries*, collections of Andean myth gathered from native sources firsthand by Spanish friars during the early sixteenth century, and translated by the Colgate University ethnographer Gary Urton, "it is said that the Huari peoples had come into this area [Cajatambo] in remote times either from the ocean, to the west, or from Lake Titicaca."

The confusion is understandable, in view of the unknown millennia that separated the *Idolatries* from the arrival of Pacific Ocean ancestors on Peruvian shores, and the subsequent occupation of Lake Titicaca by the Huari after AD 800. The elder or leading Huiracocha himself was consistently described by various tribal myths as tall, red-haired, light-eyed, and fair-skinned, much like the Huari themselves. Nor were they the only white minority in ancient South America. The *Chachapoya,* or "Cloud Warriors" (named for their occupation of the northern Andes' highest mountains) "are the whitest and most handsome of all the people that I have seen in the Indies," according to a firsthand report made by the mid-sixteenth-century conquistador chronicler Pedro Cieza de León.

His description has been borne out by their often well-preserved remains of long, fine, red hair and Caucasoid facial features recovered from abundant grave sites at Laguna de los Condores and Revash. Chachapoya and coastal Huari anthropomorphic sarcophagi—burial bundles with wooden masks—are very much alike, evidence that both peoples were probably more than culturally related, even though they eventually came to blows over the issue of empire building. In summer 2008, Peruvian archaeologists excavated the perfectly preserved remains of a Wari woman at the ruins of Huaca Pucllana, within the Lima city limits. Director Isabel Flores told the Reuter News Service that when the thirteen-hundred-year-old mummy's face was exposed, it revealed "two big, bright blue orbs in her eye sockets."[10]

The Huari and Chachapoya were joined by a third white-skinned ethnic group documented in pre-Spanish South America. Shortly after the Huari began picking up the pieces of the shattered Moche state, part of their territory was unexpectedly—and uninvitedly—occupied by a migration of fair-haired Llacuaz. Like their imposed-upon hosts, they were said to have arrived over the sea, when, as Steele relates, "the ancestress Coya Guarmi, her brother Condor Tocos, and their mother had traveled from the Pacific Ocean"—yet another migration account out of the distant west. (Endeavoring to square the anomalous existence of these caucasoid minorities in pre-Conquest Peru is a vast subject in itself, and is already examined by Frank Joseph, *The Lost Civilization of Lemuria* [Rochester, Vt.: Bear & Company, 2006].)

In any case, the Huari pursued their imperialistic agendas primarily through diplomacy, resorting to military solutions only if all else failed. Accordingly, they incorporated the Llacuaz newcomers as part of their growing hegemony, but neither absorbed nor assimilated the newcomers, allowing them to preserve their cultural integrity and identity. "Both the Huari and Llacuaz were intimately interconnected," writes Steele. "They held reciprocal festivals that performed *aillies* and *taquies* (ritual songs and dances) that narrated the arrival of each other's ancestors." Urton goes on to show that "the ritual life in the settlements of Cajatambo commemorated . . . the subsequent founding of a confederation between the two groups," which "also celebrated some rituals and festivals jointly, and they also jointly revered certain sacred objects . . ."[11]

The Llacuaz copied Huari feats of monumental irrigation, and began to build their own canal networks as important contributions to the new empire. From around AD 700, the imperial enterprise began widening its spheres of influence across the length of the Pacific coast in South America, incorporating one previously independent kingdom after another in the nonviolent conquest of Peru. The entire empire was tied together by a massive, ever-ongoing, road-building program to facilitate traders, messengers, and pilgrims, but likewise designed for consolidation of political power.

Resulting social and economic stability ballooned into unprecedented prosperity, as commercial fleets returned from Ecuador bearing the prized *Spondylus* shells by the hundreds of thousands. Although Huari administration continued to enrich, yet control the Peruvians, many increasingly longed for at least some measure of autonomy, while others beyond the fringe of the empire sought to outmaneuver the "Sea Foam People." The most serious challenge came from the megalopolis of Chan Chan, just outside Huari grasp in the north.

What eventually blossomed into pre-Columbian South America's largest metropolis of nine square miles, Chan Chan grew from a remnant of Moche imperialists still dreaming of reasserting their faded greatness. This largest adobe city on earth was a vast maze of alleys and boulevards crowded among ten thousand buildings, some of them palaces and temples fronting 30-foot-high walls adorned with elaborate friezes hundreds of feet long and great sheets of precious metals. A doorway sheeted in silver that today is worth more than two million dollars was found by Francisco Pizarro's less famous cousin, Pedro, when Chan Chan was already in ruins.

During its heyday, its sixty thousand residents were believed to have been hatched from three eggs: a copper egg (soldiers and workers); a golden egg (the most skilled craftsmen, priests, military officers, and the strictly male aristocracy); and a silver egg (their wives). Chan Chan was the capital of the Chimu people, who referred to their empire as *Chimor*. It stretched six hundred miles from just south of Ecuador into central Peru. Even before it was absorbed by the Chimu Empire, Chan Chan featured "a sophisticated network of irrigation canals and wells," according to *Smithsonian* magazine. "When a drought, coupled with movements in the Earth's crust, apparently caused the underground water-table to drop sometime around the year 1000, Chimu rulers devised a bold plan to divert water through a canal from the Chicama River fifty miles away to the north." Their massive achievement was part of a monumental engineering technology shared by many Andean cultures.

As their first move to head off Huari expansion, the Chimu took over the *Spondylus* shell trade and severed outside access to rich copper mines in the north, the metal's only source. Copper was used in native Peru as a lesser medium of exchange in the form of "ax money," known to the much later Spaniards as *naipes* or *hachuelas* for the ax shapes into which the little copper pieces were formed. Without them, *Spondylus* could not be purchased from the Ecuadorans. Implications were more than economic. Huari power had been called into question, undermining cooperation of the numerous, disparate, already restive peoples who comprised their tenuous empire.

Immediate, decisive action could alone restore confidence, but seizing Chan Chan would alarm the Ecuadorans, without whose continued good will resumption of the *Spondylus* trade was not possible. Instead, the Huari struck across the Amazonian Andes, bypassing Chan Chan and Ecuador, to seize the northern copper mines. Yet to do so, they had to violate the territory of a sovereign people. Long wary of their imperialist cousins, the Chachapoyas had years earlier built the strategically mounted fortresses of Kuélap and Gran Pajáten in anticipation of just such a contingency. The Huari invaders were numerous, abundantly equipped, skilled, and well led—but the environment was against them. The Amazonian Andes is a mountain range covered by dense, tropical woods and thick vegetation extending from the cordillera spurs up to above 10,500 feet. Moreover, this territory controlled by the Chachapoyas was extensive. "We could easily call it a kingdom," observed the half-Spanish, half-Inca, sixteenth-century historian Garcilaso de la Vega, "because it is more than fifty leagues [255 miles] long, per twenty leagues [62 miles] wide, without counting the way up to Muyupampa, thirty leagues [40 miles] long more."[12]

Prevented from conducting conventional battles by such difficult natural surroundings that favored defense, the invaders found themselves muddled in a losing war of attrition against an unremitting foe. Unable to break through the Amazonian Andes to the copper mines on the other side, Huari forces finally backed down into the coastal plains of central Peru. Political reverberations of their defeat shook the empire from end to end and to its core. As Alf Hornborg, professor of environmental studies at Sweden's Lund University, surmises, "The expansion of Chan Chan seems to have been correlated with the demise of Huari at the close of the Middle Horizon [an archaeological phase from AD 500 to 1000], perhaps by undermining its access to copper and Spondylus."[13]

With prestige severely compromised and prosperity on the wane, the Huari were decreasingly able to exert authority over client kingdoms now going their own way politically, as well as economically. The entire fabric of their imperial enterprise began to disintegrate, until the Huari found themselves in an alarmingly diminished condition that demanded some comprehensive solution before they ceased to exist altogether as a people. Particular concern lay with their enervated army increasingly unable to defend itself from potential attack by resentful client kingdoms. Of them all, only the Llacuaz were still faithful cousins. By the end of the tenth century AD, the situation for both folk had deteriorated so alarmingly that they began to regard emigration as a closing door through which they might pursue their last chance at avoiding oblivion. A northerly escape route was the logical—indeed only—option.

Some Huari refused to leave, regardless of what might come, and kept their cultural identity alive in the Andes before—just one hundred years later—it breathed its last. Equivalent to the Christian calendar year of AD 1000, Huari and Llacuaz by the tens of thousands cast their fate upon the waters in a mass migration, just as their Pacific Ocean ancestors were believed to have done millennia before. This time, their course closely skirted Peruvian shores within view of native peoples, former colonials, happy to see the failed empire builders leave. The balsa armada of refugees would have floated ever northward, passed Chan Chan, that huge stumbling block to their lost imperium. Gloating neo-Moche onlookers would not have very long to wait, however, before their own city was absorbed by a far greater power: the amoebic Chimor empire crawling inexorably toward them from the east.

For the waterborne émigrés, their Promised Land lay to the distant north, far beyond Ecuador, where they were still despised for their failed takeover of the back country's copper resources, and so they made no landfall until Central America hove into view at starboard. Even here, they stopped at ports of call along Pacific Coast Mexico for only as much time as was necessary to renew provisions or make repairs before getting underway again as soon as possible. While the voyage was long—made much longer because a convoy can travel only as fast as its slowest vessel—it was hardly the first of its kind.

The same trade route had already been in use for the previous eight hundred years, albeit never on the scale now being sailed. The migrants were by no means pioneers, but travelers along well-established sea lanes in more or less continuous operation by a number of various peoples since at least the third century AD. Approximately thirty-eight hundred miles and some four months after setting out from their faraway and forsaken homeland, the Peruvians glided into the Sea of Cortés, an elongated seven-hundred-forty-mile body of water separating the peninsula of Baja California from the Mexican mainland.

Weeks later, the oceanic phase of their voyage ended when they reached the gulf's northernmost extreme at the Colorado River delta. It was, as described by *Counterpunch* reporters Alexander Cockburn and Jeffrey St. Clair, "two million acres of wetlands, cienegas, lagoons, tidal pools, jaguars and mesquite scrublands . . . a vast wetland, teeming with more than 400 species of plants and animals," including the 4-foot-long Vacquita dolphin, the world's smallest. Tragically, that was then, this is now: "The Colorado River no longer reaches the Sea of Cortés. Just before the Colorado crosses the U.S./Mexico border, 75 percent of its flow is diverted into the All-American Canal," resulting in "a toxic soup of fertilizer and pesticide runoff."[14]

Around the turn of the eleventh century, however, the newcomers found conditions paradisiacal, but already occupied by Trincheras culture ancestors of the Copacha Indians, with whom traditionally friendly relations had to be upheld for the success of future plans. The buoyant but sturdy balsawood boats and rafts pushed onward into the delta, bobbing along the Colorado River north for sixty-five miles through the Sonora Desert to the Gila River, which took them east and north one hundred sixty miles across Arizona in the direction of Phoenix.

Where the Upper and Lower Gila Rivers part company, so did the Huari part from the Llacuaz. The latter followed the low road another sixty-five miles to a broad marshland ideally suited for settlement of the kind they intended. Meanwhile, their compatriots rode the Upper Gila eastward until it connected to river systems that no longer exist. A thousand years ago, they carried an entire people northward into New Mexico, beyond the Continental Divide, but no farther. A final sixty-five miles had to be made on foot. The environment then was not what it is today—not the killing, pitiless desert, but a more nurturing, verdant landscape of cooler temperatures and abundant rainfall.

Crossing this last leg of a very long and epic journey was the least challenging of all. A few steps more, and the émigrés stood for the first time before the towering walls of their new home, Chaco Canyon. Thus, ancient Peru's Llacuaz and Huari became the Hohokam and Anasazi of the American Southwest.

Eleven

PERUVIAN PROOFS

The suggestion that one thousand years ago virtually an entire people emigrated en masse over some forty-four hundred miles—most of it by sea—from Peru to the American Southwest, where they are remembered as the Hohokam and Anasazi, may be fantasy at its wildest for conventional scholars. But were these skeptics open-minded or even mildly curious enough to consider just a few of the intercontinental parallels at issue in such a proposal, they would find a growing body of proof as compelling as it is enlightening.

A fundamentally credible South American–Four Corners comparison begins to emerge even in the broad scheme of their relative time frames. Born in AD 200 along the Middle Gila River, the Hohokam culture was represented early on by the first wells and canals its people excavated above the Rio Grande River. Also, unlike their aboriginal neighbors, they raised cushaw (a kind of squash) and warty squash; sieva, jack, and tepary beans; cotton; and a weedy plant used as fodder for swine known appropriately enough as "pigweed," while trading in turquoise and shell as far as the Sea of Cortés. This so-called Pioneer Period coincides with another birth: northern coastal Peru's Moche culture, likewise renowned for its pioneering irrigation works, cotton production, broad use of imported turquoise, and, most tellingly, its seaborne commercial network for the harvesting of *Spondylus princeps* (whose Indian name is *pututu,* almost certainly how the Moche referred to it twelve centuries ago).

They were the first Peruvians to make use of this spiny oyster shell for their most sacred religious items and the manufacture of personal decorations, as well as for hard currency. *Pututu* was the gold standard of Andean civilization. Even today, specimens are avidly sought by serious collectors, who trade them at international auctions for competitive prices. Variations of *Spondylus* are grouped in the same superfamily as scallops, but, like true oysters (Ostreidae family) they cement themselves to rocks. While *Spondylus princeps* has always been particularly attractive for its form and brilliance, a scarlet band that edges the pearly white interior probably called special attention to itself during pre-Columbian times as symbolic of certain spiritual principles regarding blood-related themes of sacrifice, death, and birth. For example, fragments removed from the red band were used by the Moche as temple offerings. A clear indication of the shell's central importance to the Moche is its frequent portrayal throughout their art, where it was most often depicted in the company of a fisherman aboard his balsawood or reed boat. These efficient craft were essential for obtaining *Spondylus* because its nearest available sources were found off Ecuador. While relatively accessible, quantities were sparse in these waters, requiring extended retrieval efforts for modest gains.

Shell numbers increased progressively farther north along the Mexican coast, however, until they reached their maximum population where the Sea of Cortés terminated at the Colorado River delta. Here was the origin and largest concentration of *Spondylus princeps* in the Western Hemisphere. As soon as Moche sailors discovered this perpetual mother lode of the precious oyster, Peru's connection to it was unbroken until the destruction of Andean civilization by Spanish conquistadors thirteen centuries later. The Andean arrival sparked Hohokam culture, itself nothing more than an archaeological term for the impact first made by Early Intermediate Period Andeans on the American Southwest. First and foremost, interested in harvesting as much *Spondylus* from the Colorado River delta as their freighters could carry back to the capital at Cerro Blanco, the Moche established modest settlements along the Lower Gila River to form a foothold in the region.

Over the next six centuries, they represented hardly more than a series of outposts in the Sea of Cortés and Arizona. In a revealing chronological parallel (another of many), the El Niño-induced decline and fall of Moche power and its swift assumption by the Huari around AD 800 coincides with the Hohokam culture's so-called Colonial Period, which was characterized by a major, abrupt surge in population and material achievement. Work began on the colossal canal network, and trade routes opened up to the Valley of Mexico. The stimulus for this sudden transformation is easily identified. By default, the Huari had inherited the Moche monopoly on *Spondylus* in the Sea of Cortés, but they did their predecessors two better by expanding on Arizona's Middle-to-Lower Gila River area, exploiting its rich sources of turquoise and other favored minerals, while applying their prodigious irrigation skills.

So too, the Huari collapse near the close of the tenth century matches the Hohokam culture's sedentary period, when the region experienced its largest population increase. The canal network reached the height of its development and its farthest extent, bringing more land under cultivation than ever before. Rancheria-like villages grew up around common courtyards; communal activity flourished widely; capacious, community ovens were used to cook bread and meats for large numbers of artisans busily manufacturing jewelry and pottery; cotton textile work was in high gear; and the regional culture spread widely, extending from near the Mexican border to the Verde River in the north.

Everything attributed to Hohokam greatness flourished during their sedentary period because the Huari and Llacuaz had transported themselves and their civilization to Arizona. Within these comparative time parameters is contained an immense wealth of cogent affinities between Andean Peru and the American Southwest. They not only verify and describe prehistoric connections between two widely separated parts of the New World, but also they throw new light on the stubborn enigma of the Anasazi and Hohokam. Their cultural and chronological parallels to the Huari and Llacuaz uniquely complement each other in such an obvious manner that questions of identity and motive find credible answers for the first time. Indeed, there are very few known instances in the lives of civilizations anywhere in which two unrelated (or, at least, distantly related) peoples share so close a common destiny while preserving their own sense of self. A closer look at the relationship between South America's Huari-Llacuaz and North America's Anasazi-Hohokam shows that the latter are nothing more than Southwest Indian tribal names for the former. Both pairs of cultures were bonded by their pursuit of *pututu,* the spiny oyster shell *Spondylus princeps.* If Pacific coastal Peruvians used it as the basis of their exchange system, the Hohokam valued the mollusk no less highly. Shell processing was second in economic importance only to ancient Arizona's canal-spawned agriculture.

"The Hohokam regarded shell as a commodity of more than ordinary importance," Haury discovered. "It was, in fact, the basis for an industry in which many people in the society had a hand, and in which some craftsmen seem to have achieved the level of specialists. The Hohokam have frequently been characterized in the archaeological literature as the shell merchants of the Southwest, and the evidence of their far-flung groups has often been based on the presence of shell artifacts in the distinctive Hohokam idiom." He stresses that the oysters were not used for food, because they could not be properly preserved. Moreover,

> ... all parts of Snaketown, whether house-fill or trash, regardless of age, are saturated with shell manufacturing residue of various kinds. ... Shellwork occupied a special niche in the total context of the Hohokam life-way. That an inland people, several hundred kilometers from the source of supply, should have been so heavily committed to using imported marine materials, is paradoxical ... [T]he raw

supplies of shell had to be brought into an unlikely environment as a response to an intense cultural urge and demand.[1]

Every one of the tens of thousands of shells crafted into jewelry or currency at Snaketown had to be imported by the Hohokam from sources at the Colorado River delta, two hundred fifty miles away. This is no assumption, because sedentary and colonial period pottery is scattered across the eastern shores of the Sea of Cortés and other collection areas in the vicinity of Sonora's Rocky Point, while Hohokam petroglyphs have been identified along southwestern Arizona and northwestern Sonora trails leading to grounds where shell-gathering took place. These were primarily found in the Adair Bay region—most profitably at its southern indentation at Cholla Cove, where a great tidal flat made for an abundance of easy pickings.

Return transportation to Snaketown was undertaken handily via a direct water route traveling the Colorado and Gila Rivers. It was, according to archaeologist Bruce Bryan, the "best practical route from the Rocky Mountains to California across the southern desert." This well-used and vital waterway from the sea made Haury wonder if it "may reflect a maritime origin" for the Hohokam after all, and he cautiously cites a "contention occasionally heard that the Hohokam migration into their desert habitat was waterborne." His speculation was reinforced by their harvesting of genus *Glycymeris,* because these specimens are not intertidal species, but instead must be dredged at sea, requiring levels of maritime technology and skill beyond mere shell-pickers.

Glycymeris maculata and *gigantea* were most commonly used in the Snaketown shell industry, where the more rare and, hence, valuable *Spondylus princeps* was likewise worked. Although the Peruvians preferred *pututu,* it was not the only mollusk they used for currency and jewelry, just as the same diversity of collected species occurred among the Hohokam. Examples of worked *Spondylus princeps* have been found at many Anasazi sites, most commonly in Chaco Canyon, where the ruling oligarchs unquestionably obtained *pututu* from Snaketown. Its shell manufacturing suddenly mushroomed during the Colonial Period, just when the Huari lost their empire and fled to the American Southwest.

Judging from the intensity of *Glycymeris* and *Spondylus* production undertaken as soon as the Huari resettled in Arizona, they were intent on maintaining some measure of control over their forsaken homeland—however diminished from imperial days—by monopoly of select shell sources at the Colorado River delta. The usurping Chimor at Chan Chan would be confined to Ecuador, where *pututu* was far less available, for all their *Spondylus princeps*. Huari merchants sailing out of the Sea of Cortés with precious shell cargo for all the kingdoms of the Pacific coast chiefly supplied the spiny oyster as a means of exchange during pre-Inca times—that is, from the opening to the middle of the Late Intermediate Period, AD 1000 to 1320. This neo-Huari strategy appears to have been successful, given the more than two hundred years of prosperity enjoyed by the Hohokam.

Their more detailed connection with ancient Peru appears in a wealth of material evidence, including not least of all that iconic vessel of Andean civilization. "Navigation by balsa boat was known to the Hohokam," according to Haury. Although released in 1976, his *The Hohokam, Desert Farmers and Craftsmen* is still the most thorough investigation of its kind, and reveals important South American motifs that were stamped—albeit inadvertently—on Snaketown pottery.

Among its most unequivocal themes Haury reproduces belongs to "a long-snouted, many-toothed animal." Biologists recognized it at once as the *coatimundi*, a member of *Procyonidae*, the racoon family. About the size of a large housecat, the animal has a slender head with an elongated, flexible, slightly upward-turned nose (a "retroussé snout," as Haury puts it); small ears; dark feet; and a long, nonprehensile tail. Its appearance on Snaketown pottery seems slight cause for amazement, until we realize that the coatimundi was unknown in North America—including Mexico—during the Hohokam era and for centuries thereafter. The creature was not introduced into the American Southwest until historic times, perhaps as recently as the late 1700s. Before AD 1000, the coatimundi was confined to South America, mostly Brazil, where its name is reported to have originated in either the Tupi or Guarani language.

If the Hohokam were, as mainstream archaeologists insist, indigenous Arizonans, they would not have known the animal existed. Probably, they were not acquainted with it through direct trade connections from South America, because no coatimundi bones have been found at Snaketown. More likely, the Huari-Llacuaz were long familiar with the coatimundi, because it originally inhabited their Peruvian homeland. Since prehistory, the species there, *Nasua nasua,* or the red coati, has attracted the attention of native observers, who understood the creature's migration patterns. The Indians noticed two distinct bands of rovers in packs of twenty-five individuals and groups of more than one hundred. When a habitat becomes unsuitable for some reason, the animals leave en masse, sometimes over great distances, undaunted by rivers or lakes, to resettle elsewhere.

Perhaps their ability to move in large numbers as a cohesive herd struck the Huari-Llacuaz as a legitimate parallel to their own emigration experience, and they symbolized this by coatimundi imagery on Snaketown pottery. The coatimundi might have been their new cultural emblem, proclaiming themselves as South American immigrants in a foreign land. To be sure, peoples have always personified their self-perceived, leading qualities in some universal symbol, often an animal, such as the Roman eagle, Christian fish, British bulldog, French cock, and Russian bear. More certainly, the common portrayal of *Nasua nasua* by Snaketown potters establishes Peruvian origins for the Hohokam.

They also introduced the famous figure of *Kokopelli,* the long-haired flute-player. His earliest known representation is found in an Arizona petroglyph dated to AD 1000, the same year Snaketown and the rest of the American Southwest witnessed a population surge that coincided with the abrupt florescence of Hohokam and Anasazi culture and the Huari-Llacuaz emigration from Peru. He was originally a shaman, as identified by his occasional Hohokam portrayals as part insect, which indicated his shiftshaping ability. Shapeshifting signifies the altered state of consciousness achieved by a mystical adept to move from the material world into a spiritual dimension, and to return with important guidance or healing information for his society. Kokopelli's pipe is equivalent to the shaman's drum, because music—or, at any rate, repetitive sounds—assisted him in his attempts to enter a profoundly different state of mind as a means of accessing the otherworld.

The formation of his name illustrates the figure's shamanic origins: *Koko,* a Zuni *kachina,* or spiritual being, is combined with *pelli,* the so-called desert robber fly known for its prominent proboscis equivalent to Kokopelli's long pipe. At maize-grinding ceremonies, he is accompanied by or blends his identity with another flautist known as Paiyatamu, which may have been his original name, because Kokopelli is more properly a descriptive title formed from a combination of Zuni terms. If so, Paiyatamu is a philological link to north coastal Peru, where the names of sacred or powerful people typically ended in *mu*—such as Chimu (rulers of the city of Chan Chan), Taycanamu (an early culture hero), Pacatnamu (a culture-founding ruler after whom a labyrinthine building was named), and so forth. It may be appropriate here to recall that the Hopi's full name is Hopituh Shi-nu-mu, suggesting a distant connection to South American influences from their deepest past.

Kokopelli's Peruvian roots are also revealed by the animals gathering around him in Hohokam pottery art. His snakes and lizards were symbols for water in Nazca Peru, where they were portrayed as gigantic images on Peru's coastal desert floor. Kokopelli sometimes shapeshifts into a hummingbird, his flute becoming a long beak and his hair changing into wings. Hummingbirds were commonly featured on Hohokam pottery used as water vessels. So too, the Nazca bioglyphs were associated with underground water sources or were visual appeals to heaven for rain. Among them is the hummingbird, which drinks nectar from the flowers it visits. That this creature should symbolize water for both drought-plagued Peruvians and Arizona's tenth-century irrigationists is yet one more link in the long chain of evidence linking South America to the American Southwest.

Another water-related creature Hohokam artists favored was the pelican. Though none ever existed in the vicinity of Snaketown, their appearance on local pottery suggests the pelican's connection with the Sea of Cortés at the very least. In fact, the Zuni regard Kokopelli as a rainmaker, one of the *u-wan-am-mi,* the spirits of children who perished in the Great Flood. These "water monsters" can sometimes be prevailed upon to bring water to a parched earth from their realm at the bottom of the Lake of Death—located, in the minds of many Indians, at Listening Spring Lake, where the Zuni and Little Colorado Rivers meet. Identification of Kokopelli with the "water monsters" is a mythological take on the original Hohokam flautist as a shaman primarily engaged in conjuring water.

That the Hopi worship him as a god demonstrates again the process of deification they applied to Hohokam and Anasazi technologists, in this instance the water managers at Snaketown. Revealingly, Hopi flutes, at least until the broad commercialization of Kokopelli imagery beginning in the late twentieth century, do not resemble his, and have always been much smaller, hardly more than whistles. The long pipe he blows appears to be 2 or 3 feet long, a kind of bassoon missing from the prehistoric Southwest, but played by Andean musicians during Moche times and into the Inca Empire.

Some researchers wonder if Kokopelli may also represent the Hopi's Lost White Brother. Pahána may have been a personification of the fair-skinned Huari and Llacuaz émigrés, because he is described as a foreigner, the "One from Across the Water." It would seem that the Anasazi mummies of red-haired Caucasoid men and women at Utah's Grand Gulch were the same Peruvians the Hopi associated with Pahána. He, in fact, may have been Kokopelli himself, one of the *u-wan-am-mi* water wizards of the Hohokam, whose magical technology transformed the Middle Gila River region into an agricultural paradise. His subterranean home was always symbolized by a hole at the bottom of many kivas.

It was into this *sipapu* that the waters of the Great Deluge were believed to have drained, and from which the earliest Hopi ancestors emerged into the upper world as survivors. The Peruvian Llacuaz entertained the closely parallel myth of an ancestral deity, *Apu Libiac,* "Mountain Lord Lightning," who caused the Flood to empty into a hole out of which the Llacuaz forefathers appeared. Hopi variants of the same tradition have their ancestors born in a great cave, just as Urton relates that "In Cajatambo, caves were the places of origin of the ancestors of the Huari and Llacuaz *ayllu*s."

He goes on to state that these same caves were also "repositories of the mummies (*malquis*) of deceased *ayllu* members," recalling the mummified remains of Anasazi aristocrats at Grand Gulch. *Ayllu*s comprised the basic political unit of pre-Inca and Inca society. They were composed of extended family groups—again, very much reminiscent of the Anasazi system of ruling families, with their focus on ancestor worship, and replicated in the Huari-Llacuaz burial caves for mummified forefathers. *Ayllu*s were social, religious, and ritual organizations that exerted political power through a combination of kinship and territorial ties. This otherwise unique Andean system appears indistinguishable from the kind of government that controlled the Four Corners region after the turn of the eleventh century.

The Anasazi family groups that ruled Chaco Canyon's sphere of influence were likewise composed of benign masters. They had no imperialist armies to intimidate subject peoples; no secret police to spy or coerce reluctant colonials; no dungeons or torture chambers for members of the opposition. As such, they were identical to Middle Horizon Peruvians. Moseley explains:

> As in Moquegua, Huari opened a vital agrarian niche in the Carahuarazo Valley, but here there is no evidence of fortified colonization or militarism. Rather, Huari policy in Carahuarazo was apparently one of promoting cooperative innovation that motivated local ethnic tribes to build and benefit from irrigated terraces, as

well as state buildings, roads and facilities that integrated the region within the national economy.[2]

Huari policy toward Moquegua, a regional capital city in extreme southern Peru, was not unique, but repeated during another blood-less conquest at Jincamocco, located in the southern Ayacucho valley. According to Moseley, "There are no indications of fortifications, or of conflict with the Marcahuamachuco," Jincamocco's inhabitants. Instead, the Huari built a 427-by-853-foot agricultural center there to increase maize production. Moseley contrasts this gentler decentral-ization with the heavier-handed diplomacy of powerful predecessors: "Intensive states, such as coastal Moche, submerged local populations under their administrative and cultural presence. Alternatively, exten-sive regimes, such as highland Huari, established administrative nodes dispersed among local populations."

Just as the Hohokam were to do in the Arizona desert, the Huari, writes Moseley, "had developed reclamation technology that could bring into production the vast quicha zone, which had previously been underexploited." The Huari capital of the same name was likewise "sur-rounded by extensive irrigation, and a sophisticated system of conduits transported water throughout the city." In his *Atlas of World Art,* John Onions agrees that "much of its success lay in the system of irriga-tion developed during a period of severe drought in the 6th and 7th Centuries" that preceded the collapse of the Moche.

An even greater canal network was on the magnitude of Hohokam water management: as Moseley explains, "[T]he El Paso irrigation system was monumental in scale—various data sources support the contention that the Huari irrigation system was indeed extensive." Moseley uses the same language to describe the waterworks that sur-rounded the great city of Huari, located in the center of the Ayacucho basin with direct communication to the coast. Situated atop a hilly plateau, the twenty-five-acre metropolis was home to "probably as many as one hundred thousand people—including many full-time specialist workmen," according to Cambridge University archaeologist professor Glyn Daniel.[3]

While the capital's population was larger than that of Arizona's Snaketown, the two sites nonetheless resembled each other as major centers for specialized manufacturing and administrative hubs of far-flung irrigation projects. Indeed, the Huari created some particularly enlightening, even decisively convincing parallels with eleventh- and twelfth-century events in the American Southwest. Perhaps the single most important comparison is found in Huari's multistory, D-shaped buildings of imposing dimensions. The only other place on earth where the same kind of structures may be found is in Chaco Canyon, where most of the great houses were four and five stories and raised upon a D-configuration.

In early 1998, Martha Cabrera and Jose Ochatoma excavated one of the best-preserved D-shaped structures in the southern Ayacucho valley. Although Conchopata contained several hundred rooms with plastered walls of finely fitted stonework, Peruvian archaeologists determined that the expansive site was never a palace, apartment building, or administrative complex, but instead served entirely as a center for ritual activities, including offerings of turquoise and the ritual breaking of pottery.

The Huari site is a mirror image of Chaco Canyon's foremost structure, Pueblo Bonito, with its frontal mound of ceremoniously broken pots, gifts to the spirit world. The canyon's largest such earth-work contains enough smashed pottery to form a hill the size of one of its great houses. Anasazi style was black-on-white redware pottery decorated with geometric designs. In describing Huari pottery, Moseley tells how "unifying ceramic characteristics are polychrome wares with white and black paintings on red surfaces. Motifs are predominantly geometric . . ." Some specimens of Hohokam pottery are emblazoned with identifiably South American motifs. An outstanding example depicts a line of dancers, their hair stylized in braids standing out straight and level from their heads. Chile's *Gigante de Atacama,* the

Atacama Giant, etched into a desert hillside near Cerro Unitas, is not only the world's largest anthropomorphic representation at 283 feet in length but also has hair portrayed in the same, horizontal lines—a representation that occurs nowhere else.

An even larger figure connecting South and North America in prehistory is the so-called Candelabra of the Andes, its creation dated prior to AD 1000. Lying on the slope of a hillside at Pisco Bay on the Peruvian coast, the terraglyph is located north of the Nazca Plain. Here, the famous lines and drawings are etched into the arid ground, and seen to best advantage from several hundred feet in the air. They represent a diverse depiction of plants and animals—such as seaweed, trees, whales, a spider, lizards, and so forth—as well as abstract and purely geometric shapes, including spirals, trapezoids, and thin lines that run on in straight perfection over great distances. At 595 feet long, the Candelabra of the Andes is larger by far than any of its southern counterparts, but it was executed in the same unit of measurement. During the mid-1950s, the famous German archaeologist and specialist in the Nazca Lines, Maria Reiche, after extensively surveying them, determined that they were precisely laid out in a common unit of measurement: 5.95 feet.

The Candelabra is so huge that on a clear day it may be seen from about twelve miles out into the Pacific Ocean. We may assume, therefore, that it was created by a seafaring people. The geoglyph is not a maritime emblem, however, but represents a jimsomweed bush. Jimsonweed is a narcotic that has been used throughout South America from deep antiquity. Particularly important to religious practitioners, or shamans, its consciousness-expanding properties allowed their minds to soar among the heavens, from whence they returned with divine guidance for society. Narcotics were also used for healing purposes, just as they are today. Jimsomweed was revered, therefore, as a sacred plant monumentally portrayed on a simple stand by the Candelabra of the Andes.

Yet what motivated its artists to execute something of this kind on so colossal a scale? It is an exceptionally unique design. Nothing like it has ever been found anywhere else, with one cogent exception. The exact same figure, but just 4 inches high, was found during 1994 in southern California's Cleveland National Forest. The badly faded yet discernible pictograph had been very long ago applied with red pigment to a rock outcropping above a small stream. Southern California is home to a number of hallucinogenic plants, common among them the jimsonweed portrayed in both the Peruvian giant and its California miniature. Yet the western shores of South America are desert, devoid of useful plant life, narcotic or otherwise.

It would appear that Huari seafarers landed just above San Clemente in southern California, then followed the San Juan River some twenty miles into what is now the Cleveland National Forest, where they harvested jimsonweed and left a pictograph of the holy plant to mark the valuable area. Sailing back along the west coast, they knew they were home when the same symbol of their quest and sacred cargo hove into view on a hill in the Bay of Pisco, a marker that could be seen even if they were off course a dozen miles out at sea. The only correspondent to the Candelabra of the Andes is found in southern California, a comparison that shows pre-Inca Peruvians did indeed travel to the American Southwest, where they left their enduring, if faded, mark.

Turquoise offerings at the Hauris' Conchopata recall the 17-foot-long turquoise necklace found in the wall niche at Chaco Canyon's great *kiva,* Casa Rinconada. While most rooms at the Ayacucho valley site were empty, some contained evidence of mortuary practices: piles of human ash. So too, the Hohokam and Anasazi cremated their dead—with some exceptions, such as the mummified remains at Grand Gulch. There, the bodies had been contorted to sit on their haunches surrounded by funeral gifts of cloth bundles and ceramic ware. Writes Moseley, "Burying the deceased in a flexed and seated position persisted" among the Huari when they did not engage in cremation, "accompanied by cloth, pottery and other offerings."

Cabrera and Ochatoma had less than a year to conclude their investigations of Conchopata before landowners bulldozed it out of existence. Since then, however, many other D-shaped buildings have been

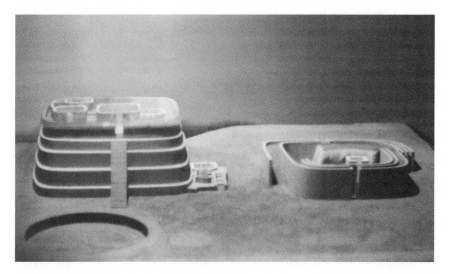

Fig. 11.1 Reconstructions of Huari buildings at Peru's National Archaeology Museum, Lima. The D-shaped structure at left rises in five stories, as did the Anasazi's Pueblo Bonito, before a kiva-like depression, while the single-story model is not unlike the Anasazi's Casa Rinconcada.

discovered throughout the central sphere of Huari influence, including the highland ceremonial center of La Galgada, contemporary with the look-alike great houses of the American Southwest and the Temple of Vegachayoq at the capital of Huari itself. Even Machu Picchu features a D-shaped building.

Not far from Huari, another contemporary Peruvian example lies in ruins northwest of Lake Titicaca, at a site known as Pukara. In size, collection of several hundred rooms, and D shape, it compares closely to New Mexico's Pueblo Bonita. Although geographically separated by many thousands of miles, both complexes self-evidently sprang from the same culture.

But why were the Huari and Anasazi great houses built to resemble a D? The answer may be found at Pueblo Bonito. There, precisely at high noon, the sun's shadow cast by the straight, north-south wall vanishes into it, splitting the day into a pair of perfect halves. The wall creates an axis bisecting the central plaza, stressing its paramount significance: "When the sun in 'the middle of the day' is over 'the middle of the earth,' the butte's glyphs commemorate this special moment in time and space."[4]

Pueblo Bonito expands this "special moment," defining the seasons exactly by separating the different paths taken from one horizon to the other by the solstices and equinoxes, from the rising and progress across the sky of the sun and moon, with architectural emphasis on their setting. This dual incorporation of solar and lunar alignments—like everything at Chaco Canyon—was multisymbolic. Combining with the great house's cosmic-spiritual significance was a political act—the vitally necessary reaffirmation of close cooperation between two groups of strangers in a strange land. These were the Huari and Llacuaz émigrés from Peru, thrown together by fate, but determined to reassert their former greatness in the American Southwest. Back in the old country, they had formed a tightly bound allegiance to one another. Urton writes:

> Each side of this two-art (moiety) confederation adopted certain rituals and ceremonies of the opposing half. That is, rituals were celebrated in a reciprocal fashion: the Guaris (Huari) celebrated rituals on behalf of the Llacuaz, and *vice versa*. . . . These people also worshipped the night-time sun—that is, the sun when it passed through the underworld, moving along its watery passage from sundown to sunrise. . . . The Llacuaz also worshipped the sun of the daytime—the sun as it passed overhead from sunrise to sunset . . .[5]

The Huari sun of the nighttime may have been a religious metaphor for the moon, or a reference to the winter solstice, when, on the shortest day of the year, the sun lingers longest in darkness, the proverbial underworld of the dead. In any case, joint honoring of these two "suns" could explain the twin solar-lunar orientations celebrated at Chaco Canyon's foremost monument. Huari-Llacuaz sun worship was a religious expression of the high-level astronomy operative in South America, most of it appropriated by the Incas, who preserved prior knowledge of celestial cycles, but added little to it. "Huari contributions to Andean civilization were far-reaching," Moseley affirms, "and lasted long after Huari collapsed."[6]

Throughout Peru, the Huari built networks of stone pylons and masonry pillars aligned with certain celestial positions. The *usnu* belonged to a special class of structures fixed exclusively on various sunsets. Usnu Capac, the great gnomon of Cuzco, the Inca capital, was a central column that marked the winter solstice just when Pueblo Bonito performed the same orientation at Chaco Canyon. The Huari operated astronomical observatories where the sun and moon appeared at calculated moments in deliberately positioned windows. Three Windows Shrine is located at Huayna Picchu, a summit adjacent to Machu Picchu, and oriented doorways in the two-story Temple to the Rising Sun look out from Llactapata, another two miles away. At Cuzco, the sun appeared on special feast days in the windows of Sunturwasi Temple, the towering "House of God."

So too, windows were accurately positioned in the Anasazi great houses and the great kiva of Casa Rinconcada for calculated solar alignments. Many of their windows are T-shaped, leading some archaeologists to assign Anasazi origins or, at least, outside influences, to Yucatán, where some religious buildings, such as those at the Honduran ceremonial city of Copán, are likewise cut with T-shaped openings. But the Maya versions are a fraction of any Four Corners counterparts, and less like windows than mere apertures. Moreover, none of them are oriented to the sun or any other astronomical fix. In Mayan hieroglyphics, *T* signifies *ik* for "breath," implying that the small, T-shaped openings were designed to allow in jungle breezes, not heavenly sunlight, to freshen the humid temple buildings of stone.

More likely, the symbol connects Chaco Canyon with contemporaneous Peru. Small, T-shaped grooves are found in the massive walls of Bolivia's Tiahuanaco. Although the capital of an independent state, the great ceremonial city had been built by either the Huari, with whom the Tiahuanacos were closely allied, or their near relatives. According to

Urton, "Many images of religious and mythological significance appear commonly in the art of both Tiahuanaco and Huari."

Tiahuanaco lies close to an even older, more ruinous site, Pumapuku, its scattered building blocks adorned with T-shaped sockets. Liquefied arsenic bronze was originally poured into them to shine like molten sunlight. Their decorative and symbolic purposes are certain, because 5-inch-long and 2-inch-deep clamps would not have been strong enough to staple together multiton stone blocks, as archaeologists once speculated. In fact, the ancient Andean construction engineers never seem to have used fasteners of any kind in their massive building projects, given the lack of evidence for clamps at Sacsuhuaman or any other Inca or pre-Inca site. The same T-shaped grooves occur among the white rock ruins at Nuestra España's Yuroc Rumi, in the Vilcabamba, and they decorate the black walls of the Coricancha.

Famed throughout the Inca empire as the "Enclosure of Gold" for its solar alignments, the Coricancha stands at the precise center of Andean civilization's most sacred site, the imperial capital of Cuzco, modified by the Incas after they seized it, but originally built by the Huari who were previously in "control of the Cuzco valley," as Urton points out. Indeed, the Huari built one of their largest, most important cities, Pikillacta, less than twenty miles southeast of Cuzco. The pink granite rhyolite of Ollantaytambo's extraordinarily massive hill temple is particularly interesting for its T-shaped sockets, because their bronze fillings show signs of having been repeatedly polished, underscoring the sunlight they symbolized. As such, Chaco Canyon's T-shaped windows oriented to the sun find their connection in the identically configured grooves of pre-Spanish Peru's foremost monuments.

When the conquistadors first visited the Coricancha in 1532, they found it "bedecked with plates of gold and silver."[7] Later, the Enclosure of Gold revealed riches of a different sort. Radiating outward like spokes of a wheel from the hub of a cosmic observatory, hundreds of sighting lines began at the Coricancha, streaming in every direction to the far horizon and beyond. Known as *ceques,* they aligned simultaneously with numerous points in the sky and connected other sacred structures and sites on the ground. The *Coricancha's* forty-one lines ran through three hundred twenty-eight *usnu*—pylons, pillars, shrines, holy places (*huacas*), major springs, and other water sources—to correspond with the same number of days in twelve sidereal lunar months. "Thus, various spatial and temporal reference points along the rays," Moseley states, "helped to organize land, water, labor and the ritual activities and festive ceremonies that initiated and closed work cycles."

His description of Cuzco forms a template for Chaco Canyon, where lines radiating from its center at the leading Great House aligned with particular celestial coordinates while connecting every other monument and sacred site. Integrating heaven and earth in an applied cosmological scheme dominated both parts of the world—but existed nowhere else. *Ceques* extending for mile after mile from their single point of origin in the *Coricancha* were identically engineered and performed the same functions undertaken by sight-lines running from centralized Pueblo Bonito throughout the Four Corners region.

A Huari center that combined leading elements of both the Anasazi and Hohokam was located at Peru's Lucre Basin in the Cuzco valley. Known in Quechua as *Pikillacta,* or "Flea Town," the ruin's real name has been lost. Its archaeological zone comprises almost 1.4 square miles once occupied by an enormous, rectangular building that contained many hundreds of separate rooms, together with larger compounds and broad courtyards. The structure's physical resemblance to a Chaco Canyon Great House deepens when we learn that Pikillacta was not a residential building, but is regarded by archaeologists as a facility for ancestor worship, the cult religion practiced by Anasazi overlords.

Gordon McEwan, professor of anthropology at New York's Wagner College, concluded, after twenty-eight years of field experience in the Cuzco area and excavations at Flea Town, that Pikillacta was a power center used by the Huari empire "to control its subjects by controlling the location and context of the Huari religious ceremonies."[8] Identical methods were duplicated in the same kind of buildings in order to impose order on the American Southwest beginning a thousand years ago. Pikillacta was also a showcase for public hydraulic works. An immense and complex series of canals, comparable in sophistication to Hohokam irrigation systems, conducted water to reservoirs, aqueducts, terraces, and cultivable fields throughout the entire Lucre Basin. Pikillacta was a kernel containing the foremost elements that went into Arizona and the Four Corners region during the eleventh century.

The Anasazi patterned their cliff dwellings at Mesa Verde and Canyon de Chelly after Cerro Baul, a fortified colony built by the Huari on top of a 1,900-foot-high mesa "with steep sides grading to vertical cliffs," according to Moseley, above the Rio Moquegua. "The architectural emphasis was on segregation rather than integration," he writes of Huari construction, "and presumably based on kin, class, rank and occupation." These words describe exactly an exclusivity similarly practiced by the ruling Anasazi families during and after Chaco Canyon's florescence, as incorporated into their buildings.

No less iconically Anasazi are the *kivas,* those circular, semi-subterranean temples that highlight the prehistoric landscape of the Four Corners region. Although archaeologists believe they evolved from local dwellings into ceremonial chambers, precisely the same type of sunken courts were built by the Huari, beginning centuries earlier with their coastal predecessors at the start of Moche expansion, around AD 200, just when the first pit houses appeared in the American Southwest.

A singular comparison of particularly enigmatic structures found exclusively in Ecuador and Arizona defines a contemporaneous relationship they shared nearly a thousand years ago. Within the city limits of Quito stands *La Olla del Panecillo,* a beehive-shaped building set in its own sunken, circular court surrounded by a retaining wall of andesite masonry. (Andesite is a black, volcanic rock.) Dug into a 600-foot-high hill, the windowless "Kettle" is 20 feet high and 10 feet in diameter at the base, and constructed of flat stone bricks finely set in mortar. Over this true-arch entrance is the sculpted representation of a solar deity—a man's face on the sun disk—the monument's only decoration. A 7-foot-long tunnel of andesite leads into the interior, a single, hollow room, its plastered walls sloping upward to the top of the dome open in an 18-inch-wide oculus.

Investigators assume La Olla was built by the Incas as a shrine or perhaps solar observatory, but no evidence for ritual activity has ever been found inside the structure, which additionally lacks any aperatures for observations of any kind. Neither its tunnel entrance nor hole at the top of the dome feature astronomical alignments. If the Incas were responsible for the Kettle, it was their sole specimen, with no parallel example throughout Andean civilization.

The same, otherwise unique type of construction is found, however, within the Hohokam sphere of influence overlooking the west side of the Lower Gila River, some twenty airline miles northeast of Florence, Arizona, a few minutes north of the 33rd parallel, near the remote ghost town of Cochran. There, visitors will find not one, but five beehive buildings standing evenly spaced in a straight line, and very similar to the site at Quito. Like their Ecuadoran counterpart, they perch on a hillside, their domes rising to an opening at the apex.

Unlike the "Kettle," the Cochran beehives are constructed without mortar, although flat stone bricks were chosen for both the Arizona structures and *La Olla del Panecillo*. The former structures, made of granite, are somewhat larger than La Olla, at 32 feet high and 15 feet across at the base and 72 feet in circumference. While they are unadorned with symbols and without tunnels, a single entrance for each one uniformally measures 3 feet wide by 6 feet high. The 3-by-5-foot oculus at the apex of the Cochran domes is rectangular. Aside from these discrepancies, they are remarkably similar to the Ecuadoran "Kettle," and hardly less mysterious. Efforts to determine the age, function, or identity of their builders have come to nothing. The guidebook writer Jim Brandon points out that "A half-mile south of Cochran is San Gregorio Taumaturgo mineral spring, which is believed by Indians to have potent magical properties. The U.S. Geologic Survey has designated this as an area of pronounced geo-magnetic anomaly."[9] Perhaps close proximity to the sacred mineral springs determined placement of the beehives at such a desolate location. Were they built by the Hohokam, in whose territory they are found, but nowhere else—except for Quito, Ecuador? While it is hardly less possible to learn who was responsible for the construction of *La Olla del Panecillo*, it and the Cochran domes nevertheless stress a unique architectural connection between northern Pacific coastal South America and the American Southwest—between Andean civilization and prehistoric Arizona.

That connection is reaffirmed by yet another comparative set of buildings. Toward the disastrous end of their culture, the Anasazi built numerous towers as a last attempt to save themselves from a rising groundswell of murderous violence overwhelming the Four Corners region. Two hundred years before, just when the Hohokam and Anasazi began their work, construction of the first *chullpa*s was undertaken along the shores of Bolivia's Lake Titicaca. These were round, square, or rectangular towers of stone averaging 30 feet in height, and therefore very similar to the round, square, or rectangular structures of equivalent demensions found at Hovenweep National Monument in Utah.

Fig. 11.2. One of Utah's Hovenweep towers

While the Andean versions are more refined and occasionally somewhat higher, their comparison to the Hovenweep towers, which were built at the same time, is inescapable. Doubtless, familiarity with *chullpa* design traveled from Lake Titicaca, where the towers originally served as mausoleums, to the American Southwest, where they were used as fortifications.

To be sure, this rather specific Andean origin is suggested by modern Pueblo Indians themselves. They claim that some of their ancestors were originally foreigners in the land who later married among native peoples to generate the tribes that today inhabit the Four Corners region: "Their kin were mingled; thus, their children were one people," relates Zuni myth.[10] These ancestral people of the pueblos are said to have come from their distant home, Palatkwapi, the "Red City of the South." Its characterization strongly implies the pre-Inca ceremonial center at Tiahuanaco with its huge blocks of red sandstone and red andesite that form the city's massive walls.

Other tribal accounts clearly refer to Andean beginnings. The Zuni Indians, who call themselves the Ashiwi, fervently believe

Fig. 11.3. A Huari chullpa near the shores of Bolivia's Lake Titicaca

that their origins lie in a location of peaceful beauty and abundance far across the sea at the "Center Place," *Itiwanna*. Interestingly, *Intihuatana* is the name of Machu Picchu's prominent monolith. Known as the "Hitching Post of the Sun," it indicates with precision the date of both equinoxes, which appear to revolve around the stone, thereby "hitching" the suns of spring and fall. The sun stands almost directly above the pillar on March 21 and September 21 at midday, creating no shadow whatsoever. Just then, the sun appears "tied" to the *Intihuatana*.

The Incas were known to have reserved such a special moment for their "Tied to the Sun" ceremony, which was aimed at halting the sun's northerly drift across the sky toward the perennially dreaded winter solstice, with its longest night of the year. The same equinoctal alignments were repeatedly stressed by the Anasazi to make Chaco Canyon the sacred center of their world. That the New Mexican Itiwanna derived from the Quechua Intihuatana is not only phililogically self-evident, but also affirmed by the astronomical functions attributed to the Hitching Post of the Sun, the Zuni Center Place, that axis created by revolving equinoxes.

The Ashiwi tribal myth of the *Enote,* or "Ancient Time," recounts an ancestral mass migration across lands and seas after the loss of *Itiwanna* to find its replacement. Here, the "Center Place" recalls the Huari-built Inca capital of Cuzco, because its name means "The Navel of the World," the place from which everything originated. For all the Japanese impact made on the Zuni language, a renowned American linguist, Morris Swadesh, concluded that Zuni was fundamentally Macro-Quechuan—an Andean dialect spoken in the Bolivian highlands. Palatkwapi's identification as the "Red City of the South," with red-walled Tiahuanaco, is complemented by Hopi oral traditions of the "Lost White Brother," *Pahána,* who arrived in New Mexico long ago from far across the ocean.

His story parallels the Andean myth of *Con-Tiki-Viracocha,* "Sea Foam": After the Great Deluge, Viracocha, desirous of learning whether or not his antediluvian commandents were still being obeyed, dispatched his sons on a fact-finding mission. Satisfied that their father's guidance had taken root among many flood survivors, Imaymana and Tocapo bestowed names on trees, flowers, fruits, and herbs, indicating which were edible or poisonous, or had medicinal properties. The Viracochas additionally imparted their knowledge of the cosmos, and showed men how to irrigate fields.

The Huari, who worshipped Con-Tiki-Viracocha, derived their national name from the god, making him a kind of totemic deity from whom they claimed their semi-divine descent, and considered themselves *Viracochas*. The Great Flood that sent him and his sons on their civilizing journey north may have been the catastrophic *El Niño* that washed away the Moche civilization, but allowed for the Huari ultimately to fulfill their destiny in the Four Corners region. There, at Chaco Canyon, archaeologists have recovered several terra-cotta representations of a man's head with tears streaming down both cheeks. Throughout the Andean World, Viracocha was known as "the weeping god," and he was sometimes depicted with falling tears, simultaneously signifying his compassion for suffering humankind and rainfall against a drought-plagued earth.

That the Huari and their close confederates, the Llacuaz, left Peru to resettle in the American Southwest, where they are still remembered as the Anasazi and Hohokam, seems clear. No other two peoples moving and working together can account for events at the Four Corners region beginning around the turn of the first millennium. Comparative cultural evidence for an explanatory connection between both parts of the world can be organized by a shared chronology between the two. In this way, the last lost civilization of America begins to reemerge from its misty obscurity after nearly a thousand years.

Afterword

IS OURS THE NEXT LOST
CIVILIZATION OF AMERICA?

It may be something of a shock to realize that our civilization is far from unique—that it has been preceded on this continent by four others, which have come and gone. Recognition of their former existence naturally draws comparison with our current effort, which, so far, is shorter lived.

Perhaps too many centuries separate them from us for any useful conclusions. After all, they lacked the technological checks and balances that grant us an infinite lease on the future. After more than a thousand years of dominating the eastern half of the continental United States, the Adena may have had more justification to regard themselves with the same self-confidence, yet little more was left of their culture than overgrown mounds that baffled early colonial Europeans passing through the Ohio Valley.

All four pre–United States civilizations, like our own, were sparked by foreigners, immigrants from Western Europe, Asia, Mexico, and South America. Each one flourished for a time, but eventually succumbed to domestic violence. Only the Mississippians beat the odds against survival by never losing control of the new world they created around AD 900. They shut it down themselves four hundred twenty years later, and walked away to Mexico; they were not driven out, because the secret of their unique power lay in their willingness to exercise authority through the agency of human sacrifice, what the mad renegade Colonel Kurtz in Francis Ford Coppola's film, *Apocalypse Now,* defined as "an act of genius." While to us such a practice seems an unthinkable atrocity, it nonetheless had the political utility of sufficiently cowing the masses of native peoples who overthrew the other pre-Columbian civilizations. The Anasazi strove to make the same impression through astronomical sleight of hand with less success.

The one-time masters of Chaco Canyon, however, might provide us with our most cogent parallel. The lifeblood of their desert society was water. As long as it gushed in unhindered abundance, the otherwise parched land blossomed, people prospered, and all was well—but when drought conditions began to turn off the flow, civility was proportionately replaced by savagery. Throngs of devout pilgrims to the sun-god were brushed aside by gangs of killers more interested in cannibalism. The Hohokam and Anasazi had made water the single prop of their economy. With its increasing unavailabilty, organized society became unsupportable. Modern dependence on another liquid could prove no less fatal: Is our addiction to oil anything like the sole reliance placed upon water in New Mexico and Arizona a thousand years ago? If so, the Four Corners microcosm might yet foreshadow our twenty-first century macrocosm.

An acquaintance with the lost civilizations of North America validates Abraham Lincoln's contention that our country is impervious to alien conquest, but vulnerable to internal collapse. So too, the Adena and Hopewell suffered extermination at the hands of other ancient Americans, not foreign invaders, while most of the Anasazi-Hohokam escaped the same fate only by emigrating.

The trouble with history, as historians themselves repeatedly point out, is that no one ever learns from it. Each generation presumes it is immune from the perils that brought down previous cultures, which are regarded as entirely unrelated to contemporary affairs. Seen from a wider perspective, the story of civilization in North America, as it is everywhere, is a recurring cycle of birth, growth, expansion, prosperity, corruption, decline, and death. We are given no reason to imagine that our civilization is less caught up in this fundamental pattern than any of the organized societies that flourished prior to our own.

As ours was not the first, it may not be the last. Those who might come after us could have as little evidence of our one-time existence as we have today of the long-neglected Great Houses at Chaco Canyon. Indeed, many of our cities are already partly in ruins. Future archaeologists sifting through the remains of a late nineteenth-century church building, abandoned one hundred years later, on Chicago's south side will be no less challenged than today's excavators trying to puzzle out the mysteries of Pueblo Bonito. Comparisons such as these may engender a sense of futility, but only if we are satisfied as spectators of history. We may be on the sidelines where the past is concerned, but the energies and influences set in motion by those who came before us reverberate into our times and beyond, even though we may be oblivious to such forces.

Our Adena, Hopewell, Mississippian, and Anasazi-Hohokam predecessors live on in us; mere recognition of their fate is enough to compel revealing comparisons to the condition of our own civilization. Will ours follow theirs into the recycling bin of history? Or will we defy the deadly pattern by learning from their mistakes while there is still time?

Appendix I

A TIMELINE FOR
ANCIENT AMERICA

1200 BC—Prolonged climate deterioration makes farming impossible in the Steppes of Central Russia, the Indo-European homeland, forcing large-scale human migrations westward across Poland, into the Balkans and southern Germany.

1000 BC—Generally and loosely known as "Kelts," the tribal immigrants are continuously on the move, until eventually they occupy most of the European continent and the British Isles. Following the example of trans-Atlantic voyagers over the previous twenty thousand years, some Kelts sail beyond Ireland to make landfall along the Eastern Seaboard of North America. Their arrival coincides with the abrupt appearance of a people that modern archaeologists refer to as the "Adena," who introduce agriculture, astronomy, ironworking, road building, and monumental architecture.

300 BC—Japanese seafarers known as the Munakata leave their mound-building Yayoi culture. They arrive on America's Pacific Northwest coast, but move into the Midwest. There, they make common cause with the Adena against threatening tribes of native peoples, while developing a highly ritualized society of effigy mounds and huge ceremonial centers. Archaeologists refer to the resulting culture as "Hopewell."

100 BC—The Adena have established themselves in large numbers from the shores of the Atlantic Ocean to the banks of the Mississippi River, although their central sphere of influence is focused in the Ohio Valley. Before the onset of the first millennium AD, however, fresh waves of immigration from Western Europe fall off, resulting in Adena population decline and inbreeding, with pathological consequences. Tensions with native peoples increase, leading to the construction of hill forts and stone towers, North American versions of Keltic Europe's *oppida* and *brochs*.

AD 400—The Hopewell culture is killed off by overwhelming attacks of native tribes.

700—After centuries of intermittent warfare against the ancestors of modern Indians, the last of the Adena are massacred at the falls of the Ohio River near Louisville, Kentucky.

900—Following the dictates of a sacred calendar, the Maya abandon their city-states across Yucatán and Central America. Some relocate to west-central Illinois and eastern Missouri, where they build the megalopolis of Cahokia, capital of the Mississippian culture.

1000—Two distinct but affiliated peoples, the Huari and Llacuaz, emigrate from Peru. Landing at the Colorado River delta in the Sea of Cortés, they move into Arizona and New Mexico. On the banks of the Lower Gila River, the Llacuaz build Snaketown, capital of an irrigation empire, while the Huari dominate the Four Corners region from their Great Houses at Chaco Canyon. Archaeologists refer to both peoples, respectively, as the Hohokam and Anasazi, or "ancestal puebloans."

1200—Aztalan, the Mississippians' last and most northerly outpost, is built in southern Wisconsin.

1240—The onset of prolonged drought triggers popular loss of faith in the ruling Hohokam and Anasazi, leading to deteriorating social conditions. Snaketown is burned to the ground, and Chaco Canyon is abandoned.

1320—The neo-Mayas, once again at the behest of their sacred calendar, evacuate the Mississippi valley, migrating south toward the Valley of Mexico.

1340—Under threats of escalating violence, most Hohokam and Anasazi undertake a mass migration from the American Southwest to Paquimé, in northern Mexico. A minority repairs to places such as Mesa Verde and Canyon de Chelly, where they are remembered as the doomed cliff dwellers.

Appendix 2

A COMPARISON OF KELTIC AND PLAINS INDIANS TERMS

As some measure of the enduring impact made by Iron Age Europeans on Native America, a brief comparison of Keltic (Gaelic) and Plains Indian terms is listed here. These are drawn from John Hewson's book *A Computer-Generated Dictionary of Proto-Algonquin*[1] and A. MacBain's work *Etymological Dictionary of the Gaelic Language.*[2] Known as *loan words,* their profusion defies coincidence, and underscores the lingering influence of ancient Old World visitors on our continent's indigenous inhabitants.

ammonoosuc: Algonquian for "small fishing river"
am-min-a-sugh: Gaelic for "small river for taking out fish"

amoskeag: Algonquian for "one who takes small fish"
ammo-iasgag: Gaelic for "small fish stream"

asquam: Algonquian for "pleasant watering place"
uisge-amail: Gaelic for "seasonable waters"

attilah: Algonquian for "blueberries"
aiteal: Gaelic for "juniper berries"

bhanem: Algonquian for "woman"
ban: Gaelic for "woman"

cabassauk: Algonquian for "place of sturgeon"
cabach-sugh: Gaelic for "sturgeon"

coos or *cohas:* Algonquian for "pine tree"
ghiuthas: Gaelic for "pine tree"

cowisse-waschook: Algonquian for "proud peak"
cuise-achstuce: Gaelic for "proud peak"

cuiche: Algonquian for "gorge"
cuithe: Gaelic for "gorge"

Kaskaashadi: Algonquian name for the Merrimack River
guisgesiadi: Gaelic for "slow flowing waters"

kladen: Algonquian for "snowflake"
claden: Gaelic for "snowflake"

merrimack: Algonquian for "deep fishing"
mor-riomach: Gaelic for "of great depth"

monad: Algonquian for "mountain"
monadh: Gaelic for "mountain"

monomonock: Algonquian for "island lookout place"
moine-managh-ach: Gaelic for "boggy lookout place"

munt: Algonquian for "people"
muintear: Gaelic for "people"

nashaway: Algonquian for "land between"
naisguir: Gaelic for "land connecting"

natukko: Algonquian for "cleared place or land"
neo-tugha: Gaelic for "not covered by vegetation"

nock: Algonquian suffix denoting hills and mountains
cnoc: Gaelic for "hill or rocky outcrop"

Ottauquechee: Algonquian name for the river that flows through a
   162-foot-deep gorge
otha-cuithe: Gaelic for "waters of the gorge"

pados: Algonquian for "boat"
bata: Gaelic for "boat"

piscataqua: Algonquian for "white stone"
pioscatacua: Gaelic for "pieces of snow-white stone"

pontanipo-pond: Algonquian for "cold water"
punntaine-pol: Gaelic for "numbingly cold pool"

quechee: Algonquian for "pit"
qui: Gaelic for "chasm"

seminenal: Algonquian for "grains of rock"
semenaill: Gaelic for "grains of rock"

wadjak: Algonquian for "on top"
uachdar: Gaelic for "on top"

Appendix 3

A COMPARISON OF ZUNI INDIAN AND JAPANESE TERMS

ENGLISH	ZUNI	JAPANESE
ancestors	*kokko*	*kojin*
back	*si*	*se*
be inside of	*uchi*	*uchi*
beginning	*chimi*	*hajime*
clown	*newe*	*niwaka*
east	*tema*	*tema-koha*
Flute Mountain	*Shoko Yalana*	*shakuhachi* (flute), *yamma* (mountain)
keeper of the Creation rituals	*k'yaklu*	*kaibyaku* (creation)
leaf	*ha*	*ha*
man	*osu*	*osu*
mean	*sani*	*samu*
meeting	*kwai*	*kwe*
middle	*wannaka*	*mannaka*
sparrow	*uzuas*	*uzume*
spherical object	*mo*	*mo*
stomach	*zu*	*zo* (viscera)
supernatural	*koko*	*koko*
wake up	*okwi*	*oki*
wide	*kappa*	*hapa* (width)
west	*nishi*	*kal-ishi*
woman	*oka*	*oka*
Zuni priest	*shiwani*	*shawani* (Shinto priest)

Source: These are drawn from S. Izuru's *Kenkyusha's New Dictionary of the Japanese Language*[1] and Stanley S. Newman's *Zuni Grammar*.[2]

NOTES

INTRODUCTION.
OUR CULTURAL AMNESIA

1. Edmund J. Ladd, quoted by Nancy Yaw Davis in *The Zuni Enigma: A Native American People's Possible Japanese Connection* (New York: W. W. Norton and Company, 2001).
2. Arthur C. Clarke, *Visions of Future Past* (London: Biddle and Sons, Ltd., 1977).
3. Emil W. Haury, *The Hohokam: Desert Farmers and Craftsmen* (Tucson, Ariz.: University of Arizona Press, 1978).

CHAPTER ONE.
ADENA, FIRST CIVILIZERS OF NORTH AMERICA

1. Henry Rowe Schoolcraft, *Historical and Statistical Information Respecting the Indian Tribes of the United States* (Washington, D.C.: Society for the Investigation of North American Antiquities, 1859).
2. Robert Silverberg, *The Mound Builders* (Athens, Ohio: Ohio University Press, 1986).
3. James H. Kellar, "The C. L. Lewis Stone Mound and the Stone Mound Problem in Eastern United States Prehistory," Ph.D. Dissertation, publication 19,494 (Ann Arbor, Mich.: University Microfilms, 1956); and *Prehistory Research Series* 3, no. 4 (June 1960).
4. William S. Webb and Raymond S. Baby, eds. *The Adena People* (Knoxville, Tenn.: University of Tennessee Press, 1974).

5. Charles C. Jones, Jr., "Aboriginal Structures in Georgia," *Smithsonian Annual Report,* 1877. In William R. Corliss, *Ancient Man: A Handbook of Puzzling Artifacts* (Glen Arm, Md.: The Sourcebook Project, 1978).

6. Ibid.

7. Kellar, "The C. L. Lewis Stone Mound and the Stone Mound Problem in Eastern United States Prehistory" and *Prehistory Research Series* 3, no. 4 (June 1960).

8. Webb and Baby, *The Adena People.*

9. Ibid.

CHAPTER TWO.
WHO WERE THE ADENA?

1. Diodorus Siculus, *The Geography,* translated by C. H. Oldfather (London: Heinemann, 1968).

2. Julius Caesar, *The Gallic War,* translated by William Richter (Dallas: University of Texas Press, 1979).

3. Don W. Dragoo, *Mounds for the Dead: An Analysis of the Adena Culture* (Pittsburgh, Pa.: Carnegie Museum of Natural History, 1989).

4. J. W. Mavor and B. E. Dix, "The Pearson Stone Chamber," in Corliss, *Ancient Man: A Handbook of Puzzling Artifacts.*

5. Corliss, *Ancient Man: A Handbook of Puzzling Artifacts.*

6. Scott A. Browne, "The Mysterious Stone Structures of New England," *Ancient American* 5, no. 33 (June 2000).

7. Andrew E. Rothovius, "Connecticut's Unfolding Mystery," *Ancient American* 1, no. 4 (August 2004).

8. Corliss, *Ancient Man: A Handbook of Puzzling Artifacts.*

9. Rothovius, "Connecticut's Unfolding Mystery."

10. William Conner, "Visiting Ohio's Spruce Hil Fort," *Ancient American* 10, no. 64 (August 2005).

11. Arlington Mallery, *The Rediscovery of Lost America* (New York: E. P. Dutton, 1979).

12. William Conner, "The Legendary Azgens: A White People in Prehistoric Kentucky," *Ancient American* 12, no. 76 (December 2007).

13. Miranda J. Green, *The Celtic World* (London: Routledge, 1995).

14. John J. White III, "Mills Found the Adena Pipe, not Baby," *Ancient American* 6, no. 38 (April 2001).

15. Cyrus Thomas, "Iron from North Carolina Mounds," *Science,* 1884. In Corliss, *Ancient Man: A Handbook of Puzzling Artifacts.*

16. Dr. Gunnar Thompson, *American Discovery, the Real Story* (Seattle, Wash.: Argonauts Misty Isles Press, 1994).

17. William Conner, "Visiting Ohio's Spruce Hill Fort," *Ancient American* 10, no. 64 (August 2005).

18. John Haywood, in "Ancient Iron-Smelting Furnaces in Ohio," Clyde E. Keeler and Bennet E. Kelley. *NEARA Newsletter,* 1971. In Corliss, *Ancient Man: A Handbook of Puzzling Artifacts.*

19. William Conner, "The Legendary Azgens: A White People in Prehistoric Kentucky," *Ancient American* 12, no. 76 (December 2007).

20. W. W. Holmes, "Traces of Aboriginal Operations in an Iron Mine near Leslie, Missouri." *Smithsonian Institution Annual Report,* 1904. In Corliss, *Ancient Man: A Handbook of Puzzling Artifacts.*

21. Thompson, *American Discovery, the Real Story.*

CHAPTER THREE.
THE KELTIC FINGERPRINT ON PREHISTORIC AMERICA

1. William R. Corliss, "The Scottish Brochs," *Ancient Structures* (Glen Arm, Md.: The Sourcebook Project, 2001).

2. Pere Marquette quoted in "What was the Monster of Alton, Illinois?" by Clara Kern Bayless, *Ancient American* 6, no. 40 (July–August 2001).

3. Peter B. Cattlett quoted in "Inscribed Stone of Grave Creek Mound," by M. C. Reid, *American Antiquarian,* 1879. In Corliss, *Ancient Man: A Handbook of Puzzling Artifacts.*

4. J. E. Wharton quoted in "Inscribed Stone of Grave Creek Mound," by M. C. Reid, *American Antiquarian,* 1879. In Corliss, *Ancient Man: A Handbook of Puzzling Artifacts.*

5. Fell, *America B.C.*

6. Donal Buchanan, "Report on the Morristown Tablet," *Early Sites Research Society Bulletin* 10, no. 1 (1982).

7. Fell, *America B.C.*

8. Ibid.

9. Conner, "The Legendary Azgens: A White People in Prehistoric Kentucky," *Ancient American* 12, no. 76 (December 2007).

10. Ross Hamilton with Patricia Mason, "North American Warfare and a Tradition of Giants," *Ancient American* 5, no. 36 (December 2000).

11. Thomas Cole, ed. *The Wonders of the World* (Boston: The John Adams Lee Publishing Company, 1882).

CHAPTER FOUR.
HOPEWELL MASTERS OF CEREMONY

1. James D. Middleton, "Ohio Mounds," *Science,* 1887. In Corliss, *Ancient Man: A Handbook of Puzzling Artifacts.*

2. Ross Hamilton, "Ancient Ohio's Great Hopewell Highway," *Ancient American* 4, no. 29 (October–November 1999).

3. George Ephriam Squier, *Ancient Monuments of the Mississippi Valley* (New York: Compshire House Publishers, 1848).

4. Bradley T. Lepper and Cornelius Cadle, "A Remarkable Prehistoric Ceremonial Pipe," *Ancient American* 9, no. 56 (April 2004).

5. Ross Hamilton, "Ancient Ohio's Great Hopewell Highway."

6. David Cain, "The Hopewell Highway to Heaven," *Ancient American* 6, no. 40 (July–August 2001).

7. J. E. Cirlot, *A Dictionary of Symbols* (New York: Philosophical Library, 1962).

8. Martin Hill, *Indiana's Wyandotte Cave* (Indianapolis, Ind.: University of Indiana Press, 1977).

9. Ibid.

10. Clark R. Mallam, "Effigy Mounds in Iowa, Ideology from the Earth" (Harper's Ferry, Iowa: Effigy Mounds National Monument Museum, 1980).

11. Jan Beaver, "Wisconsin's Gigantic Eagle Mound," *Ancient American* 1, no. 2 (September–October 1993).

CHAPTER FIVE.
WHO WERE THE HOPEWELL?

1. Richard J. Pearson, *Ancient Japan* (New York: George Brazilier Publishers, 1992).

2. Gunnar Thompson, "Japanese Voyagers," *American Discovery, the Real Story* (Seattle: Argonauts Misty Isles Press, 1994).

3. Nancy Yaw Davis, *The Zuni Enigma: A Native American People's Possible Japanese Connection* (New York: W. W. Norton and Company, 2001).

4. Wanatabe Hitoshi, *Possibilities for Ancient Migrations* (Urbana: University of Illinois Press, 1993).

5. Patrick Huyghe, *Columbus was Last* (New York: Hyperion Books, 1992).

6. John Erlandson, www.google.com/search?source=ig&hl=en&rlz=&q=oyu+c ircle+japan&btnG=oogle+Search.

7. Dr. Theodore Schurr, "DNA Reveals Diverse Native American Heritage," http://macdonnellofleinster.org/page_7h.htm.

8. John Heckewelder. In Robert Silverberg's *Mound Builders of Ancient America: The Archaeology of a Myth* (Norwalk, Conn.: New York Graphic Society, 1968).

9. Dragoo, *Mounds for the Dead: An Analysis of the Adena Culture.*

10. Francis Hamilton in Corliss, *Ancient Man: A Handbook of Puzzling Artifacts.*

11. Dragoo, *Mounds for the Dead: An Analysis of the Adena Culture.*

12. Hamilton and Mason, "North American Warfare and a Tradition of Giants."

CHAPTER SIX.
MISSISSIPPIANS REIGNITE THE TORCH OF CIVILIZATION

1. Stephen D. Peet, "The Great Cahokia Mound," *American Antiquarian,* 1891. In Corliss, *Ancient Man: A Handbook of Puzzling Artifacts.*

2. Dilg, Charles. www.earlychicago.com/encyclopedia.php?letter=D.

3. Ibid.

4. Ibid.

5. Ibid.

6. Thomas Jeffers, "Indian Mound Yielded Ancient Treasures," Tulsa: *Oklahoma Star,* vol. 19, no. 8, July 10, 1937.

7. Iron Thunderhorse, *Return of the Thunderbeings* (Rochester, Vt.: Bear and Company, 1990).

8. Lyn Chamberlain, "Alabama: Mound State Monument," in *Sacred Sites, A*

Guidebook to Sacred Centers and Mysterious Places in the United States, by Frank Joseph (St. Paul, Minn.: Llewellyn Publications, 1992).

9. Patricia Galloway, *The Southeastern Ceremonial Complex: Artifacts and Analysis (Indians of the Southeast)* (Lincoln: University of Nebraska Press, 1989).

10. Chamberlain, "Alabama: Mound State Monument."

11. Thunderhorse, *Return of the Thunderbeings.*

CHAPTER SEVEN.
WHO WERE THE MISSISSIPPIANS?

1. William L. Iseminger, Michael Nance, Madeline Winslow, and Marilyn Gass, *Cahokia Mounds State Historical Site Nature/Culture Hike Guidebook,* fourth revised edition (Collinsville, Ill.: Cahokia Mounds Museum Society, 2004).

2. Henry M. Brackenridge, quoted in *Jefferson the Scientist,* by Henry W. Powell (New York: Crosstown Books, Inc., 1943).

3. Chamberlain, "Alabama: Mound State Monument."

4. Dragoo, *Mounds for the Dead: An Analysis of the Adena Culture.*

5. Forrest E. Clements and Alfred Reed, "Eccentric Flints of Oklahoma," *American Antiquity,* 1939. In Corliss. *Ancient Man: A Handbook of Puzzling Artifacts.*

6. Jim Iler, "Oklahoma's Buried Maya Treasure," *Ancient American* 3, no. 13 (April–May 1996).

7. *Science Newsletter* quote from "The Objective Existence of Large-Scale Order," *Ancient Structures,* by William R. Corliss (Glen Arm, Md.: The Sourcebook Project, 2001).

8. Bruce C. Hunter, *A Guide to Ancient Mexican Ruins* (Norman: University of Oklahoma Press, 1978).

9. *Science Newsletter* quote from "The Objective Existence of Large-Scale Order."

CHAPTER EIGHT.
THE SORCERERS OF CHACO CANYON

1. Hu Fan San, *Ancient Chinese Chronicles,* translated by Edward Bruzinski (Chicago: University of Chicago Press, 1969).

2. Tom Windes in *House of Rain: Tracking a Vanished Civilization Across the American Southwest,* by Craig Childs (New York: Little, Brown and Company, 2007).

3. Childs, *House of Rain: Tracking a Vanished Civilization Across the American Southwest.*

4. Richard Friedman in *House of Rain: Tracking a Vanished Civilization Across the American Southwest.*

5. John Bruno Hare, *Early British Trackways, Moats, Mounds, Camps and Sites by Alfred Watkins* (London: BiblioBazaar, 2008).

6. Anna Sofaer with Rolf M. Sinclair, "From Astronomy and Ceremony in the Prehistoric Southwest." In John B. Carlson and W. James Judge, eds. *Anthropological Papers,* no. 2, Maxwell Museum of Anthropology, 1983.

7. D. D. Gaillard, "A Gigantic Earthwork in New Mexico." *American Anthropologist,* 1896. In Corliss. *Ancient Man: A Handbook of Puzzling Artifacts.*

8. Wilbur C. Knight, "Prehistoric Quartzite Quarries in Central Eastern Wyoming," *Science,* 7:308-311, 1898. In Corliss, *Ancient Man: A Handbook of Puzzling Artifacts.*

CHAPTER NINE.
LIQUID GOLD

1. Richard B. Woodbury, "The Hohokam Canals at Pueblo Grande, Arizona." *American Antiquity,* 1960. In Corliss, *Ancient Man: A Handbook of Puzzling Artifacts.*

2. Todd W. Bostwick and John P. Andrews, "Desert Farmers at the River's Edge," *Pueblo Grande Museum Profiles,* no. 12, www.ci.phoenix.az.us/PUEBLO/dfharves.html.

3. Jerry B. Howard and Gary Huckleberry, "The Operation and Evolution of an Irrigation System: The East Papago Canal Study" (Phoenix: *Soil Systems Publications in Archaeology,* No. 18, 1991).

4. Frank Midvale, "Prehistoric Irrigation in the Salt River Valley, Arizona," *Science,* 1968. In Corliss, *Ancient Man: A Handbook of Puzzling Artifacts.*

5. Emil Haury in "First Masters of the American Desert: The Hohokam." *National Geographic,* May 1967. In Corliss, *Ancient Man: A Handbook of Puzzling Artifacts.*

6. Robert D. Hicks III, "Astronomy in the Ancient Americas," *Sky and Telescope*, 51:372, 1976.

7. Clarke, *Visions of Future Past.*

8. Corliss, *Ancient Structures.*

9. Charles B. Gallenkamp, "New Mexico's Vanished Tower Dwellers," *Natural History*, 62:312, 1953.

10. Michael F. Aveni, *Stairways to the Stars: Skywatching in Three Great Ancient Cultures* (New York: Wiley, 1999).

11. Childs, *House of Rain: Tracking a Vanished Civilization Across the American Southwest.*

CHAPTER TEN.
WHO WERE THE LOST OTHERS?

1. "Tse Diyil, the Old Woman of Fajada Butte." Adapted from a Navajo couple's interpretation of Fajada Butte. www.angelfire.com/indie/anna_jones1/old-woman.html.

2. Childs, *House of Rain: Tracking a Vanished Civilization Across the American Southwest.*

3. Frank C. Hibben, "The Mystery of the Stone Towers," *Art and Archaeology*, 7:353, 1918. In Corless, *Ancient Structures.*

4. Charles B. Gallenkamp, "New Mexico's Vanished Tower Dwellers."

5. Haury, *The Hohokam: Desert Farmers and Craftsmen.*

6. Donnan quoted by Mary A. Dempsey's "Treasure of the Moche Lords," *Ancient American* 2, no. 10 (July–August 1995).

7. Mary A. Dempsey, "Treasure of the Moche Lords," *Ancient American* 2, no. 10 (July–August 1995).

8. Michael E. Moseley, *The Incas and Their Ancestors* (London: Thames and Hudson, 1992).

9. Ibid.

10. Dana Ford, "Pre-Incan female Wari mummy unearthed in Peru,"August 2008, http://in.reuters.com/article/lifestyleMolt/idINN2636587520080826.

11. Paul R. Steele, *Handbook of Inca Mythology* (Santa Barbara, Calif.: ABC Clio, 2004).

12. Garcilaso de la Vega in *Dictionary of Literary Biography,* by Bryant Creel, vol. 318: *Sixteenth-Century Spanish Writers.* A Bruccoli Clark Layman

Book. Edited by Gregory B. Kaplan (Gale, Tenn.: University of Tennessee, 2005).

13. Alf Hornborg, *The Power of the Machine: The Peoples and Cultures of Ancient Peru* (Washington, D.C.: Smithsonian Institution Press, 1994).

14. Alexander Cockburn and Jeffrey St. Clair. "To the Last Drop: Why the Colorado River Doesn't Meet the Sea." www.counterpunch.org/colorado.html, March 14, 2001.

CHAPTER ELEVEN.
PERUVIAN PROOFS

1. Haury, *The Hohokam: Desert Farmers and Craftsmen*.

2. Moseley, *The Incas and Their Ancestors*.

3. Glyn Daniel, *The Illustrated Encyclopedia of Archaeology* (New York: Thomas Y. Crowell Company, 1977).

4. Moseley, *The Incas and Their Ancestors*.

5. Gary Urton, *Inca Myths* (Austin, Tex.: University of Texas Press, 1999).

6. Moseley, *The Incas and Their Ancestors*.

7. Francisco Pizzaro quoted by Pedro de Cieza de Leon in *The Travels of Pedro de Cieza Leon, Contained in the First Part of his Chronicle of Peru* (London: Hakluyt Society, 1864).

8. William Harris Isbell and Gordon McEwan, *Huari Political Organization* (Washington, D.C: Dumbarton Oaks, 1991).

9. Jim Brandon, *Weird America* (New York: E. P. Dutton, 1978).

10. Julian H. Steward, ed., *Handbook of South American Indians* (Washington, D.C.: Smithsonian Institution, Bureau of American Ethnology, 1950).

APPENDIX 2.
A COMPARISON OF KELTIC AND
PLAINS INDIAN TERMS

1. John Hewson, *A Computer-Generated Dictionary of Proto-Algonquian* (Toronto: Canadian Museum of Civilization, 1993).

2. A. MacBain, *Etymological Dictionary of the Gaelic Language* (New York: French and European Publishing, 1991).

APPENDIX 3.
A COMPARISON OF ZUNI INDIAN
AND JAPANESE TERMS

1. S. Izuru, *Kenkyusha's New Dictionary of the Japanese Language* (Tokyo: Kenkyusha, 2001).

2. Stanley S. Newman, *Zuni Grammar* (Tucson, Ariz.: University of New Mexico Press, 1965).

BIBLIOGRAPHY

Ackerly, Neal W., Jerry B. Howard, and Randall H. McGuire. "La Ciudad Canals: A Study of Hohokam Irrigation Systems at the Community Level." Tempe, Ariz.: Arizona State University *Anthropological Field Studies,* no. 17, 1987.

Anders, Martha. "Dual Organization and Calendars Inferred from the Planned Site of Azangaro: Wari Administrative Strategies," Ph.D. dissertation, Cornell University, 1986.

Anderson, Oz. "Bandelier National Monument." In Frank Joseph, ed., *Sacred Sites, A Guidebook to Sacred Centers and Mysterious Places in the United States.* St. Paul, Minn.: Llewellyn Publications, 1992.

Anonymous. "Fire-Swept City of Ancient Man in Tennessee." *Science,* 1923. In William R. Corliss, *Ancient Man: A Handbook of Puzzling Artifacts.* Glen Arm, Md.: The Sourcebook Project, 1978.

Anonymous. "The Piasa," *American Antiquarian,* 1906. In William R. Corliss, *Ancient Man: A Handbook of Puzzling Artifacts,* Glen Arm, Md: The Sourcebook Project, 1978.

Aveni, Anthony. *Skywatchers of Ancient Mexico.* Austin, Tex.: University of Texas Press, 1980.

Aveni, Michael F., *Stairways to the Stars: Skywatching in Three Great Ancient Cultures.* New York: Wiley, 1999.

Avil, Fr. Francisco de. *A Narrative of the Errors, False Gods, and Other Superstitions and Diabolical Rites in which the Indians lived in Ancient Times.* Edited and translated by Clements R. Markham. London: Hakluyt Society, 1873.

Baby, Raymond S. "Prehistoric Ohio." In *American Heritage* 4, no. 3 (June 1954).

Baelz, E. "Prehistoric Japan." *Smithsonian Institution Annual Report,* 1907. In William R. Corliss, *Ancient Man: A Handbook of Puzzling Artifacts.* Glen Arm, Md.: The Sourcebook Project, 1978.

Barrowes, Edwin, and Wayne May. "Unveiling the Secrets of Mound PK-5." In *Ancient American* 12, no. 74 (July 2007).

Barth, F. E., J. Biel, et al. *Vierrädrige Wagen der Hallstattzeit* [The Hallstatt Four-wheeled Wagons at Mainz]. Mainz: Römisch-Germanisches Zentralmuseum, 1987.

Bauer, Brian S., and Dearborn, D. S. *Astronomy and Empire in the Ancient Andes.* Austin, Tex.: University of Texas Press, 1995.

Baum, Henry Mason. "Monuments in the Mississippi River Valley." In *Ancient American* 11, no. 69 (August 2006).

Bayless, Clara Kern. "What was the Monster of Alton, Illinois?" In *Ancient American* 6, no. 40 (July–August 2001).

Beaver, Jan. "Wisconsin's Gigantic Eagle Mound." In *Ancient American* 1, no. 2 (September–October 1993).

Benedict, Ruth Fulton. "Tales of the Cochiti Indians." *Bureau of American Ethnology Bulletin* 98, 1931. In William R. Corliss, *Ancient Man: A Handbook of Puzzling Artifacts.* Glen Arm. Md.: The Sourcebook Project, 1978.

Bergquist, A. K., and T. F. Taylor. "The Origin of the Gundestrup Cauldron." In *Antiquity* 61, no. 87 (1950).

Berry, Michael S. *Time, Space and Transition in Anasazi Prehistory.* Salt Lake City, Utah: University of Utah Press, 1982.

Bichler, P., ed. "Hallstatt textiles: technical analysis, scientific investigation and experiment on Iron Age textiles." Oxford: Archaeopress, 2002.

Blake, William P. "Aboriginal Turquoise Mining in Arizona and New Mexico." *American Antiquarian,* 1899. In William R. Corliss, *Ancient Man: A Handbook of Puzzling Artifacts.* Glen Arm, Md.: The Sourcebook Project, 1978.

Bornus, David S. "Ohio's Magical Mounds." In *Ancient American* 4, no.17 (March–April 1997).

Bostwick, Todd W., and John P. Andrews. "Desert Farmers at the River's Edge." *Pueblo Grande Museum Profiles,* no. 12, www.ci.phoenix.az.us/PUEBLO/dfharves.html.

Brackenridge, Henry M., quoted in *Jefferson the Scientist,* by Henry W. Powell. New York: Crosstown Books, Inc., 1943.

Brand, D. *Aboriginal Trade for Seashells in the Southwest.* Yearbook of the Association of Pacific Coast Geographers, 1938. In William R. Corliss, *Ancient Man: A Handbook of Puzzling Artifacts.* Glen Arm, Md.: The Sourcebook Project, 1978.

Brandon, Jim. *Weird America.* New York: E. P. Dutton, 1978.

Breternitz, Cory D., ed. "Prehistoric Irrigation in Arizona." Symposium: "Soil Systems Publications in Archaeology," no. 17. Phoenix: 1999.

Brower, Jacob V. In Frank Joseph, "Crystal Eagles of Ancient America." *Ancient American* 7, no. 44 (March–April 2002).

Brown, Herbert. "Stone Squares in Arizona." *American Antiquarian,* 1899. In William R. Corliss, *Ancient Man: A Handbook of Puzzling Artifacts.* Glen Arm, Md.: The Sourcebook Project, 1978.

Brown, M. G. *Blue Gold: The Turquoise Story.* Anaheim, Calif.: Main Street Press, 1975.

Browne, Scott A. "The Mysterious Stone Structures of New England." In *Ancient American* 5, no. 33 (June 2000).

Bryant, Alice. "Chaco Canyon National Monument." In Frank Joseph, ed. *Sacred Sites, A Guidebook to Sacred Centers and Mysterious Places in the United States.* St. Paul, Minn.: Llewellyn Publications, 1992.

Buchanan, Donal. "Report on the Morristown Tablet." In *Early Sites Research Society Bulletin* 10, no. 1 (1982).

Burchell, James H. "The Gaelic Connection with Southeastern Kentucky." In *Ancient American* 11, no. 69 (August 2006).

Bushnell, G. H. S. *The Ancient People of the Andes.* New York: Penguin, 1949.

Cadle, Cornelius. "A Remarkable Prehistoric Ceremonial Pipe." In *Ancient American* 9, no. 56 (April 2004).

Cain, David. "Cities of the Hopewell." In *Ancient American* 6, no. 40 (July–August 2001).

———. "The Hopewell Highway to Heaven." In *Ancient American* 6, no. 40 (July–August 2001).

———. "Ohio's Ancient Metal Cast?" In *Ancient American* 10, no. 64 (August 2005).

Cattlett, Peter B. quoted in "Inscribed Stone of Grave Creek Mound," by M. C. Reid, *American Antiquarian,* 1879. In William R. Corliss, *Ancient Man: A Handbook of Puzzling Artifacts.* Glen Arm, Md.: The Sourcebook Project, 1978.

Chamberlain, Lyn. "Alabama: Mound State Monument." In Frank Joseph, ed., *Sacred Sites, A Guidebook to Sacred Centers and Mysterious Places in the United States.* St. Paul, Minn.: Llewellyn Publications, 1992.

Childress, David Hatcher. *The Mystery of the Olmecs.* Kempton, Ill.: Adventures Unlimited Press, 2007.

Childs, Craig. *House of Rain: Tracking a Vanished Civilization Across the American Southwest.* New York: Little, Brown and Company, 2007.

Chouinard, Pat. "Enigmatic Ruins of the Chachapoyas." In *Ancient American* 8, no. 50 (March–April 2003).

Ciampa, Frank G. "Temple of Chachapoyan." In *Ancient American* 3, no. 22 (January–February 1998).

Cieza de Leon, Pedro de. *The Incas.* Translated by Harriet de Onis. Norman: University of Oklahoma Press, 1996.

———. *The Travels of Pedo de Cieza Leon, Contained in the First Part of his Chronicle of Peru.* London: Hakluyt Society, 1864.

———. *The Travels of Pedo de Cieza Leon, Contained in the Second Part of his Chronicle of Peru.* London: Hakluyt Society, 1883.

Cirlot, J. E. *A Dictionary of Symbols.* New York: Philosophical Library, 1962.

Clarke, Arthur C. *Visions of Future Past.* London: Biddle and Sons, Ltd., 1977.

Clements, Forrest E., and Alfred Reed. "Eccentric Flints of Oklahoma," *American Antiquity,* 1939. In William R. Corliss, *Ancient Man: A Handbook of Puzzling Artifacts.* Glen Arm, Md.: The Sourcebook Project, 1978.

Cockburn, Alexander, and Jeffrey St. Clair. "To the Last Drop: Why the Colorado River Doesn't Meet the Sea." www.counterpunch.org/colorado.html, March 14, 2001.

Coe, Michael. *The Olmecs.* New York: Alfred Knopf, 1982.

Cole, Thomas, ed. *The Wonders of the World.* Boston: The John Adams Lee Publishing Company, 1882.

Collis, John. *The Celts: Origins, Myths and Inventions.* Stroud, Gloucestershire, England: Tempus Publishing, 2003.

Conner, William. "The Legendary Azgens: A White People in Prehistoric Kentucky." In *Ancient American* 12, no. 76 (December 2007).

———. "Visiting Ohio's Spruce Hill Fort." In *Ancient American* 10, no. 64 (August 2005).

Cordell, Linda S. *Ancient Pueblo Peoples.* Washington, D.C.: St. Remy Press and Smithsonian Institution, 1994.

———. *Prehistory of the Southwest.* New York: Academic Press, 1984.

Corliss, William R. *Ancient Man: A Handbook of Puzzling Artifacts.* Glen Arm, Md.: The Sourcebook Project, 1978.

———. "Ancient Surgery and Dentistry; The Cannibalism Signature." In *Archaeological Anomalies.* Glen Arm, Md.: The Sourcebook Project, 2001.

———. "Incongruous Towers in the North American Southwest; Tiahuanaco; Ecuador." In *Ancient Structures.* Glen Arm, Md.: The Sourcebook Project, 2001.

———. "Mystery Hill: America's Stonehenge; The Gungywamp Lithic Complex; Ohio's Furnace-Like Structures; Notable Ancient Stone Forts: A Survey; Hilltop Forts." In *Ancient Structures.* Glen Arm, Md.: The Sourcebook Project, 2001.

———. "New Mexico; the Great Houses." In *Ancient Structures.* Glen Arm, Md.: The Sourcebook Project, 2001.

———. "North America; Arizona." In *Ancient Structures.* Glen Arm, Md.: The Sourcebook Project, 2001.

———. "The Objective Existence of Large-Scale Order." In *Ancient Structures.* Glen Arm, Md.: The Sourcebook Project, 2001.

———. "The Scottish Brochs." In *Ancient Structures.* Glen Arm, Md.: The Sourcebook Project, 2001.

Crevier, Benoit. "Niagra's Ancient Cemetary of Giants." In *Ancient American* 6, no. 41 (September–October 2001).

Cunliffe, Barry. *The Ancient Celts.* Oxford: Oxford University Press, 1997.

Cushing, Frank M. *Zuni Folk Tales.* New York: Alfred A. Knopf, 1979.

Dancey, William. "The Enigmatic Hopewell of the Eastern Woodlands." In Timothy R. Pauketat and Diana DiPaolo Loren, eds. *North American Archaeology.* Malden, Mass.: Blackwell Studies in Global Archaeology, 2005.

Daniel, Glyn. *The Illustrated Encyclopedia of Archaeology.* New York: Thomas Y. Crowell Company, 1977.

Davis, Nancy Yaw. *The Zuni Enigma: A Native American People's Possible Japanese Connection.* New York: W. W. Norton and Company, 2001.

Deal, David Allen. "Spruce Hill Fort: A Bird's Eye View." In *Ancient American* 10, no. 64 (August 2005).

Dean, Darrick. "Ohio's Ancient Smelters." In *Ancient American* 12, no. 78 (May–June 2007).

De la Vega, Garcilaso in *Dictionary of Literary Biography.* Bryant Creel, Volume 318: *Sixteenth-Century Spanish Writers.* A Bruccoli Clark Layman Book. Edited by Gregory B. Kaplan. Gale: University of Tennessee, 2005.

———. *Royal Commentaries of the Incas.* Translated by Patricia J. Lyon. Bloomington, Ind.: Indiana University Press, 1994.

Demarest, A. A. *Viracocha: The Nature and Antiquity of the Andean High God.* Cambridge, Mass.: Harvard University Press, 1984.

Dempsey, Mary A. "Treasure of the Moche Lords." In *Ancient American* 2, no. 10 (July–August 1995).

Dilg, Charles A. www.earlychicago.com/encyclopedia.php?letter=D.

Diodorus Siculus. *The Geography.* Translated by C. H. Oldfather. London: Heinemann, 1968.

Donnan quoted by Mary A. Dempsey. "Treasure of the Moche Lords." In *Ancient American* 2, no. 10 (July–August 1995).

Dragoo, Don W. *Mounds for the Dead: An Analysis of the Adena Culture.* Pittsburgh, Pa.: Carnegie Museum of Natural History, 1989.

Duff, U. Francis. "Prehistoric Ruins of the Southwest." In *Ancient American* 9, no. 55 (February 2004).

Emerson, Iseminger, L. Michael Nance, Madeline Winslow, and Marilyn Gass. *Cahokia Mounds State Historical Site Nature/Culture Hike Guidebook,* fourth revised edition. Collinsville, Ill.: Cahokia Mounds Museum Society, 2004.

Emerson, Thomas. *Cahokia and the Archaeology of Power.* Tuscaloosa, Ala.: University of Alabama Press, 1997.

Emerson, Thomas, and Barry Lewis. *Cahokia and the Hinterlands: Middle Mississipian Cultures of the Midwest.* Urbana, Ill.: University of Illinois Press, 1999.

Erlandson, John. www.google.com/search?source=ig&hl=en&rlz=&q=oyu+circle +japan&btnG=oogle+Search.

Eschborn, Archie. "Michigan's Heritage Park Stone Enigmas." In *Ancient American* 12, no. 78 (May–June 2007).

Everhart, Dr. J. T. "The Discovery of Ohio's Brush Creek Tablet." In *Ancient American* 6, no. 38 (April 2001).

Fagan, Brian M. *Ancient North America: The Archaeology of a Continent.* London: Thames and Hudson, 1995.

Fan San, Hu, *Ancient Chinese Chronicles.* Translated by Edward Bruzinski. Chicago: University of Chicago Press, 1969.

Farquharson, R. J. "The Elephant Pipe." *American Antiquarian,* 1879. In William R. Corliss, *Ancient Man: A Handbook of Puzzling Artifacts.* Glen Arm, Md.: The Sourcebook Project, 1978.

Faulkner, Charles. *The Old Stone Fort: Exploring an Archaeological Mystery.* Knoxville, Tenn.: University of Tennessee Press, 1971.

Fell, Barry. *America B.C.*, New York: Simon and Schuster, 1994.

Fewkes, J. W. *Casa Grande.* 28th Report of the Bureau of American Ethnology, Washington, D.C.: 1912. In William R. Corliss, *Ancient Man: A Handbook of Puzzling Artifacts.* Glen Arm, Md.: The Sourcebook Project, 1978.

———. *The Mimbres: Art and Archaeology.* Albuquerque: Avanyu Publishing, 1993.

———. "Prehistoric Towers and Castles of the Southwest." *Art and Archaeology,* 1918. In William R. Corliss, *Ancient Man: A Handbook of Puzzling Artifacts.* Glen Arm, Md.: The Sourcebook Project, 1978.

Ford, Dana. "Pre-Incan female Wari mummy unearthed in Peru," August 2008. www.//in.reuters.com/article/lifestyleMolt/idINN2636587520080826.

Freeman, Philip Mitchell. *The Earliest Classical Sources on the Celts: A Linguistic and Historical Study.* Cambridge, Mass.: Harvard University Press, 1994.

Gaillard, D. D. "A Gigantic Earthwork in New Mexico." *American Anthropologist,* 1896. In William R. Corliss, *Ancient Man: A Handbook of Puzzling Artifacts.* Glen Arm. Md.: The Sourcebook Project, 1978.

Gallagher, Ida Jane. "Grave Creek Tablet is Genuine." In *Ancient American* 12, no. 78 (May–June 2007).

Gallenkamp, Charles B. "New Mexico's Vanished Tower Dwellers." In *Natural History*, 62:312, 1953.

Galloway, Patricia. *The Southeastern Ceremonial Complex: Artifacts and Analysis (Indians of the Southeast)*. Lincoln: University of Nebraska Press, 1989.

Gelles, Paul. *Water and Power in Highland Peru: The Cultural Politics of Irrigation and Development*. Piscataway, N.J.: Rutgers University Press, 2000.

Glynn, Frank. "The Effigy Mound: A Covered Cairn Burial Site in Andover, Massachusetts." *NEARA Newsletter*, 1969. In William R. Corliss, *Ancient Man: A Handbook of Puzzling Artifacts*. Glen Arm, Md.: The Sourcebook Project, 1978.

Green, Miranda J. *The Celtic World*. London: Routledge, 1995.

Greene, Don. "West Virginia's Prehistoric Mounds Discovered." In *Ancient American* 5, no. 31 (February 2000).

Grzimek, Bernard. *Grzimek's Animal Life Encyclopedia,* vol. 12. New York: Van Nostrand Reinhold, 1975.

Hamilton, Francis. In William R. Corliss, *Ancient Man: A Handbook of Puzzling Artifacts*. Glen Arm, Md.: The Sourcebook Project, 1978.

Hamilton, Ross. "Ancient Ohio's Great Hopewell Highway." In *Ancient American* 4, no. 29 (October–November 1999).

———. "Giants in the Ancient Ohio Valley." In *Ancient American* 12, no. 76 (December 2007).

———. "Holocaust of Giants." In *Ancient American* 6, no. 40 (July–August 2001).

Hamilton, Ross, with Patricia Mason. "North American Warfare and a Tradition of Giants." In *Ancient American* 5, no. 36 (December 2000).

Hare, John Bruno. *Early British Trackways, Moats, Mounds, Camps and Sites by Alfred Watkins*. London: BiblioBazaar, 2008.

Harrington, M. R. "Ancient Salt Mines of the Indians." *Scientific American*, 1926. In William R. Corliss, *Ancient Man: A Handbook of Puzzling Artifacts*. Glen Arm, Md.: The Sourcebook Project, 1978.

Hathaway, Bruce. "Chan Chan, Peru: End of an Empire." In *Smithsonian* 39, no. 12 (March, 2009).

Haury, Emil W. "First Masters of the American Desert: The Hohokam." *National*

Geographic, May 1967. In William R. Corliss, *Ancient Man: A Handbook of Puzzling Artifacts.* Glen Arm, Md.: The Sourcebook Project, 1978.

———. *The Hohokam: Desert Farmers and Craftsmen.* Tucson, Ariz.: University of Arizona Press, 1978.

Haywood, John. "Ancient Iron-Smelting Furnaces in Ohio." In Keeler, Clyde E., and Bennet E. Kelley. *NEARA Newsletter,* 1971. In William R. Corliss, *Ancient Man: A Handbook of Puzzling Artifacts.* Glen Arm, Md.: The Sourcebook Project, 1978.

Heckewelder, John. In Robert Silverberg, *Mound Builders of Ancient America: The Archaeology of a Myth.* Norwalk, Conn.: New York Graphic Society, 1968.

Hemming, John. *Conquest of the Incas.* New York: Harcourt, 1970.

Hewson, John. *A Computer-Generated Dictionary of Proto-Algonquian.* Toronto: Canadian Museum of Civilization, 1993.

Hibben, Frank C., "The Mystery of the Stone Towers," *Art and Archaeology,* 7:353, 1918. In William R. Corless, *Ancient Structures.* Glen Arm, Md: The Sourcebook Project, 2001.

Hicks, Robert D., III. "Astronomy in the Ancient Americas," *Sky and Telescope,* 51:372, 1976.

Highsmith, Hugh. *The Mounds of Koshkonong and Rock River.* Fort Atkinson, Wisc.: Highsmith Press, 1997.

Hill, Martin. *Indiana's Wyandotte Cave.* Indianapolis, Ind.: University of Indiana Press, 1977.

Hitoshi, Wanatabe. *Possibilities for Ancient Migrations.* Urbana: University of Illinois Press, 1993.

Hodge, F. W. "Prehistoric Irrigation in Arizona." *American Anthropologist,* 1893. In William R. Corliss. *Ancient Man: A Handbook of Puzzling Artifacts.* Glen Arm, Md.: The Sourcebook Project, 1978.

Holmes, W. W. "Traces of Aboriginal Operations in an Iron Mine near Leslie, Missouri." *Smithsonian Institution Annual Report,* 1904. In William R. Corliss, *Ancient Man: A Handbook of Puzzling Artifacts.* Glen Arm, Md.: The Sourcebook Project, 1978.

Hornborg, Alf. *The Power of the Machine: The Peoples and Cultures of Ancient Peru.* Washington, D.C.: Smithsonian Institution Press, 1994.

Hothem, Lars. *Treasures of the Mound Builders: Adena and Hopewell Artifacts of Ohio.* Lancaster, Ohio: Hothem House Books, 1989.

Howard, Jerry B. "Hohokam Legacy: Desert Canals." www.waterhistory.org/ histories/hohokam2/.

Howard, Jerry B., and Gary Huckleberry. "The Operation and Evolution of an Irrigation System: The East Papago Canal Study," *Soil Systems Publications in Archaeology,* no. 18. Phoenix: 1991.

Hunter, Bruce C. *A Guide to Ancient Mexican Ruins.* Norman: University of Oklahoma Press, 1978.

Huyghe, Patrick. *Columbus was Last.* New York: Hyperion Books, 1992.

Iler, Jim. "Oklahoma's Buried Maya Treasure." In *Ancient American* 3, no. 13 (April–May 1996).

Isbell, W. H. "Emergency Excavations at Conchapata Huari Temple Architecture and Iconography in Ayacucho, Peru." In Dumbarton Oaks Research Report, State University of New York, Binghamton, 2000.

Isbell, W. H., and A. Cook. "Huari D-shaped Structures, Sacrificial Offerings and Divine Kingship." In Betty Benson and Anita Cook, *Ritual Sacrifice in Ancient Peru: New Discoveries and Interpretations.* Austin, Tex.: University of Texas Press, 1999.

Isbell, W. H., and Gordon McEwan. *Huari Political Organization.* Washington, D.C: Dumbarton Oaks, 1991.

———. "Ideological Origins of an Andean Conquest State." In *Archaeology* 40, no. 4 (1987).

Iseminger, William, L. Michael Nance, Madeline Winslow, and Marilyn Gass. *Cahokia Mounds State Historical Site Nature/Culture Hike Guidebook,* fourth revised edition. Collinsville, Ill.: Cahokia Mounds Museum Society, 2004.

Izurin, S. *Kenkyusha's New Dictionary of the Japanese Language.* Tokoyo: Kenkyusha, 2001.

James, Simon. *The Atlantic Celts: Ancient People or Modern Invention?* Madison, Wisc.: University of Wisconsin Press, 1999.

Jeffers, Thomas. "Indian Mound Yielded Ancient Treasures," *Oklahoma Star,* vol. 19, no. 8. Tulsa: 10 July 1937.

Jennings, Jesse D. *Glen Canyon: An Archaeological Summary.* Salt Lake City: University of Utah Press, 1966.

Jewell, G. Iudhael. "The Brockville 'Giants': Twelve Skeletons from the St. Lawrence River." In *Ancient American* 8, no. 54 (December 2003).

Jones, Charles C. Jr. "Aboriginal Structures in Georgia." *Smithsonian Annual Report,* 1877. In William R. Corliss, *Ancient Man: A Handbook of Puzzling Artifacts.* Glen Arm, Md.: The Sourcebook Project, 1978.

———. *Smithsonian Annual Report.* In William R. Corliss, *Ancient Man: A Handbook of Puzzling Artifacts.* Glen Arm, Md.: The Sourcebook Project, 1978.

Joseph, Frank. "America's Oldest Pyramid." In *Ancient American* 10, no. 61 (February 2005).

———. "Ancient Mound Builders of Japan." In *Ancient American* 1, no. 4 (January–February 1994).

———. "Angel Mounds and the Great Circle: Forgotten Monuments of Ancient Indiana." In *Ancient American* 9, no. 58 (August 2004).

———. *Atlantis in Wisconsin.* Lakeville, Minn.: Galde Press, Inc., 1995.

———. "Forgotten Earthworks of the Prehistoric Midwest." In *Ancient American* 9, no. 60 (December 2004).

———. "Illinois: Cahokia (Monks Mounds);" "Indiana: The Great Circle Mound;" "Ohio: Seip Mound;" "Tennessee: Saul's Mound (Pinson Mounds);" "Wisconsin: Lizard Mounds." St. Paul, Minn.: Llewellyn Publications, 1993.

———. *The Lost Pyramids of Rock Lake,* revised edition. Lakeville, Minn.: Galde Press, Inc., 2003.

———. "Prehistoric 'Forts' or 'Observatories' in Ohio and Tennessee?" In *Ancient American* 9, no. 57 (June 2004).

———. "Pre-Inca City Found in Peruvian Jungle." In *Ancient American* 9, no. 59 (October 2004).

———. "The Viking and the Indian." In *Ancient American* 1, no. 6 (May–June 1994).

Joseph, Frank, ed. "Angel Mounds." In *Sacred Sites, A Guidebook to Sacred Centers and Mysterious Places in the United States.* St. Paul, Minn.: Llewellyn Publications, 1992.

Julius Caesar. *The Gallic War.* Translated by William Richter. Dallas: University of Texas Press, 1979.

Keeler, Clyde E., and Bennet E. Kelley. "Ancient Iron Smelting Furnaces in

Ohio." *NEARA Newsletter,* 1971. In William R. Corliss, *Ancient Man: A Handbook of Puzzling Artifacts.* Glen Arm, Md.: The Sourcebook Project, 1978.

Kellar, James H. "The C. L. Lewis Stone Mound and the Stone Mound Problem in Eastern United States Prehistory," Ph.D. Dissertation, publication 19,494. Ann Arbor, Mich.: University Microfilms, 1956; and *Prehistory Research Series* 3, no. 4 (June 1960).

Kincaid, Chris, ed. "Chaco Roads Project Phase 1." Albuquerque: Bureau of Land Management, 1983.

Klindt-Jensen, O. "The Gundestrup Bowl, A Reassessment." In *Antiquity* 33, no. 55 (1946).

Knight, Wilbur C. "Prehistoric Quartzite Quarries in Central Eastern Wyoming." *Science,* 1898. In William R. Corliss, *Ancient Man: A Handbook of Puzzling Artifacts.* Glen Arm. Md.: The Sourcebook Project, 1978.

Knobloch, Patricia. "Huari Administrative Structure: Prehistoric Monumental Architecture and State Government." Washington, D.C.: Dumbarton Oaks, 1991.

Kolata, Alan Louis. *The Tiawanaku.* Malden, Mass.: Blackwell Studies in Global Archaeology, 1993.

Korp, Maureen. *The Sacred Geography of the American Mound Builders.* New York: E. Mellen Press, 1990.

Krupp, E. C. *In Search of Ancient Astronomies.* New York: Doubleday, 1977.

Kruta, V., O. Frey, Barry Raftery, and M. Szabo. *The Celts.* New York: Thames and Hudson, 1991.

Ladd, Edmund J. quoted by Nancy Yaw Davis. *The Zuni Enigma: A Native American People's Possible Japanese Connection.* New York: W. W. Norton and Company, 2001.

Laing, Lloyd. *The Archaeology of Late Celtic Britain and Ireland c. 400–1200 AD.* London: Methuen, 1975.

Laing, Lloyd, and Jennifer Laing. *Art of the Celts.* London: Thames and Hudson, 1992.

Lange, Charles M. *Echoes of the Ancient Skies.* New York: Harper and Row, 1983.

LeBlanc, Steven A. *Prehistoric Warfare in the American Southwest.* Salt Lake City, Utah: University of Utah Press, 1999.

Lekson, Stephen. "Great Pueblo Architecture of Chaco Canyon, New Mexico." Albuquerque, N. Mex.: National Park Service Publications in Archaeology 18B, 2002.

Lepper, Bradley T. and Cornelius Cadle. "A Remarkable Prehistoric Ceremonial Pipe." In *Ancient American* 9, no. 56 (April 2004).

Lewis, T. H. "The Camel and Elephant Mounds at Prairie du Chien." *American Antiquarian,* 1884. In William R. Corliss. *Ancient Man: A Handbook of Puzzling Artifacts.* Glen Arm, Md.: The Sourcebook Project, 1978.

Little, Curtis J. "Chickasawaba Mound, Mississippi Valley." In *Ancient American* 12, no. 73 (May 2007).

Livy. *The History of Rome from its Foundation,* Books XI–X. London: Penguin Books, 1982.

Lough, Glenn D. "Ohio's Prehistoric Village Site." In *Ancient American* 10, no. 62 (April 2005).

MacBain, A. *Etymological Dictionary of the Gaelic Language.* New York: French and European Publishing, 1991.

MacCullough, John A., and Louis H. Gray. *The Mythology of All Races,* 13 vols. New York: Cooper Square Publishers, 1922.

MacKillop, James. *A Dictionary of Celtic Mythology.* Oxford: Oxford University Press, 1998.

Magrath, Willis H. "The Temple of the Effigy." In *Scientific American* (August 1940).

Mallam, Clark R. "Effigy Mounds in Iowa, Ideology from the Earth." Harper's Ferry, Iowa: Effigy Mounds National Monument Museum, 1980.

Mallery, Arlington. *The Rediscovery of Lost America.* New York: E. P. Dutton, 1979.

Malsberry, John. "The Discovery and Loss of Ohio's 'Hopewell Age' Mound." In *Ancient American* 8, no. 51 (May–June 2003).

Masse, Bruce. "Prehistoric Irrigation Systems in the Salt River Valley, Arizona." *Science* 214, no. 23 (1981).

Mavor, J. W., and B. E. Dix. "The Pearson Stone Chamber." In William R. Corliss, *Ancient Man: A Handbook of Puzzling Artifacts.* Glen Arm, Md.: The Sourcebook Project, 1978.

———. "The Upton Stone Chamber." In William R. Corliss, *Ancient Man: A*

Handbook of Puzzling Artifacts. Glen Arm, Md.: The Sourcebook Project, 1978.

May, Wayne. "Ohio's Ancient City?" In *Ancient American* 6, no. 37 (February 2001).

———. "Visiting Ohio's Spruce Hil Fort." In *Ancient American* 10, no. 64 (August 2005).

Maybury-Lewis, D. *The Attraction of Opposites: Thought and Society in the Dualistic Mode.* Ann Arbor: University of Michigan Press, 1989.

McClain, Florence W. "Hovenweep." In Frank Joseph, ed. *Sacred Sites, A Guidebook to Sacred Centers and Mysterious Places in the United States.* St. Paul, Minn.: Llewellyn Publications, 1992.

McGlone, William R., and Phillip M. Leonard. *Ancient Celtic America.* Ohio: America Panorama West Press, 1990.

Meddens, Frank, and Anita G. Cook. "Archaeological Investigations at Pikillacta, a Wari Site in Peru." In *Journal of Field Archaeology* 23, no. 2 (1996).

Menzel, Dorothy. "Huari Administration and the Cult of the Dead Yako D-shaped Structures in the South Central Highlands." In Luis Millones and Enrique González Carré, eds. *Wari el Primer Estado Imperial Andino.* El Monte, Seville: Spain.

Middleton, James D. "Ohio Mounds." *Science*, 1887. In William R. Corliss. *Ancient Man: A Handbook of Puzzling Artifacts.* Glen Arm, Md: The Sourcebook Project, 1978.

Midvale, Frank. "Prehistoric Irrigation in the Salt River Valley, Arizona," *Science*, 1968. In William R. Corliss, *Ancient Man: A Handbook of Puzzling Artifacts.* Glen Arm. Md.: The Sourcebook Project, 1978.

Mills, William C. "America's Oldest Pyramid." In *Ancient American* 9, no. 60 (December 2004).

———. "Excavation of an Adena Mound." In *Ancient American* 12, no. 74 (July 2007).

———. "Ohio's Ancient Adena Mound." In *Ancient American* 8, no. 54 (December 2003).

Milner, George R. *The Moundbuilders: Ancient Peoples of Eastern North America.* London: Thames and Hudson, 2004.

Mink, Claudia Gellman. *Cahokia, City of the Sun: Prehistoric Urban Center in* the American Bottom. Collinsville, Ill.: Cahokia Mounds Museum Society, 1992.

Molina, Cristobal de. *The Fables and Rites of the Yncas.* Translated and edited by Clements R. Markham. London: Hakluyt Society, 1873.

Moore, Dennis J. "An Iberian Mortuary Complex in Ancient Michigan?" In *Ancient American* 6, no. 40 (July–August 2001).

Moseley, Michael E. *The Incas and their Ancestors.* London: Thames and Hudson, 1992.

Muscutt, Keith. *Warriors of the Clouds.* Albuquerque, N. Mex.: University of New Mexico Press, 1998.

Newberry, J. S. "Ancient Mining in North America." *American Antiquarian,* 1889. In William R. Corliss, *Ancient Man: A Handbook of Puzzling Artifacts.* Glen Arm, Md.: The Sourcebook Project, 1978.

Newman, Stanley S. *Zuni Grammar.* Tucson, Ariz.: University of New Mexico Press, 1965.

Nickerson, William Baker. "Burial Mounds of Albany, Illinois." In *Ancient American* 11, no. 70 (October 2006).

Norton, Jonathan Leonard. *Early Japan.* New York: Time-Life Books, 1974.

O'Donnell, James H., III. *Ohio's First Peoples.* Athens, Ohio: Ohio University Press, 2004.

O'Keefe, Christine. "Scottish Legends." www.tartanplace.com/tartanlegend/celtictribeseur.html.

Onians, John. *Atlas of World Art.* New York: Oxford University Press, 2004.

Osborne, Harold. *South American Mythology.* London: Hamlyn Publishing Group, 1975.

Pauketat, Timothy. *The Ascent of Chiefs: Cahokia and Mississippian Politics in Native North America.* Tuscaloosa, Ala.: University of Alabama Press, 1994.

Peale, T. R. "Prehistoric Ruins of the Southwest." In *Ancient American* 9, no. 55 (February 2004).

Pearson, Richard J. *Ancient Japan.* New York: George Brazilier Publishers, 1992.

———. *Archaeology of the Ryukyu Islands.* Honolulu: University of Hawaii Press, 1969.

Peet, Stephan D. "Defensive Works of the Mound-Builders." *American*

Antiquarian, 1891. In William R. Corliss, *Ancient Man: A Handbook of Puzzling Artifacts.* Glen Arm, Md.: The Sourcebook Project, 1978.

———. "The Great Cahokia Mound." *American Antiquarian,* 1891. In William R. Corliss, *Ancient Man: A Handbook of Puzzling Artifacts.* Glen Arm, Md.: The Sourcebook Project, 1978.

———. "Stone Circles in Europe and America," *American Antiquarian,* 1901. In William R. Corliss, *Ancient Man: A Handbook of Puzzling Artifacts.* Glen Arm, Md.: The Sourcebook Project, 1978.

Pere Marquette. Quoted in "What was the Monster of Alton, Illinois?" by Bayless, Clara Kern. *Ancient American* 6, no. 40 (July–August 2001).

Pizzaro, Francisco. Quoted by Pedro de Cieza de Leon in *The Travels of Pedo de Cieza de Leon, Contained in the First Part of his Chronicle of Peru.* London: Hakluyt Society, 1864.

Plog, Stephen. *Ancient Peoples of the American Southwest.* London: Thames and Hudson, 1997.

Potter, Martha. "Ohio's Most Unusual Pipe." In *Ancient American* 9, no. 58 (August 2004).

Powell, T. G. E. *The Celts.* New York: Thames and Hudson, 1997.

Prescott, William H. *History of the Conquest of Peru.* London: Everyman Library, 1963.

Radin, Paul. *The Winnebago Tribe.* Lincoln: University of Nebraska Press, 1970.

Raftery, Barry. *Pagan Celtic Ireland: The Enigma of the Irish Iron Age.* London: Thames and Hudson, 1994.

Reid, M. C. "Inscribed Stone of Grave Creek Mound." *American Antiquarian,* 1879. In William R. Corliss. *Ancient Man: A Handbook of Puzzling Artifacts.* Glen Arm, Md.: The Sourcebook Project, 1978.

Reyman, Jonathan E. "Astronomy, Architecture, and Adaptation at Pueblo Bonito." *Science,* 1976. In William R. Corliss. *Ancient Man: A Handbook of Puzzling Artifacts.* Glen Arm, Md.: The Sourcebook Project, 1978.

Ricky, Donald B., ed. *Encyclopedia of Ohio Indians.* St. Clair Shores, Mich.: Somerset Publishers, 1998.

Riotte, Louise. "Spiro Mounds." In Frank Joseph, ed. *Sacred Sites, A Guidebook to Sacred Centers and Mysterious Places in the United States.* St. Paul, Minn.: Llewellyn Publications, 1992.

Ritchie, William A. "The Stone Chambers of Northeastern North America." In William Corliss, *Ancient Structures*. Glen Arm, Md.: The Sourcebook Project, 2001.

Roberts, David D. *In Search of the Old Ones: Exploring the Anasazi World of the Southwest*. New York: Simon and Schuster, 1996.

Rothovius, Andrew E. "Connecticut's Unfolding Mystery." In *Ancient American* 1, no. 4 (August 2004).

Salomon, Frank, and George Urisotem, trans. *The Huarochiri Manuscript*. Austin, Tex.: University of Texas Press, 1991.

Sanders, Barry, and Paul Shepherd. *The Sacred Paw, the Bear in Nature, Myth and Literature*. New York: Doubleday, 1985.

Savoy, Gene. *Antisuyo: The Search for the Lost Cities of the Andes*. New York: Simon and Schuster, 1970.

Scherz, James P. "The Kingman Coins." In *Ancient American* 1, no. 7 (September–October 2004).

Schoolcraft, Henry Rowe. *Historical and Statistical Information Respecting the Indian Tribes of the United States*. Washington, D.C.: Society for the Investigation of North American Antiquities, 1859.

Schreiber, Katharina. *Conchopata: A Community of Potters in Huari Administrative Structure and State Government*. Washington, D.C.: Dumbarton Oaks, 1991.

Schurr, Dr. Theodore. "DNA Reveals Diverse Native American Heritage," http://macdonnellofleinster.org/page_7h.htm.

Scofield, Bruce. "Mystery Hill: America's Stonehenge." In Frank Joseph, ed. *Sacred Sites, A Guidebook to Sacred Centers and Mysterious Places in the United States*. St. Paul, Minn.: Llewellyn Publications, 1992.

Science Newsletter quote from "The Objective Existence of Large-Scale Order." In *Ancient Structures,* by William R. Corliss. Glen Arm, Md.: The Sourcebook Project, 2001.

Silverberg, Robert. *The Mound Builders*. Athens, Ohio. Ohio University Press, 1986.

Smith, Colette Thomas. "Legends of White Indians in the Americas." In *Ancient American* 12, no. 77 (February 2008).

Smithsana, Don. "Japanese Place-Names in Ancient America." In *Ancient American* 2, no. 10 (July–August 1995).

Sofaer, Anna. "Mystery of Chaco Canyon." DVD/VHS, Bullfrog Films, 1999.

Sofaer, Anna, with J. Crotty. "Survey of Rock Art on Fajada Butte." Ms. on file, Albuquerque, Chaco Center, University of New Mexico, 1977.

Sofaer, Anna, with R. M. Sinclair. "From Astronomy and Ceremony in the Prehistoric Southwest." In John B. Carlson and W. James Judge, eds. *Anthropological Papers,* no. 2, Maxwell Museum of Anthropology, 1983.

Sofaer, Anna, with R. M. Sinclair, and L. E. Doggett. "Lunar Markings on Fajada Butte." In A. Aveni, ed. *Archaeoastronomy in the New World.* New York: Cambridge University Press, 1982.

Sofaer, Anna, with R. M. Sinclair and M. P. Marshall. "Cosmographic Expression in the Road System of the Chaco Culture of Northwestern New Mexico." Paper presented at the Second Oxford Conference on Archaeoastronomy, Merida (Yucatán), Mexico, 1979.

Solarzano, Brian. "Prehistoric Chicago." In *Ancient American* 3, no. 12 (February–March 1996).

Squire, Ephraim George. *Ancient Monuments of the Mississippi Valley.* New York: Compshire House Publishers, 1848.

———. In Sydney J. Tanner, "Celtic Script in New Hampshire," *Ancient American* 9, no. 58 (January–February 1994).

———. "The Primeval Monuments of Peru Compared with Those in Other Parts of the World," *American Naturalist,* 1870. In William R. Corliss, *Ancient Man: A Handbook of Puzzling Artifacts.* Glen Arm, Md.: The Sourcebook Project, 1978.

Steel, Duncan. "Probability of Cosmic Collisions in the Late Bronze Age." In Palmer, Trevor, and Mark E. Bailey, eds., *Natural Catastrophes During Bronze Age Civilizations: Archaeological, Geological, Astronomical and Cultural Perspectives.* Oxford, England: Archaeo Press, 1998.

Steele, Paul R. *Handbook of Inca Mythology.* Santa Barbara, Calif.: ABC Clio, 2004.

Steward, Julian H., ed. *Handbook of South American Indians.* Washington, D.C.: Smithsonian Institution, Bureau of American Ethnology, 1950.

Taylor, Timothy. "The Gundestrup Cauldron." In *Scientific American* 98. no. 12 (March 1992).

Tchiffely, A. S. *Coricancha.* London: Hodder and Stoughton, 1949.

Thomas, Cyrus. "Iron from North Carolina Mounds." *Science,* 1884. In William R. Corliss, *Ancient Man: A Handbook of Puzzling Artifacts.* Glen Arm, Md.: The Sourcebook Project, 1978.

———. "Mound Works at Hales Place, Jackson County, Illinois." In *Ancient American* 12, no. 77 (February 2008).

Thompson, Dr. Gunnar. *American Discovery, the Real Story.* Seattle, Wash.: Argonauts Misty Isles Press, 1994.

———. "Japanese Voyagers." In *American Discovery, the Real Story.* Seattle, Wash.: Argonauts Misty Isles Press, 1994.

Thunderhorse, Iron. *Return of the Thunderbeings.* Rochester, Vt.: Bear and Company, 1990.

Titiev, Mischa. "Old Oraibi: A Study of the Hopi Indians of Third Mesa." Paper of the Peabody Museum of American Archaeology and Ethnology 22, no. 1. Cambridge, Mass.: Harvard University, 1944.

———. "The Story of Kokopelli." In *American Anthropologist* 41, no. 1 (1939).

Trento, Salvatore Michael. *Keltic Cultural Development from 1000 B.C. to 100 A.D.* New York: MacMillan, 1979.

Trotti, Hugh H. "America's Stonehenge." In *Fate* 45, no. 6 (June 1992).

"Tse Diyil, the Old Woman of Fajada Butte." Adapted from a Navajo couple's interpretation of Fajada Butte. www.angelfire.com/indie/anna_jones1/oldwoman.html.

Turk, Jon. "New World's First Dwellers Japanese?" *Japan Times,* Aug. 16, 2007.

Turney, Omar. "Prehistoric Irrigation in Arizona." Phoenix, Ariz.: Arizona Historical Review, 1929. In William R. Corliss, *Ancient Man: A Handbook of Puzzling Artifacts.* Glen Arm. Md.: The Sourcebook Project, 1978.

Tyler, Hamilton A. *Pueblo Gods and Myths.* Norman: University of Oklahoma Press, 1964.

Urton, Gary. *At the Crossroads of Earth and Sky: An Andean Cosmology.* Austin, Tex.: University of Texas Press, 1981.

———. *Inca Myths.* Austin, Tex.: University of Texas Press, 1999.

Von Hagen, Adriana. *Wari Imperialism in Middle Horizon Peru.* Ann Arbor, Mich.: University of Michigan Press, 1992.

Von Hagen, Victor W. *The Ancient Sun Kingdoms.* London: Thames and Hudson, 1962.

————. *The Desert Kingdoms of Peru.* London: Weidenfeld and Nicolson, 1965.

Walters, Edwin. In William R. Corliss. *Ancient Man: A Handbook of Puzzling Artifacts.* Glen Arm, Md.: The Sourcebook Project, 1978.

Warner, Jared. "Hopewellian Mound Builders." In *Ancient American* 10, no. 61 (February 2005).

Webb, William S., and Raymond S. Baby, eds. *The Adena People.* Knoxville: University of Tennessee Press, 1974.

Welsh, L. B., and J. M. Richardson. "The Discovery of Ohio's Adena/Hopewell Tablet." Reprinted from Prehistoric Relics found near Wilmington, Ohio, 1879. In *Ancient American* 4, no. 28 (June–July 1999).

"What 'Unknown Race' Built the Monuments of Prehistoric America?" Reprinted from the *Manitoba Daily Free Press.* Winnipeg, Canada. November 9, 1877. In *Ancient American* 6, no. 39 (June 2001).

White, Brian. "Underworld Cult of the Pueblo People." In *Ancient American* 6, no. 42 (November–December 2001).

White, John J., III. "Mills Found the Adena Pipe, not Baby." In *Ancient American* 6, no. 38 (April 2001).

Whittal, James P. "A Report on the Pearson Stone Chamber, Upton, Massachusetts." *Early Sites Research Society Bulletin,* 1973. In William R. Corliss, *Ancient Man: A Handbook of Puzzling Artifacts.* Glen Arm, Md.: The Sourcebook Project, 1978.

Wilcox, David R., C. Sternberg, and T. R. McGuire. "Hohokam Ballcourts and Their Interpretation." Tempe: Arizona State Museum Archaeological Series 160, University of Arizona. 1983.

————. *Snaketown Revisited.* Tempe: Arizona State Museum Archaeological Series 155, University of Arizona, 1981.

Windes, Tom. In *House of Rain: Tracking a Vanished Civilization Across the American Southwest,* by Craig Childs. New York: Little, Brown and Company, 2007.

Woodbury, Richard B. "The Hohokam Canals at Pueblo Grande, Arizona." *American Antiquity,* 1960. In William R. Corliss. *Ancient Man: A Handbook of Puzzling Artifacts.* Glen Arm, Md.: The Sourcebook Project, 1978.

Woodward, Susan L., and Jerry N. McDonald. *Indian Mounds of the Middle Ohio Valley: A Guide to Mounds and Earthworks of the Adena, Hopewell, Cole, and Fort Ancient People.* Lincoln, Neb.: University of Nebraska Press, 2002.

Yamashita, Hiroshi. *Eastward Ancient Japan*. Westport, Conn.: Cornell College Press, 1990.

Yoshida, Professor Nobuhiro. "An Ancient Japan-Wisconsin Connection?" In *Ancient American* 5, no. 36 (December 2000).

———. "Ancient American and Japanese Dragons: Related or Coincidental?" In *Ancient American* 12, no. 76 (December 2007).

———. "Japan's Megalithic Links to America and Europe." In *Ancient American* 3, no. 23 (April–May 1998).

Young, Biloine. *Cahokia: The Great Native American Metropolis*. Urbana, Ill.: University of Illinois Press, 2000.

Xu, H. Mike. *Origin of the Olmec Civilization*. Edmond, Okla.: University of Central Oklahoma Press, 1996.

Ziegler, Gary R. "Inca Architecture, The 'T' Groove: Symbol, Gold or Bronze." www.adventurespecialists.org/tgroove.html.

Zimmermann, Fritz. "Cultural and Physical Similarities of the Beaker People and the Adena." In *Ancient American* 9, no. 58 (August 2004).

INDEX

Page numbers in *italics* refer to figures.

BOOKS OF RELATED INTEREST

Atlantis and the Coming Ice Age
The Lost Civilization—A Mirror of Our World
by Frank Joseph

Before Atlantis
20 Million Years of Human and Pre-Human Cultures
by Frank Joseph

The Lost Civilization of Lemuria
The Rise and Fall of the World's Oldest Culture
by Frank Joseph

Our Dolphin Ancestors
Keepers of Lost Knowledge and Healing Wisdom
by Frank Joseph

Ancient Giants Who Ruled America
The Missing Skeletons and the Great Smithsonian Cover-Up
by Richard J. Dewhurst

The Suppressed History of America
The Murder of Meriwether Lewis and the Mysterious Discoveries
of the Lewis and Clark Expedition
by Paul Schrag and Xaviant Haze

Secrets of Ancient America
Archaeoastronomy and the Legacy of the Phoenicians,
Celts, and Other Forgotten Explorers
by Carl Lehrburger

There Were Giants Upon the Earth
Gods, Demigods, and Human Ancestry: The Evidence of Alien DNA
by Zecharia Sitchin

Inner Traditions • Bear & Company
P.O. Box 388
Rochester, VT 05767
1-800-246-8648
www.InnerTraditions.com

Or contact your local bookseller